Becoming Vancouver

MAP OF THE CITY OF VANCOUVER B.C.

Published by THE VANCOUVER TOURIST ASSOCIATION. 1903

DANIEL FRANCIS

Becoming Vancouver: A History

HARBOUR
PUBLISHING

CONTENTS

• • •

Introduction · 1

Naming Names · 7

CHAPTER ONE · Birth, and Rebirth · 13

CHAPTER TWO · Railtown · 45

CHAPTER THREE · Intolerance · 69

CHAPTER FOUR · War, and Postwar · 91

CHAPTER FIVE · Protest · 123

CHAPTER SIX · The Modernist City · 151

CHAPTER SEVEN · The City of Grass · 179

CHAPTER EIGHT · Vancouverism and its Discontents · 209

AFTERWORD · Next Vancouver · 232

Acknowledgements · 238
Notes · 241
Sources · 252
Index · 258

Sometimes the sea-gulls fly over the city streets, and their mewing cries disturb the busy or distracted minds of the townspeople going about their business. Something shakes for an instant the calm of a man crossing the street when he hears the cry of a gull above the traffic, something that is not a sound but a disturbing, forgotten, unnamed desire, a memory... The cry of the wheeling gulls in the city streets.

—ETHEL WILSON, *The Innocent Traveller*

Introduction

VANCOUVER IS BLESSED with one of the most stunning locations in the world. Lying at the mouth of a major river in the shadow of a majestic range of snow-capped mountains on a picturesque inland sea, with a mild climate and boasting one of the best deep-water ports in the world, Vancouver consistently finishes near the top of any ranking of the world's most beautiful cities. Yet residents of the place have never agreed about how best to exploit the advantages that their location has conferred upon them.

Another way of saying this is that Vancouver exists in tension between competing ideas of itself. On the one hand it is a "world-class city" striving for a size and a sophistication that might rank it on a par with any of the great metropolises of the world. On the other hand, it is a "liveable city" maintaining a slower lifestyle and keeping development to a human scale while making the most of its privileged natural assets. This tension plays out in almost every aspect of urban life: preservation versus redevelopment; density versus suburban sprawl; bike paths versus car culture; lotus land versus global metropolis; Green City versus City of Glass.

There is nothing new about such choices. Since the city was created in 1886, different images of its future have contended for predominance. To take just one example: In the spring of 1899 on a tiny island in Vancouver's inner harbour, war was declared. At issue was control of the city's showpiece, Stanley Park. Who did it belong to? Who had the right to say what went on within its borders? And there were other issues at stake as well. Should the preservation of green space take precedence over economic development? Did the interests of the west side's social elite carry more weight than the needs of the east side's working class? Ultimately, what kind of place was Vancouver going to be? Such a weight of significance for such a small scrap of land.

The conflict began almost comically, with no indication that it would drag on for forty years and require resolution in Canada's highest court. Early in 1899 the federal government gave a Seattle lumberman named Theodore Ludgate a twenty-five-year lease on Deadman's Island, a 2.8-hectare chunk of rock in Coal Harbour that at low tide wasn't even an island at all. Originally the local Indigenous people had used it as a burial ground, hence its name. More recently it was home to a community of squatters. For $500 a year, Ludgate had permission to clear-cut the site and build a sawmill.[1] But the city believed that it owned the island, which it considered to be part of Stanley Park. One April morning, when Ludgate and his logging crew arrived to begin work, they found their way blocked by the mayor, the appropriately named James Garden, and a troop of twenty-five police officers. The moment Ludgate and his men started felling trees, the police arrested them. The first shot in "the Battle for Deadman's Island" had been fired.

"Time after time the matter has come up in the City Council," wrote a reporter in the Daily World, "and on countless occasions has the burning question been discussed on the street corners of Vancouver."[2] Opposition to Ludgate's plans was led by prominent residents of the city's West End who wished to protect the park, and their neighbourhood, from industrial development. On the other hand, Ludgate's supporters included many working people who saw the employment opportunities presented by a new mill. For them, jobs were more important than a small piece of parkland. "The City would never prosper," argued one alderman, "unless it made good use of every foot of land it possessed."[3] But that gave rise to another question, the still unresolved issue of who actually owned Stanley Park: the city or the federal government.

Three weeks after the initial skirmish, Ludgate returned and managed to supervise the clear-cutting of half the island before police again received orders to stop him. When Ludgate refused to withdraw, the police forcibly handcuffed him and hauled him off to jail. After a reading of the riot act, the rest of the men dispersed.[4] Subsequently the province sued the federal government, claiming ownership of the island on behalf of the city. In 1901 the BC Supreme Court ruled in favour of the province, but that was just the beginning of the legal battle. On appeal the federal government won its case for jurisdiction over the park. Then in 1906 the final authority, the Judicial Committee of the Privy Council, ruled again in Ottawa's favour, meaning that Ludgate's lease was confirmed and work could go ahead.

In the end the Battle for Deadman's Island turned into a war of attrition. About 150 squatters occupied shacks and floathomes along the shore and many refused to leave, despite Ludgate's best efforts to evict them. There was yet another court case, and in the end no mill was ever built. Following Ludgate's death in 1918, ownership of the island reverted to the federal government. In 1930 the city's Parks Board gained jurisdiction over the site and evicted its tiny village of squatters. During World War II the Department of National Defence took control, and since 1944 it has been the site of HMCS *Discovery*, a naval cadet training facility.

As inconsequential as the Battle for Deadman's Island might appear in retrospect, it was an early manifestation of the tension that has always animated Vancouver's history. The urban geographer Walter Hardwick made the point in his 1974 book *Vancouver,* when he wrote that there is a "conflict in images of the region" between it being a place of opportunity for development/exploitation and a place of quality that must be protected from the forces of international capitalism.[5] As a member of city council in the early 1970s, Hardwick played a key role in the deindustrialization of the south side of False Creek and the development of the human-scale residential community that was built there, including the transformation of Granville Island into an urban showpiece. Compare False Creek South to its north side, which was sold to a Hong Kong developer following Expo 86 and is now a forest of glittering high-rises. These two neighbourhoods look across the creek at each other and are linked by a bicycle path, but they are worlds apart. They represent Vancouver's contradictory impulses. One impulse wants to protect its location in order to build an affordable, green, "liveable" city. Another wants to leverage its location to make the city ever more attractive to the forces of global capitalism. Vancouver is an antithesis looking for its synthesis; it is a city with a split personality.

NOT SURPRISINGLY for a place that prides itself on its setting, Vancouver has always been about real estate. The early settlers appropriated the land from its First Nations inhabitants. Then most of it was handed over to a private railway company in a transfer that was generous even by the standards of its time. The Canadian Pacific Railway received the grant in return for locating its Pacific terminus on Burrard Inlet, and the company has been selling it back piece by piece ever since. In the city's early days, speculating in property was the source of many personal fortunes, as well as a popular recreational pastime. Now, in our own day, the affordability crisis of the 2010s is the latest example of the way that the property market preoccupies the city. Along with the weather, real estate has always been the main topic of conversation in Vancouver.

Running a close third as a reliable source of contention in the city's history has been the question of race. Because of developments since the 1960s, Vancouver now finds itself an ethnically diverse community with more residents of Asian heritage per capita than any other city in the world outside Asia. But for most of its first century, the population was overwhelmingly white and western European in background, and distinctly unfriendly to newcomers who weren't. Before the city was a year old its residents had mobilized to drive the Chinese inhabitants out of town. Barely two years old and the First Nations of Stanley Park had been sent packing. Rioting and racism stained the years that followed, from the 1907 anti-Asian violence to the *Komagata Maru* incident, to the apartheid-like partitioning of the city into ethnic ghettos, to the shameful displacement of Japanese Canadians during World War II. It took many decades for the city to shed its white supremacist ideology and to become the multi-ethnic community that now presents itself to the world.

But a city is more than the sum of its faults. Vancouver wouldn't be worth a book if its history were just a litany of greed and injustice. It may be home to what journalists insist on calling the poorest postal code in the country, the Downtown Eastside, but it is also home to some of the most attractive neighbourhoods of any city in North America. That is not something that happens by accident, and the way Vancouver handled the transition from industrial to post-industrial city, while becoming a model for downtown liveability, is a story worth telling as well.

Like most modern cities, Vancouver devours its own history. Buildings that are here today are gone tomorrow. Historic old business blocks are replaced by gleaming new glass and steel high-rises. Tudor homes that have stood for a century are replaced by angular, architect-designed mega-houses for the mega-rich. Newcomers to the city, arriving by the tens of thousands every year, find few physical reminders of what has gone before. Vancouver has been called a city without a history, partly because of its youth but also because of the way that it seems to change so quickly that it leaves no trace of itself behind.[6] It exists only in the present; it's "instant urbanism" in the words of Lance Berelowitz.[7] According to this view, Vancouver has reinvented itself as a global city full of "knowledge workers" and "world citizens," replacing its own past with a gleaming, high-tech version of the future. From this perspective, history is mainly an impediment. Old neighbourhoods should be gentrified; old jobs are out-moded in the creative economy; old paradigms need "recalibrating."[8] The artist Douglas Coupland writes that he has a theory that Vancouver becomes a new city every ten years.[9] In such a vortex of change, as the city rushes headlong into its future, there is no room for history, only for amnesia.

Not surprisingly, as a historian I am unsympathetic to this exercise in urban memory loss. Of course Vancouver has a past, and it is an important one that has shaped the city's geography, its economy, its ethnic relations, its atmosphere and its politics. Presenting Vancouver as a place outside of history—drunk on the possibilities of the future; indifferent to the events of the past—is a way of handing over the city to the forces of global con-sumerism that sometimes threaten to overwhelm it but in no way should be allowed to define it. It is in large part to insist on Vancouver's past that I have written this book.

August Jack Khahtsahlano, his wife and
a child in a canoe at Kitsilano Point, ca. 1907.
August Jack was one of the most important
informants about the early, Indigenous
history of the Vancouver area.
W. Chapman photo, City of Vancouver Archives,
AM1376-: CVA 1376-203

Naming Names

AUGUST JACK KHAHTSAHLANO was born in the village of Sen-ákw, or Snauq, near the mouth of False Creek, around 1877. His grandfather was Chief Khahtsahlanogh, who had moved down to Chaythoos, just inside the First Narrows in what is now Stanley Park, early in the nineteenth century, from Titamook up the Squamish River. His great uncle was Chief Chip-kay-um, known also as Chief George, who came to Burrard Inlet at the same time as his brother Khahtsahlanogh but chose to establish his own community at Sen-ákw, a good fishing spot. August Jack's father was Supple Jack (Khaytulk), son of Khahtsahlanogh, who divided his time between the two village sites. As a boy, August Jack stood on the shores of False Creek and watched the billowing smoke from the great fire that destroyed the new city of Vancouver in 1886. As a young man in 1913, he was one of the people displaced from Sen-ákw when the government forcibly removed its residents and dispersed them to other communities. "The orchard went to ruin, the fences fell down and the houses were destroyed."[10] From his new home on the Capilano Reserve on the North Shore, August Jack worked as a millhand, a longshoreman and a logger. He could not read or write but he listened attentively to the stories that the elders told him about life in the inlet before the white man came.

In 1932, August Jack began to share his stories with Major James Matthews, the city archivist. The two men sat chatting in the backyard of

The map of Burrard Inlet place names
prepared by Major Matthews with the help
of local Indigenous informants, 1933.
Major James Skitt Matthews, *Conversations with
Khahtsahlano 1932-1954*, (Vancouver: Vancouver
City Archives, 1955), 515

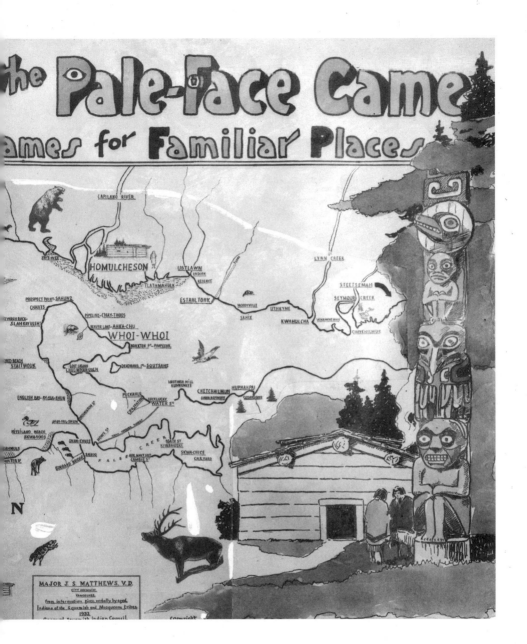

Matthews's house on Kitsilano Point—in an area of the city not far from August Jack's boyhood home and named for his grandfather, the old chief—drinking tea and eating cake. Or they met more formally at the offices of the Vancouver Archives in city hall. "August is dependable," declared the Major. "He is the most reliable historian of Indian life in these parts."[11]

Matthews himself was a diligent collector and defender of Vancouver's historical record. By most accounts an unpleasant man—quick to take offence, stubborn as a mule, a complainer, a bully—he was also, in the estimation of historian Jean Barman, "arguably the single most important individual in the history of Vancouver" because of his single-minded devotion to preserving its past.[12] One of his more admirable qualities, rare for the time, was his interest in the original inhabitants. Matthews recognized that a world had existed before the city and he wanted to know what it was. For that he consulted Khahtsahlano.

Major Matthews asked, "How many Indians do you suppose lived around Burrard Inlet and English Bay before the white man came?" Without a pause August Jack responded: "About a million!" He may have been exaggerating for effect, but his point was made. "There was a settlement at E-yal-mough (Jericho)," he reeled off the names, "another at Snauq (Burrard Bridge), at Ay-yul-shun (English Bay Beach), at Stait-wouk (Second Beach), at Chay-thoos (Prospect Point), at Xway'xway (Lumberman's Arch), at Homulcheson (Capilano), at Ustlawn (North Vancouver), at Chay-chil-wuk (Seymour Creek)—there was nothing at Lynn Creek—and more settlements up the inlet besides the one at Kum-kum-lye (Hastings Sawmill)."[13]

The litany of names he could hardly pronounce piqued Matthews's curiosity, and he extended his inquiries to other Squamish and Musqueam elders. He also consulted prominent local ethnologists Charles Hill-Tout and the Reverend Charles Tate, and eventually he compiled an illustrated map of Burrard Inlet, the North Shore and the peninsula that comprises the city of Vancouver. The map, titled *Indian Names for Familiar Places*, contained the Squamish names for sixty-five village sites and physical features. On January 13, 1933, Matthews convened a meeting of Squamish chiefs at the Rogers Building on Granville Street downtown to confirm his findings. Also in attendance were Frederick Ball, the Indian agent, and Andy Paull (Qoitchetahl), the secretary of the Squamish council. The chiefs put their stamp of approval on the map and thanked Major Matthews. "It is a story of our history which had been lost," said Chief Mathias Joe from the Capilano Reserve, "and is now largely recovered."[14]

The Squamish and the other Coast Salish nations had been insisting on title to their lands for many years. In 1906 Chief Joe Capilano from the North Shore, father of Mathias Joe, made a celebrated trip to England with two other BC chiefs to meet with King Edward VII. The purpose of the trip was to go over the heads of local politicians and appeal directly to the British crown to defend the rights of the Indigenous people. "We have no vote," Chief Capilano explained. "If we had it might be different, but as it is we are at the mercy of those who have the vote, and alas! They have no mercy."[15] The delegation travelled by train to eastern Canada and then by ship to Europe. On their way to the train station, the chiefs marched through the Vancouver streets accompanied by dozens of prominent Indigenous leaders and led by a brass band.[16] Once in London they had an audience with the king. Whether or not they presented their petition to him, and whether he made commitments to support their grievances, is a matter of debate. What is not debatable is that the First Nations' struggle to have their territorial rights recognized was a long one and it included assisting in the creation of the 1933 map.

Along with their own place names, the First Nations had stories that explained many physical features shown on the map. The Mohawk poet and performer Pauline Johnson collected some of these stories from Joe Capilano and published them in her book *Legends of Vancouver*. According to these tales, the Lions, the pair of peaks overlooking Burrard Inlet, are twin sisters, daughters of an ancient chief whose potlatch led to an enduring peace with nations from the northern coast; Siwash Rock, the tall stone pinnacle at the entrance to the harbour, is a young man who was turned to stone because he defied the most powerful god; and Deadman's Island in Coal Harbour was the site of a formidable battle between the local people and their northern enemies. The map reflects not just a different version of history but also a different understanding of the way the world worked.

Water Street was the core of old Gastown and Vancouver's "Main Street" when the city was incorporated in 1886.

CHAPTER ONE

Birth, and Rebirth

DEPENDING ON ONE'S POINT OF VIEW, the "founder" of the city of Vancouver might be a combative sawmill manager, a voluble saloon keeper or an arrogant railway tycoon. The sawmill owner was Edward Stamp, a sea captain from Northumberland who, impressed by what appeared to be the limitless abundance of the coastal forest, launched the British Columbia and Vancouver Island Spar, Lumber and Saw Mill Company on the south shore of Burrard Inlet in 1865. More succinctly known as Hastings Mill, this enterprise provided the economic lifeblood for the tiny community of loggers and drinkers that eventually became the city.

The saloon keeper was John Deighton, known to his customers as Gassy Jack for his tendency to run off at the mouth. "He was a man without education," remarked the historian F.W. Howay, "but that did not prevent him from airing his views on any and every subject . . ."[17] Deighton arrived by canoe from New Westminster in September 1867, washing up not far from Stamp's mill with his young Squamish wife, Quahail-ya, a barrel of whiskey and a primitive business plan. Offering free drinks to anyone who would help him, he soon had his Globe House saloon up and running, serving the thirsty millhands. Gastown, the jerry-built settlement that grew up around Deighton's establishment, was the original core of what emerged as downtown Vancouver.

At the other end of the social spectrum to Gassy Jack was the railway tycoon William Cornelius Van Horne, plump, prosperous and ever so much the man in charge. It was Van Horne, the general manager of the Canadian Pacific Railway, who selected Vancouver as the western terminus for his transcontinental line—he even chose its name—thereby ensuring the city's future as Canada's entrepôt on the Pacific and gateway to the great world beyond. Any one of this disparate trio might reasonably lay claim to being the "founding father" of Vancouver.

Unless, of course, you consider August Jack's people, the Indigenous residents, who, as the 1933 map made clear, populated the inlet in significant numbers long before the arrival of outsiders. These Coast Salish people—known today as the Musqueam, Squamish and Tsleil-Waututh First Nations—used the waters of the Fraser River and Burrard Inlet to fish, hunt seals and waterfowl, and gather shellfish. In the dense forest and open marshes that covered the site of the future city, they tracked deer, bear and smaller animals, and gathered fruits and edible plants. The temperate climate nurtured the tall trees that provided the wood they used to manufacture their lodges, canoes, utensils and monumental art. Again, as the map made clear, they named all the major landmarks, from Siwash Rock (Slah-kay-ulsh) to Kitsilano Beach (Skwayoos) to Point Grey (Ulksen) to Brockton Point (Paapee-ak), and they inhabited several villages and seasonal camps within what are now the city limits.

When the twenty-three-year-old Spanish navigator José María Narváez appeared off Point Grey in the summer of 1791, several canoes of Musqueam came out from a village at the mouth of the Fraser River to trade. Narváez's expedition, which consisted of forty-one officers and crew aboard the 11-metre sloop *Santa Saturnina* and an accompanying longboat, was the first European venture into what the Spanish called the Gran Canal de Nuestra Señora del Rosario la Marinera, what came to be known as the Strait of Georgia or, more recently, the Salish Sea. The Gran Canal held out the possibility that it was the entrance to the fabled Northwest Passage—the Spanish called it the Strait of Anián—connecting the Pacific and Atlantic Oceans across the top of North America. Such a passage, if it existed, would allow Europeans to access more easily the rich trade of the Far East. The Musqueam, knowing as they did the convoluted geography of the coast, could have told Narváez that he was on a wild goose chase, but the language barrier made an exchange of information difficult. The *Santa Saturnina* continued on its way around the tip of Point Grey into Burrard Inlet, where Narváez anchored briefly off Spanish Banks and then again off the northern shore just outside the narrow entrance to what appeared to be a long channel. The passage looked like it might lead some-where promising, but Narváez was impatient to continue his investigations of the Gran Canal so he pushed on to the northwest, leaving the future site of Vancouver unexamined.

A year later it was the turn of British mariners. Captain George Vancouver had been sent to the northwest coast to achieve two objectives: first, to negotiate a truce with the Spanish, and second, to settle one way or another whether the rumoured northwest passage actually existed. He had two vessels under his command, the *Discovery* and the *Chatham,* with a total of 145 sailors and marines. After a year-long voyage from England, the two ships arrived off northern California in mid-April 1792 to begin their survey of the coastline. Initially Vancouver worked from the ships, but once his vessels entered the Strait of Juan de Fuca, the coast became more complicated, and the meticulous inlet-by-inlet investigation was carried out by the men in longboats. On June 12, two of these boats, one containing Vancouver himself, rowed around Point Grey into Burrard Inlet (named during the visit after Captain Harry Burrard of the Royal Navy). Crossing to the northern shore, they located and entered the narrow opening that Narváez had seen the summer before. The accounts left by the British are not exact, but it seems that the boats were welcomed by two groups of First Nations in canoes. One group were Squamish people from Homulcheson, their village at the mouth of the Capilano River. The other were Musqueam from Xway'xway, a beachfront site known today as Lumberman's Arch in Stanley Park. Many years later Andy Paull described the scene to Major Matthews as he had heard it from the elders: "Our people threw in greeting before him [Vancouver] clouds of snow white feathers which rose, wafted in the air aimlessly about, then fell like flurries of snow to the water's surface, and rested there like white rose petals scattered before a bride. It must have been a pretty welcome."[18]

As it opened before him, the inner harbour would have seemed an auspicious lead in Vancouver's search for a passage. To his right the land was low and wooded right down to the shoreline. To his left a wall of forested mountains rose almost from the water's edge, their flanks broken by a series of rivers and streams tumbling down to the sea. Vancouver must have recognized the value of the dense forest that one day would provide stout timbers for his own navy and fuel an industry to support a community that would take his name. For the moment, however, he had to admit that the inlet was a dead end, as chimerical as all the other nooks and crannies he had investigated. After camping for one night on the south shore opposite the entrance to Indian Arm, the two boats returned through the narrows and continued their survey into Howe Sound and as far north as Jervis Inlet, before heading back to the mother ships, which were waiting in Birch Bay.

By this time it was June 21, and as they neared Point Grey they encountered, much to their surprise, a pair of vessels flying Spanish colours. These were the *Sutil*, commanded by Dionisio Alcalá-Galiano, and the *Mexicana* under Cayetano Valdés. The Spanish were back in the Gran Canal conducting their own follow-up of Narváez's visit. Captain Vancouver boarded the *Sutil* and shared breakfast with Galiano and his officers. The two commanders agreed to pursue their exploration of the coast together. But before the Europeans set sail for the north, the Spanish sent a pair of boats to assure themselves that Burrard Inlet, which they called Canal de Floridablanca, did indeed lead nowhere. Nine days had passed since Vancouver's reconnaissance. The Spanish made their way through the First Narrows and as far as the head of the inlet. Unlike the British, they investigated the length of Indian Arm, where they encountered a camp of Tsleil-Waututh people with whom they had a short meeting. Then they retraced their steps and departed the main inlet after recording that the local people called it "Sasamat."

The world that these European mariners entered in the 1790s was not the same world they would have seen had they arrived even a few years earlier. George Vancouver remarked on the number of deserted villages he and his officers observed. A smallpox epidemic had swept through the southern coast in the 1780s, killing as much as 80 per cent of the population in some areas. (Another epidemic may have followed in about 1800, and subsequent ones came later in the century, culminating in the smallpox outbreak of 1862, which claimed an estimated one-third of the First Nations population of coastal BC.) When August Jack Khahtsahlano told Major Matthews that "about a million" First Nations people once lived in the area, he was estimating—overestimating, actually—the much larger population that had existed before the white man's diseases took their toll. In Burrard Inlet, for example, the Tsleil-Waututh by some accounts numbered about ten thousand people pre-contact, a total that had plummeted to one hundred individuals by the 1830s. The Squamish suffered a comparable decline.

One of the largest settlements on the future site of Vancouver was an ancient Musqueam village and cemetery on the opposite side of the Point Grey peninsula, on the north arm of the Fraser River. Known to the Musqueam as c̓əsnaʔəm, and to outsiders as the Marpole Midden, or the Great Fraser Midden, it dates back several thousand years, though its presence only became known to archaeologists and historians when a road-building gang "rediscovered" it in 1884. The site contained an extensive shell midden, which, when excavated by archaeologists, revealed stone and bone tools, human and animal remains, and other artifacts. In 1933 it was declared a National Historic Site.

The midden site is located upstream from a village encountered by Simon Fraser when he arrived in early July 1808. Fraser was a Nor'Wester, an employee of the Montreal-based North West Company of fur traders. In their quest for furs the traders had pushed across the continent and were now seeking a navigable route between their interior posts and the Pacific. Thinking that the river (which now bears his name) might offer such a route, Fraser had set off from Fort George (Prince George) to explore it all the way to the sea. According to his own account, when he landed at the Musqueam village he found "but a few old men and women; the others fled into the woods upon our approach." Fraser was investigating the shed-style plank dwellings occupied by the Musqueam when one of the people who had been showing him around warned him that he should get away before the others returned. "Having spent one hour looking about this place we went to embark," he recorded in his journal, "when we found the tide had ebbed, and left our canoe on dry land. We had, therefore, to drag it out to the water some distance. The Natives, no doubt seeing our difficulty, assumed courage, and began to make their appearance from every direction [...] howling like so many wolves and brandishing their war clubs. At last we got into deep water, and embarked."[19] After continuing downstream to within sight of the open ocean, Fraser decided to turn back and returned up the river to the interior without further hostility. It is possible that the Musqueam were so hostile because word had reached them that days earlier Fraser had stolen a canoe from some First Nations people near the future site of New Westminster. His own canoes were so battered they had become useless, and Fraser may simply have been borrowing a replacement that he meant to return. Whatever the case, it was not encouraging that relations between the Musqueam and outsiders began with a theft.

The Musqueam ranged widely across the peninsula between the river and Burrard Inlet that we now know as Point Grey, which Major Matthews's map of place names called Ulksen. They made seasonal visits to English Bay, where they had resource sites at Spanish Banks and Jericho, and Stanley Park. And they occupied Xway'xway, the substantial village site at Lumberman's Arch. In 1888 road builders discovered a large midden of crushed shells covering a 1.6-hectare site at Xway'xway to a depth of up to 2.5 metres. Evidence suggests that Indigenous people occupied the site for thousands of years before contact, and that other sites in what is now the park were also used for gathering food, for spiritual practices and for burying the dead. The territories of the Musqueam, Squamish and Tsleil-Waututh First Nations overlapped each other so that members of the latter two nations also frequented the park and other sites around what is now Vancouver. In the words of the geographer Cole Harris, the Lower Mainland was "a Native place": an ancient homeland with a long history.[20]

FOLLOWING THE VISITS BY GEORGE VANCOUVER, the Spanish and Simon Fraser, outsiders did not return to Point Grey and Burrard Inlet for several decades. The Hudson's Bay Company built Fort Langley in 1827, about 50 kilometres from the mouth of the Fraser, and the coastal people travelled upriver to trade there. The discovery of gold in the gravel bars of the Fraser Canyon brought thousands of prospectors to the interior, an influx that led to the creation of the colony of British Columbia in 1858 and its capital city, Queensborough (New Westminster), located on the north side of the Fraser about 20 kilometres inland from its mouth. But Burrard Inlet was distant from all this activity, off the beaten path for the traders and gold seekers. As a result, outside interest did not refocus on the future site of Vancouver until the end of the 1850s.

In 1859 Captain George Henry Richards, in command of the steam sloop HMS *Plumper*, carried out a survey of Burrard Inlet for the British Admiralty. The vessel's chief engineer, Francis Brockton, acting on a report from local First Nations, located a seam of coal on the south shore of the inner harbour near the foot of what is now Bute Street. Richards named the spot "Coal Harbour" and, on his map, labelled the entire future downtown as the "Coal Peninsula." The Admiralty was keen on locating sources of coal to fuel its steam vessels. The seam turned out to be of inferior quality and was never mined. Nonetheless, a few years later it attracted the interest of the first people who actually pre-empted land on the future site of Vancouver. John Morton had arrived in New Westminster from England, in 1862, along with his cousin, Samuel Brighouse, and a friend, William Hailstone, intending to make for the goldfields upriver. The three Englishmen instead heard about the coal deposits and, under the terms of the Pre-emption Proclamation issued two years earlier, they obtained rights to more than 200 hectares of land next door to Stanley Park, encompassing most of what became the West End. Under the terms of the pre-emption, the trio had to build and occupy a habitation on the lot, formally designated District Lot 185, which they did, planning to mine the coal to make bricks—and the site became known as the "Brickmaker's Claim." The cabin, occupied by John Morton, was located on Burrard Inlet just west of what is now Burrard Street. Thought to be hopelessly naïve for investing in land so distant from settlement, the speculators were ridiculed as "the Three Greenhorns." Although they did not develop the site themselves, time and the escalation of real estate values gave them the last laugh.

Earlier a detachment of Royal Engineers, under the command of Colonel Richard Moody, had arrived in British Columbia to carry out public works and maintain the peace in the new colony. Stationed at New Westminster on the Fraser River, Moody decided that it was important to secure his "back door" from possible attack. To this end he had his men build two trails to Burrard Inlet, one to the future Port Moody and a second to English Bay, and he set aside several chunks of land as government reserves for future townsites and defensive installations. These included the site of what is now Stanley Park, the core of what became Vancouver's downtown, and naval reserves at Jericho and the tip of Point Grey, where the University of British Columbia now stands. With his eye on the main chance, Moody also pre-empted lots in the vicinity of these reserves and shared them with several friends—what historian Fred Howay characterized as "the land-grabbing activities of the Colonel"[21]—though none of these lots were settled by their original owners, whose tenure eventually lapsed.

The Three Greenhorns—*(left to right)* William Hailstone, Sam Brighouse, John Morton—were the original owners of what is now the West End.
J.D. Hall photo, City of Vancouver Archives, AM54-S4-: Port P775

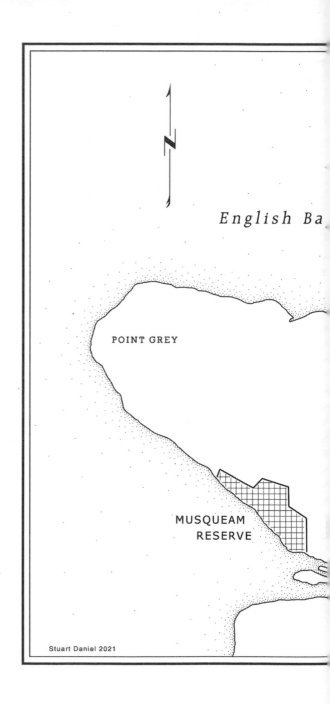

Stuart Daniel 2021

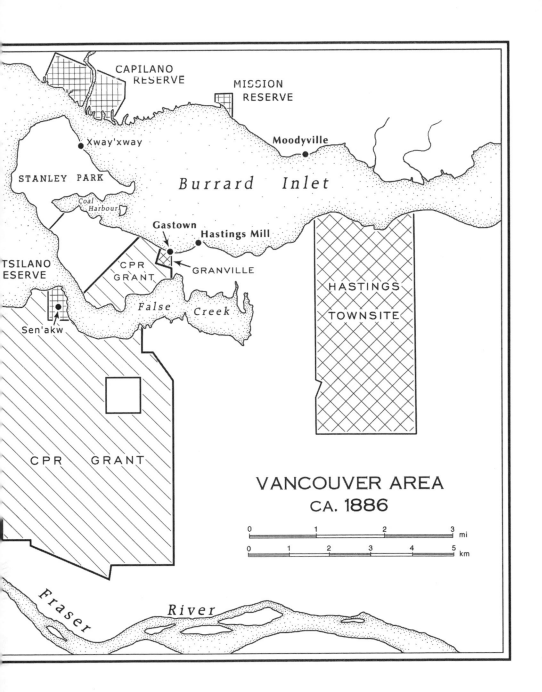

CAPILANO
RESERVE

MISSION
RESERVE

Xway'xway

Moodyville

STANLEY PARK

Burrard Inlet

Coal
Harbour

Gastown

Hastings Mill

TSILANO
ESERVE

CPR
GRANT

GRANVILLE

Sen'akw

False   Creek

HASTINGS

TOWNSITE

CPR   GRANT

VANCOUVER AREA
CA. 1886

0   1   2   3 mi

0   1   2   3   4   5 km

Fraser   River

The early pre-emptors included Robert Burnaby, Moody's private secretary and a member of the colonial legislature, and Henry Crease, the colony's attorney general. These officials and their cronies took it for granted that they were speculating with empty land. Robert Preston, one of the men hired to clear a site for Edward Stamp's mill, described what he saw when he arrived in Burrard Inlet in 1865: "On the south side of the inlet there was not a single habitation or white man, or, in fact, in any part of the peninsula. A solid unbroken belt of timber extended from Stanley Park, or the Naval Reserve, to Port Moody. Not a single tree had been cut nor was there the mark of the axe upon any trees standing or lying."[22] Of course this was not true. There was "not a single habitation" only if the First Nations' villages and resource sites were ignored. But eventually almost all these native places were built over or otherwise destroyed, replaced by waterfront industry, parks and residential development.

By 1865, Captain Stamp had raised enough capital in England to launch his new sawmill company. He selected a site for the mill just inside the First Narrows on the south shore of Burrard Inlet near Brockton Point. This was one of the lots earlier set aside as a military reserve, but the colonial government agreed to allow Stamp a chunk of it for his logging and milling operation. When a surveyor, J.B. Launders, arrived to lay out Stamp's property, he discovered that part of it overlapped the village of Xway'xway, whose residents, he reported, were "very distrustful of my purpose."[23] As things turned out, Xway'xway was spared, at least for the moment. Stamp decided that the tidal current at the initial site was too strong and the shoals too dangerous, so he requested, and received, another site about 3 kilometres to the east, at the foot of what would become Dunlevy Street. The beach was a Coast Salish seasonal camp known as Kumkumalay ("big leaf maple trees"). By November his new mill—known locally as Stamp's Mill—was in business. Delays in the delivery of equipment meant that Stamp could not produce sawn lumber for a couple of years, but he was able to export spars, the long, heavy timbers used for ships' masts. This wood came from a camp established by the logging contractor Jeremiah (Jerry) Rogers on the south shore of English Bay near the Musqueam site at E-yal-mough. The place became known as Jerry's Cove, later Jericho. With the permission of the colonial governor, Frederick Seymour, Rogers logged the government naval reserve at Jericho and at a second camp at Kitsilano Beach, and his timber was shipped by Stamp to distant ports in Great Britain, France, China and Russia. Across Burrard Inlet on the North Shore, another mill had been producing lumber off and on for two years. It began to flourish under the ownership of Sewell Moody, who took over early in 1865, and also began exporting lumber to various foreign ports. With the emergence of the two mills, Burrard Inlet's economic future as a centre of logging and international shipping was set.

Edward Stamp's role in the economic opportunities that he did so much to stimulate was terminated abruptly at the beginning of 1869. By all accounts he was not an easy man to get along with. (He "seems to have been a somewhat difficult character," is how his biographer, W. Kaye Lamb, delicately put it.[24]) Stamp and his suppliers, including Jerry Rogers, began a litigious feud over who owned the timber rights to the reserves; in truth, the government may have promised them to both sides. Then Stamp's London backers grew impatient with him as well, and he lost control of the mill. He returned to England to raise money for new ventures and died there of a heart attack, aged fifty-eight. The mill passed into the hands of a new consortium, which incorporated as the Hastings Mill Company and installed a new manager, Captain James Raymur. Less tolerant of the boozy community at Gastown, Raymur wanted the place cleaned up and squatters like Jack Deighton evicted. Instead the colonial government dispatched a survey crew to make the community official. On March 1, 1870, Gastown became the townsite of Granville, named for the British colonial secretary.

The new town encompassed 15 hectares of land stretching from today's Cambie Street on the west to Carrall Street on the east between Hastings and Water Streets. Six weeks later, lots were offered at auction. Among the bidders was Deighton, who bought the southwest corner of Water and Carrall, where he erected a new hotel, the two-storey Deighton House. Gassy Jack, the unofficial "mayor" of Granville, had gone from being an unsavoury squatter to one of the town's leading businessmen. When he died five years later, at just forty-four years old, his obituary read: "Although uncouth occasionally in his language, he possessed a good heart."[25] His wife Quahail-ya may not have agreed. According to Squamish accounts, she fled her husband and went to live on the North Shore.

Granville, with a population of 243 people in 1881, was a diverse community of millhands, fishermen, saloon keepers, sailors, sex workers and loggers. The main thoroughfare, the only one at first, was Water Street, which hugged the shoreline so closely that at high tide the seawater ran in beneath its plank surface. William Gallagher, an early resident, described it as nothing more than "a wagon trail which corkscrewed a sinuous way in and out among the stumps."[26] Deer passed through the tiny settlement at night, their hooves softly tapping on the boards.[27] The clearing at the corner of Carrall, today called Maple Tree Square but known to the Squamish as

1

2

1 The earliest photograph of the Hastings Mill, 1872. For many years the mill was Vancouver's main employer and most significant enterprise. City of Vancouver Archives, AM54-S4-: CVA 371-3178

2 This painting of historic Gastown by Gordon Miller shows the buildings along Water Street and the Hastings Mill in the background. The mill was one of the few buildings that survived the horrific fire of 1886. The other structures in the painting would have been consumed by the flames. Painting courtesy Gordon Miller

Luk'luk'I ("grove of maple trees"), was the low ground where the Indigenous people portaged their canoes between the Inlet and False Creek. At its western end, Water Street dwindled to a rough trail leading through the forest to the bluff at what is now Burrard Street. At night the frogs in the surrounding swamps set up a noisy chorus; locals called them "British Columbia nightingales."

Granville boasted several drinking spots and a brothel managed by Vancouver's first madam, Birdie Stewart. Residents originated from all points of the globe. William Gallagher recalled that one block behind Water Street there "was a row of Chinese cabins and some other occupants of ill repute."[28] Portuguese Joe Silvey, a whaler and fisherman from the Azores, owned a saloon, and across the street his countryman Gregorio Fernandez ran a general store, as did Louis Gold and his wife Emma, the first Jewish residents. Josephine and Philip Sullivan, an African-American couple from California, operated a restaurant. George Black, a Scot, kept a pet bear chained outside his butcher shop. Logger Jerry Rogers hailed from New Brunswick. Eihu, a Kanaka from the Hawaiian Islands, lived with his family in what is now Coal Harbour. Chinook Jargon—the lingua franca of the coastal fur trade, which was a mixture of French and several Indigenous languages—was more likely than English to be spoken in the street, and in the barroom.

Like every frontier community, Granville had a lawman, Constable Jonathan Miller. He was appointed in 1871, at the same time that the town acquired a courthouse, erected next door to Deighton's hotel. Miller had been a logger, supplying Stamp's mill with wood from the Stanley Park peninsula. Once appointed constable, he lived in the courthouse with his family. A two-room log jail stood next door, its cells often filled but never locked.

IT SEEMED UNLIKELY that this beachside huddle of shabby saloons, tilting shacks and rutted streets would ever achieve anything beyond its status as a service provider for the sawmill that supported most of its inhabitants. But then the railway came to town, and everything changed. A transcontinental rail link with eastern Canada was the promise that lured British Columbia into Confederation in 1871. Residents waited impatiently for the Canadian Pacific Railway (CPR) to be completed, and finally it was, on November 7, 1885, when a party of dignitaries drove home the "last spike" at Craigellachie in the mountains west of Revelstoke. Eight months later the first scheduled passenger train from the East rumbled into Port Moody at the head of Burrard Inlet, the designated terminus of the line. Or so it had been supposed. But for the previous four years

Cornelius Van Horne, the railway company's managing director, had been busy negotiating behind the scenes to obtain a different site, 20 kilometres farther down the inlet at Granville. Port Moody did not suit the railway for several reasons. It did not have the space required for extensive waterfront development. To reach it, ships had to navigate the tidal currents at the First and Second Narrows. And most important, the land was already owned by speculators, whereas at the Granville site Van Horne hoped to persuade the province to give him what land he needed, plus plenty more with which to speculate. Vancouver had begun with a giant real estate deal—and property speculation has been a major source of wealth ever since.

In 1885, Van Horne made a deal with the provincial government to locate the terminus at Granville in return for a land grant of 6,275 acres (2,539.4 ha) covering most of the downtown peninsula and a vast swath of forest south of False Creek. (In today's terms the grant ran from Burrard Inlet to False Creek between Burrard and Carrall Streets, and south of False Creek between Trafalgar and Ontario Streets almost as far as Southwest Marine Drive.) As well, the CPR convinced private landowners on either side of the grant to kick in some of their lands, raising the total to 2,610.2 hectares. It was standard practice for the railway to secure grants of public land in return for building its facilities, but nowhere else in western Canada was the grant as generous as it was in Vancouver.[29]

Initially Van Horne wished to route his rail line across False Creek and out to a terminal on the south shore of English Bay at Jericho. To this end, the company tried to obtain land on the naval reserve there and to expropriate additional land on Kitsilano Point that had been designated a Squamish Indian Reserve. In the case of the Indian Reserve, the CPR offered to pay $1,800 for the entire 80-acre plot, a derisory amount compared to the $60,000 that Indian Department officials thought was fair. To their credit, these officials, on behalf of the Squamish, rejected the CPR offer.[30] At this point the city offered the railway tax concessions if it would locate its yards and shops on the north side of False Creek, and the company put aside its plans for Kits Point.[31]

Speculators who had backed the wrong horse by investing in Port Moody were outraged that their town had been "robbed" of the terminus. They tried to block the railway's acquisition of the properties it needed to extend the line along the south shore of the inlet to Granville. It took several court cases and some high-pressure arm-twisting by Van Horne, but in the end the railway was allowed to expropriate the land it needed.[32]

Van Horne's land deal had enormous implications for the future of the city. For many years it was, if not a company town, a company-influenced town. "It is the CPR's town," remarked one American visitor in 1893. "The railroad controls everything . . ."[33] Because of the railway, an economy once reliant on logging and sawmilling flourished as a transportation hub. Vancouver emerged as Canada's portal to the Pacific and one of the most significant ports on the west coast of the continent. It was also the gateway to a vast coastal hinterland: as the forest and fishing industries expanded along the BC coast, Vancouver would emerge as the corporate headquarters for this industrial outback.

For decades the CPR was Vancouver's major employer. Many of its downtown streets bear the names of prominent company executives, and at least one company representative always managed to get elected to city council to ensure that corporate interests were protected. Much of the waterfront, in both Burrard Inlet and False Creek, was occupied by rail-related operations. The company developed residential districts on its own properties and influenced every significant public land use decision in the city, an influence that continued, however diminished, all the way into the twenty-first century.

With the imminent arrival of the railway, residents expected great things for their community. At a public meeting in mid-January 1886, they decided to incorporate as a city so as to better manage the development that was sure to come. The meeting attendees chose a committee to draw up terms of incorporation, which were submitted to the provincial legislature. The chief impediment to city status was the proposed name, Vancouver, which earlier had been suggested by William Van Horne and endorsed by the incorporation committee. According to R.H. Alexander, manager of the Hastings Mill and chair of the committee, Van Horne was convinced that the association with Vancouver Island would help people to locate the city, as well as linking it with the famous British mariner who had visited the site in 1792. "The name Vancouver strikes everybody in Ottawa and elsewhere most favourably in approximately locating the point at once," he wrote to a colleague.[34] In his arrogance, Van Horne did not consider that anyone would take offence at his appropriating the right to christen the city. Or perhaps he just didn't care.

During the incorporation debate in the legislature on March 19, several elected members wondered what was wrong with retaining the name Granville. Robert Beaven, a former provincial premier, was miffed that "an American citizen who had set his foot for the first time in British Columbia two years ago [i.e., Van Horne] proposed to alter the name to Vancouver."

Theodore Davie, a Victoria lawyer and future premier, expressed the common view that the new name would occasion "endless confusion" with Vancouver Island and with two communities of the same name in Washington State. Other members were chagrined that the people's representatives had less power to name the city than a private corporation. Perhaps, suggested one member, the city should be called not Vancouver but Van Horne. Speaking in favour of incorporation, John Robson, the influential member from New Westminster, warned that the residents of Granville wanted the new name and by not accepting it the legislature would be refusing incorporation. It was quite appropriate, Robson argued, to name the new city after the "great navigator who had discovered Burrard Inlet."[35] In the end the legislature agreed to the request and on April 6, 1886, the City of Vancouver was incorporated. It encompassed an area bounded on the north by Burrard Inlet, on the south by Sixteenth Avenue, on the east by Nanaimo Street and on the west by Alma Street. A pedestrian could stroll across it in less than an hour. Beyond these limits, only a few scattered homesteads and logging camps interrupted the unbroken forest that First Nations people had occupied for centuries.

The exception was the Hastings Townsite, located to the east, where the government had set aside a land reserve at the Second Narrows early in the 1860s. Settlement began in 1865, when contractor John Scott completed the Douglas Road from New Westminster. Uncomfortable as the muddy track was to travel, the shores of Burrard Inlet began to attract beach-goers that summer, and John Robson, a newspaper editor as well as a politician, suggested that the spot be called Brighton, after the famous British resort town. (The Tsleil-Waututh people from the North Shore knew the site as Khanamoot, where they left their canoes while they followed a trail to Burnaby Lake and across to the Fraser.) Accepting the new name, Oliver Hocking and Fred Houston opened the Brighton Hotel in a clearing beside the water—the first hotel on Burrard Inlet. For two years the humble resort catered to swimming parties, excursionists and the few travellers who used the Douglas Road.

By the summer of 1867, traffic was heavy enough that W.R. Lewis, a New Westminster hotelier, began operating a scheduled stagecoach service to Brighton. In 1869 another hotelier, Maximilian Michaud, purchased the Brighton Hotel, and it was not long before the small community became known locally as Maxie's. Michaud advertised his hotel as "the Most Fashionable Watering Place in British Columbia." His wife Frisadie was part Aboriginal, part Kanaka, a common intermixing on the coast.

The Brighton Hotel in the Hastings Townsite was the first hotel on Burrard Inlet when it opened in 1865.
City of Vancouver Archives, AM54-S4-: Dist P13

That summer, the first lots were sold in the newly surveyed townsite, which stretched between Nanaimo Street and Boundary Road, and south from the inlet to Twenty-ninth Avenue. Officially the site was called Hastings after the retiring naval admiral G.F. Hastings. Only a winding path connected it to Captain Stamp's sawmill and the community of Gastown/ Granville—until 1876, when the provincial government contracted Arthur Herring to build a wagon road roughly following the shoreline. Before that, travellers had to use the new steam ferry, *Sea Foam*, launched by Captain James van Bramer to connect the three nodes of activity on the Inlet: Moodyville, Stamp's Mill and Hastings. When Vancouver was created in 1886, the Hastings Townsite kept itself separate and remained so for over two decades. A bit of an anomaly was Hastings Park, a large chunk of land located in the townsite which belonged to the city as of 1889, when the province transferred it. Hastings was Vancouver's second largest park, after Stanley Park, and in 1910 it became home to the Vancouver Exhibition, an annual agricultural/industrial fair, known since 1947 as the Pacific National Exhibition (PNE).

ON MAY 3, 1886, Vancouverites turned out to elect their first mayor and council. The mechanisms of electoral democracy were not yet in place. There was no list of electors and no real way of determining who could vote. As a result, fraud and intimidation were commonplace. It was not necessary to be a resident to vote, only to be at least twenty years of age and to own or lease property in the city, which meant that an absentee landowner could cast a ballot.[36] (Similarly, candidates for public office—mayor and aldermen—were required to own property worth $1,000 or lease property worth $2,000.) The "establishment" candidate was R.H. Alexander. He had come out to BC from Ontario in 1862 with a party of Overlanders to try his luck in the Cariboo goldfields. He had started work at the Hastings Mill as a storekeeper and worked his way up to manager. As a long-time resident with ties to business interests in Victoria, he looked like a shoo-in for mayor, especially since his opponent, Malcolm MacLean, a real estate agent, had been in the city for less than four months. But unhappily for Alexander and his supporters, the mill was embroiled in a contentious labour dispute. Millhands had gone on strike for a ten-hour day (instead of the usual twelve), and Alexander had alienated the workers with his determination not to give in to their demands. On election day a boatload of voters arrived from Victoria to support Alexander. He also mustered sixty of his Chinese employees to walk over from the mill to the polling station. But these were not enough to counter the pro-MacLean faction, who chased the Chinese employees back to the mill—according to the city's charter, neither "Chinese" nor "Aboriginals" were allowed to vote anyway—and used their own dirty tricks to influence the outcome. "One man had a lease to a portion of a building on Cordova Street, and came down to vote with the lease in his hand, and voted on it," explained William Gallagher. "Mr. MacLean's committee persuaded him to leave the lease with them; it was drawn up on the usual form with a space for the name, and I think fifty men must have voted on that lease. After one man had voted, the next voter's name was written on a slip of paper, and pasted in the space on the lease where the name appeared."[37] When the ballots were counted, MacLean had outpolled Alexander 242 to 227.

Once the results were known—ten aldermen were also elected, two from each of the five wards—the mayor-elect made his way to the Sunnyside Hotel on Water Street, where his supporters had been imbibing glasses of "artificial enthusiasm" all afternoon. He spoke from the balcony to a boisterous crowd, then climbed into the back of an open wagon to begin a triumphal procession around Gastown. On Cordova Street the parade encountered a fallen log across its path; the men simply lifted the wagon, with MacLean in it, over the log and continued on their way back to the hotel, where celebrations went on into the night.[38] Not everyone was happy, of course. Some of Alexander's supporters fired off a petition to Victoria alleging voter fraud. But before anything came of their complaints, catastrophe struck the city, forcing political rivalries into the background.

MID-MORNING ON SUNDAY, June 13, 1886, a crew was clearing land to make way for the construction of a railway roundhouse on False Creek, at what is now the foot of Drake Street. Vancouver was sweltering in a heat wave. Lack of rain and unseasonably high temperatures rendered the bush tinder dry. As the men worked, a breeze blowing across the peninsula from the west gusted into a small gale. Sparks swirled up from a clearing fire and blew into the adjacent underbrush, which burst into flame. Defying the men's efforts to beat back the fire with buckets of water and blankets, the blaze swept across the peninsula toward Gastown, feeding on the slash and fallen timber that littered the ground. At 1:30 p.m. the alarm went up: a fire is coming, run for your lives![39] "The city did not burn," said William Gallagher, who was an eyewitness to the frightening events. "It was consumed by flame; the buildings simply melted before the fiery blast." The flames blew down Cambie hill and rushed upon the settlement, devouring everything in their path as they raced eastward down Water Street. "Never was there such a fire before," reported the *Vancouver Advertiser.* "No one ever saw anything so frantically rapid or terribly complete. The startled populace barely heard the cry of 'fire' when they were compelled to flee for their lives."[40] Gallagher recalled that "the fire went down the sidewalk on old Hastings Road so rapidly that people flying before it had to leave the burning sidewalk and take to the road; and the fire travelled down that wooden sidewalk faster than a man could run." Everyone remarked on how quickly the flames had spread.

As the city burned, people fled south across False Creek or north into the waters of Burrard Inlet. Some clambered into boats or canoes; others fashioned rafts out of anything that would float and paddled out to the *Robert Kerr*, a sailing barque blown eastward from its anchorage in Coal Harbour by the strong wind. Purchased at auction by Captain William Soule, it was more or less derelict, and at first the resident caretaker refused to allow anyone to board. "The stupid man said he had orders to keep people off, that was what he was paid for," recalled Mrs. Emily Strathie, one of the refugees.

"Threats were made to throw him in the water before he could be induced to let the rope ladder down."[41] Eventually the *Kerr* provided a haven for three hundred or so people, including Mayor MacLean, who escaped the inferno in a dugout canoe. Many others were rescued by Squamish paddlers who came by canoe from their villages on the North Shore, or by vessels from Moodyville.

As suddenly as it had begun, it was over. As the flames whipped through Gastown and bore down on the Hastings Mill, the wind suddenly dropped and shifted direction. By three o'clock the fire had petered out, leaving Vancouver a smoking wasteland of ash. Along Water Street only one building survived, the Regina Hotel, perhaps because its quick-witted owner, Ed Cosgrove, managed to cover the roof of the three-storey building with wet blankets. More than twenty people died, some of whose bodies had burned beyond recognition. Remains were brought to a building next door to the Bridge Hotel on Westminster Avenue (Main Street), where they were wrapped in blankets and laid out on a makeshift table. A note was attached to each parcel identifying where the contents had been discovered.

Late in the afternoon Mayor MacLean rowed from the *Kerr* over to the dock at the mill to begin to assess the damage. He dispatched city clerk Thomas McGuigan on horseback to New Westminster with a message to be cabled to Prime Minister John A. Macdonald in Ottawa: "Our city is ashes. Three thousand people homeless. Can you send us any government aid?"[42] (Two weeks later Macdonald finally answered that his government would contribute $5,000. The CPR, who in today's more litigious environment might be held responsible for the blaze, committed $3,000.) MacLean may have been a surprise mayor but he responded to the crisis with energy and determination. He ordered that survivors in need should congregate at the south end of the Westminster Bridge to meet three wagons bringing emergency supplies from New Westminster. The wagons arrived that evening to distribute relief to the small tent community of evacuees that sprang up on the shore of False Creek. As darkness fell, Gallagher described "a mass of glimmering lights in the darkness of the night, smouldering embers and smoke. The city had been swept clean . . ."[43]

News of the fire flashed across the continent. On Wednesday a first-hand report appeared on the front page of the *New York Times*, emphasizing how quickly the city had been overwhelmed. The flames seemed to fill the air and "even after leaving the houses the danger was not over, for every road had become an avenue of fire, the falling timbers and stumps on each side of the road glowing with fire and proving as serious a menace to the fugitives as the burning houses of the doomed city."[44] Four days after the fire, James Ross, editor of the *Vancouver Daily News*, published a special edition of his newspaper. "Probably never since the days of Pompeii and

Herculaneum," Ross grandiloquently informed his readers, "was a town WIPED OUT OF EXISTENCE so completely and suddenly as was Vancouver on Sunday." The *News* had been burned out of its Gastown office, but Ross had borrowed the presses of the *British Columbian* in New Westminster to print his single-page "fire" edition.

Much like the enterprising Ross, the city itself did not pause to lament its fate. George H. Keefer, who was clearing the CPR right of way when the fire struck, recalled that "the day after the fire I saw a burned out hotel keeper selling whiskey from a bottle on his hip pocket and a glass in his hand, his counter being a sack of potatoes."[45] Donald McGregor, an early historian of the disaster, notes that "the fire was a tragedy but it was not a defeat. At three o'clock on Monday morning teams were delivering lumber on the ash-strewn streets and by daybreak the city was rising again." And why not? Lives were lost and buildings destroyed, but the assets that had brought about the creation of Vancouver in the first place remained: a capacious harbour, a plentiful supply of rich timber and a railway connection to the East. "Though disfigured," boasted the *Advertiser*, "we are still in the ring."[46] (Many years later a man named John Mole Keefer claimed to be the person responsible for the Great Fire. When he died in 1953, the *Sun* reported that Keefer had earlier confessed to setting the small fire that had sparked the blaze, then leaving it unattended. When they realized what they had done, Keefer and two companions swore never to tell anyone, a promise that he kept until late in his life.[47])

Given that the settlement was such a ramshackle place to begin with, it wasn't so difficult to get it back on its feet. In spite of the deaths of two dozen or so victims, the fire came to seem like a golden opportunity to transform the frontier outpost into a modern city. "The fire seemed to be a positive benefit," according to an article in the *West Shore*, a Portland-based magazine that reported on the city in May 1889, "and in a few weeks all traces of it had been removed and the town presented a vastly better appearance." Residents rebuilt with amazing speed. The shores of the inlet echoed with the sounds of hammer and saw as houses and business establishments went up almost overnight. One hotel on Hastings Street reportedly took just three days to construct. Before the fire Vancouver's population had numbered a few hundred. By the end of 1886 it had climbed to 2,000, and by the official census of 1891 it was 13,709. There is a famous photograph of city council convened at two tables arranged in front of a tent on Water Street with a hand-scrawled sign reading "City Hall" affixed to the tent post. The photograph is staged; by the time it was taken, three months after the fire, city government had already found lodgings for itself in a warehouse on Powell Street. But the image symbolizes the determination with which the community got back to work in the wake of its worst disaster, transforming itself in a few short years from a roughneck logging village at the edge of nowhere into a modern city in touch with the world.

The recovery rode a wave of optimism generated by the imminent arrival of the railway. "It was the 'end of steel', the beginning of the Pacific, and people thought that possibly the place had a future," wrote the novelist Ethel Wilson, who came to live in the West End as a young girl.[48] When the steam locomotive Engine 374 hauled the first passenger train into town on May 23, 1887, eleven months after the fire, an enthusiastic populace turned out to welcome it. (Among the welcoming party was Malcolm MacLean, who had been re-elected mayor the previous December, not least because he had steered the city through its great crisis.) The engine was draped in banners and flags along with a picture of Queen Victoria, whose official birthday was the next day. "Vancouver gave me the grandest reception," marvelled a bemused John Ems, who was one of the passengers

The famous staged photograph of city council after the 1886 fire. Mayor Malcolm MacLean is seated in the middle.
H.T. Devine photograph, Vancouver Public Library 1089

on the train. "Why, they had a fire brigade, and a band, down to meet me when I came in. Wasn't much of a fire brigade; just a few men and a couple of hose reels, and the band was only five or six musicians, but ... they could not have given the Prince of Wales a finer reception."[49] The first depot was a simple wooden structure built on piles near the foot of what is now Howe Street at the base of a steep bluff. According to Major Matthews, the Squamish knew the place as Puckahls.[50] There was a wharf next to the station and three weeks after the inaugural train, on June 14, the *Abyssinia,* the first of the steamships that the CPR had chartered to inaugurate its trans-Pacific trade, arrived with a cargo of tea, silk and other merchandise bound for eastern Canada and the United States. As much as the arrival of the first train, the arrival of the *Abyssinia* was seen as a harbinger of the prosperity to come, since it completed the link to East Asia that turned Burrard Inlet into a significant international port. When word came that the ship was due, a great crowd gathered at the waterfront to get a glimpse of it. "Men felt," observed the *News-Advertiser,* "that the period of suspense and difficulty which beset the earlier months of the existence of the city was at an end."[51]

As the city's preeminent landowner and major employer, the CPR was the engine that drove the local economy. Along with the Burrard Inlet depot and wharves, the company erected a rail trestle across False Creek to allow its trains to access the south shore of English Bay, where Van Horne initially wanted to locate his main terminal. Land clearing on the downtown peninsula proceeded with speed. The forest was so dense that loggers employed "the bowling pin method," cutting partway through the trunks of the smaller trees so that one of the giants, when it fell, could knock the rest over like bowling pins. It was said that five acres could be felled at one time with a sound like thunder.[52] During the summer of 1887, crews working for the CPR transformed a skid road that once hauled logs to the inlet into a graded thoroughfare that became Granville Street. The original Granville Street bridge, a wooden trestle with a swing section that opened to allow water traffic to pass through, spanned False Creek early in 1889, linking the CPR's downtown lands to its "suburban" holdings to the south. Known originally as Centre Street, Granville stretched to the city limits at Sixteenth Avenue before dwindling to a narrow track, the North Arm Road, that made its way through the forest all the way to the Fraser River.

When its plans for a Kitsilano terminal did not materialize, the CPR welcomed an offer from the city to locate its yards on the north shore of False Creek in return for not having to pay taxes on the property. Soon the shoreline between Granville and Westminster Avenue (Main Street) emerged as an industrial heartland with a variety of mills, brickyards, shipyards and other plants joining the railway. Chief among these was the Royal City Planing Mills, which began operations early in 1886 where Carrall Street met the creek. Spared by the fire that June, the mill profited handsomely by producing much of the lumber used to rebuild the city. In 1889 Royal City purchased the Hastings Mill and reorganized as the BC Mills, Timber and Trading Company, with John Hendry, one of the RCPM's founders, as president. Hendry ranked among the most successful entrepreneurs in the province. He had arrived in 1872 from New Brunswick and within four years had established sawmills in Nanaimo and New Westminster. Working from headquarters in New Westminster, he expanded his operations steadily until he owned not just Royal City and the Hastings Mill but the mill in Moodyville on the north shore as well. He is credited with assembling the first forest industry conglomerate in BC and dominated the industry between 1890 and 1910, while diversifying into railway construction, mining and hydroelectric development. When he retired from BC Mills in 1913, he turned the operation over to his son-in-law, the future lieutenant governor Eric Hamber.

False Creek was just one of the neighbourhoods where the CPR's rail and real estate activities reconfigured the geography of the city. Beginning in the fall of 1885, the company's chief surveyor, Lachlan Hamilton, led a crew across the forested peninsula, scrambling over fallen trees and hacking through the undergrowth, hammering stakes to mark the future pattern of streets. It was Hamilton who named most of these future thoroughfares after various company executives (Abbott, Beatty, Cambie), British naval officers (Hornby, Howe, Nelson) and provincial politicians (Robson, Smithe), and to the south of False Creek after battles (Trafalgar, Balaclava, Waterloo) and trees (Arbutus, Fir, Oak), not neglecting to name one of the streets after himself. Subsequently Hamilton's survey came to be mythologized as the city's founding moment. In 1952 the Parks Board installed a brass plaque on a building at the corner of Hastings and Hamilton. The inscription, which conveniently ignores the presence of the First Nations people, declared grandly: "Here stood Hamilton, first land commissioner, Canadian Pacific Railway, 1885. In the silent solitude of the primeval forest he drove a wooden stake in the earth and commenced to measure an empty land into the streets of Vancouver."

Once the bare bones of the new city were laid out, the CPR set about shifting the commercial core away from "old" Gastown to the centre of its own land grant. In the spring of 1888 the company opened a hotel at the top of the rise on Granville Street. The Hotel Vancouver, the first of three to bear the name, was intended to cater to rail passengers. Despite its unprepossessing appearance—one newspaper called it a "monument of external ugliness"—the company hoped the hotel would anchor a new business district for the city. The erection of a 1,200-seat opera house next door to the hotel in 1891, and the decision by the Hudson's Bay Company to locate a new store across the street in 1892, encouraged the westerly migration of commerce. At the same time, members of the city's wealthy elite began building homes along West Hastings Street and its western extension, Seaton Street, on the bluff overlooking Burrard Inlet. Known locally as Blueblood Alley, this neighbourhood attracted prominent residents such as Harry Abbott, the railway's general superintendent, CPR solicitor and land developer Colonel Alfred St. George Hamersley, salmon canner Henry Bell-Irving, and Edward Mahon, principal partner in an investment company that developed the townsite of North Vancouver. During the next decade, as the West End—the former Brickmaker's Claim—was cleared of its forest cover and subdivided into building lots, it became the most prestigious residential neighbourhood in the city.

Another significant landowner was the Vancouver Improvement Company (VIC), a group of investors based initially in Victoria and led by the Oppenheimer brothers, David and Isaac. While Isaac focused on the family's wholesale grocery business, David engaged in land speculation and promoted a wide variety of civic improvements, including street railways, a water system, electric street lighting, wharves and parks. David Oppenheimer had persuaded the Three Greenhorns to sell him a piece of their West End claim, which they laid out as a subdivision dubbed "New Liverpool." This was in 1882, and nothing came of the plan. Once Vancouver was incorporated, Oppenheimer played a major role in local politics. Following the fire, he made available the family warehouse on Powell Street as the site for the temporary city hall. More significantly he served a term as alderman, followed by four terms as city mayor, mixing civic affairs and his own business interests in a way that today would be considered inappropriate, if not scandalous. The VIC was the third-largest landowner in the city, after the CPR and the Hastings Mill. Much of its land was located on the city's east side, land that had been logged over by the mill. Strathcona, as it came to be called, was the city's first residential neighbourhood. As the years passed, it filled with a heterogeneous population of immigrant newcomers, including Jews, Italians and eastern Europeans. Many of the men found jobs at the sawmill or at the various waterfront industries. There were also a number of African-Americans, many of whom came from the Prairies or from Vancouver Island. They congregated

in the southwestern corner of Strathcona where a Black neighbourhood, casually known as Hogan's Alley, emerged.

The close connections between the CPR and other corporate interests in the new city are embodied in the story of the BC Sugar Refining Company, sometimes called Vancouver's first manufacturer outside the forest industry. The company was created by Benjamin Tingley Rogers, son of an American sugar refiner. Having grown up in the business, Benjamin Tingley saw the possibilities afforded by the CPR's new Pacific terminus and shared with Cornelius Van Horne his plans for a refinery in Vancouver. Van Horne invested in the project, along with other CPR directors, and used his influence to see that city council passed a motion approving the city's purchase of land for the refinery. As well, the city agreed to provide free water to the facility and to grant a tax exemption and a municipal loan; in return Rogers promised not to employ any Chinese workers. The person instrumental in winning these concessions for Rogers's project was John M. Browning, chair of the city's finance committee and, not coincidentally, a land commissioner for the CPR. Once the deal was done, Browning became the sugar company's first president. The twenty-four-year-old Rogers moved to the city and got the refinery up and running by early in 1891. He lived with his family—his wife, Mary Isabella, was a generous supporter of the arts—in a splendid mansion called Gabriola (still standing) on Davie Street in the West End.

EARLY VANCOUVER was a pungent place to live. The air was filled with a smoky haze from the clearing fires dotting the downtown peninsula. Smoke burned the throat, irritated the eyes and on many days was thick enough to obscure the view of the North Shore mountains. Even more insistent than the smell of burning wood was the stench of sewage and rotting garbage. Homes were served by outdoor privies, and droppings from horses, oxen, pigs, turkeys and chickens littered every street and backyard. (The 1891 census recorded 13,706 chickens, as many as there were humans in the city.) Drains were open and refuse was burned or left to rot outside. "The whole refuse of the town, solid and liquid, is thrown out on the face of the earth," one resident complained.[53] Burrard Inlet was a convenient garbage dump where residents and businesses threw their trash and discharged their sewage. As the stench became unbearable, especially at low tide, the city contracted with the Union Steamship Company to haul garbage by the scowful out to deeper water. In the short term at least, that seemed to solve the trash problem.[54]

Within the first few years of incorporation most of the other amenities of a modern city were put in place. Fire protection was an obvious priority, given the catastrophic blaze that had devoured Gastown. The origins of the fire department actually predate the great fire by a couple of weeks, but the equipment did not arrive until afterward. The first wagon was a horse-drawn steam pumper with four hose reels and 760 metres of hose, based at a new firehall on Water Street. For another decade most members of the brigade were volunteers. The first chief, Sam Pedgrift, skipped town with money that had been raised at a minstrel show to pay for the department's expenses, but his successor, John Carlisle, proved more reliable, remaining on the job for the next forty-two years. To maintain the peace, council appointed a chief constable, John Stewart, assisted by three officers and a one-armed jailer named John Clough who doubled as the city's lamplighter. (The original Granville constable, Jonathan Miller, decided he would rather be postmaster.) The lockup consisted of four cells in the basement of the new city hall on Powell Street. For the most part the cells were filled with drunks drying out after a night in one of Gastown's several bars. Fines imposed on its brothel keepers were a mainstay of the city's budget in the early years.

With public safety seen to, a reliable supply of drinking water moved to the top of the city's to-do list. Wells were easily contaminated, and cases of cholera, typhoid and other water-borne diseases were common. "People drinking [well water] are drinking poison," declared the same correspondent in the *News-Advertiser*[55]—not to mention the firefighters' need for a reliable water supply. The city was blessed by its proximity to the coastal mountains, down the flanks of which flowed many rivers and streams carrying pure meltwater to the sea. During the winter of 1885–86, an Ontario-born engineer named George Alexander Keefer ascended the Capilano River with a small survey party and decided that it would do nicely for the city's purpose. Along with H.O. Smith, the city's chief engineer, Keefer created the Vancouver Water Works Company, and offered to deliver clean drinking water from the North Shore across Burrard Inlet via the First Narrows, a daunting engineering challenge. Following a public vote, city council agreed to award the franchise to Keefer's company and work began on a dam 10.5 kilometres from the river's mouth. Supplies arrived by mule team up a wagon road that more or less followed the route of today's Capilano Road. Water was carried from the reservoir behind the dam through wooden mains to the First Narrows, where the company laid a flexible joint pipe across the ocean bottom to the other side. This was the most difficult part of the project. The narrows was a shipping lane with heavy tidal currents. Would the submerged pipe stand up to the stress, and if it broke, could it be repaired? After one false start, Keefer and his team managed to lay the pipe without mishap. A 40.5-centimetre main continued across Stanley Park and beneath Coal Harbour to the corner of Georgia and Granville Streets, where, on March 26, 1889, water flowed for the first time. Within three weeks, water was gushing from taps and fire hydrants all over the city. Eight months later, as city council prepared to purchase the new water system and make it a public utility, the main beneath First Narrows broke, leaving residents without water for several days. The city put its takeover plans on hold while the vwwc hurriedly laid a second pipe across the channel. Once the improved system had proven itself, the city purchased the company for $400,000.

Clean water was a great boon, but it did not eliminate all threats to public health. Outbreaks of smallpox were periodic. Jessie Greer Hall, whose father Sam Greer homesteaded in Kitsilano, recalled for Major Matthews an outbreak that occurred in the summer and fall of 1892. The infection was said to have arrived aboard one of the CPR liners from Asia. "People were quarantined all over the city," Mrs. Hall said. "It was the custom to put those stricken in an express wagon, and with the driver ringing a bell to keep people away, warning them, the load of sick, frequently girls from Dupont Street [i.e., sex workers], who had been visited by the sailors from the *Empresses*, would be driven down to the dock, and taken by boat to Deadman's Island." A small pesthouse, or quarantine station, was erected on the island to handle the sick.[56] Hall was perhaps referring to the infamous "War of the Hoses." Early that year, word had spread that a CPR steamship was trying to land smallpox-infected passengers down in the harbour. A crowd gathered on the wharf to turn away the vessel and the fire brigade was called in to turn its hoses on the ship. The captain ordered his own hoses into action and several people were injured before someone cut the ship's lines and it drifted out into the harbour, at which point the captain decided to look elsewhere for a landing spot and steamed away.[57]

By this time electric lights were illuminating the city streets. It had been a toss-up whether to go with gas or electric street lighting to replace the outmoded gas lamps, but in the end, council chose a proposal from the Vancouver Electric Illuminating Company, and in August 1887 the first lights were switched on. "Vancouver is better lighted," declared the News-Advertiser, "than any other city of her size in the world."[58] Ten years later the electrical system became part of the BC Electric Railway Company's operation. Initially the BCER generated power from a small steam plant on Union Street. At the end of 1903 the company switched to hydroelectricity produced at a power plant at Buntzen Lake in Coquitlam and carried across Burrard Inlet and into the city along a 27-kilometre pole line.

One of the most far-sighted steps taken by the new city council was also one of its first. Colonial authorities had designated the peninsula of land west of Coal Harbour a government reserve, though subsequently they were willing to allow logging to take place, chiefly by Jonathan Miller before he became Gastown's constable.[59] At its second meeting following incorporation, city council received a letter from A.W. Ross, a real estate speculator from Winnipeg and a close associate of the CPR. Ross proposed that the city ask the government in Ottawa to set aside the reserve at the First Narrows as a public park. Alderman Lachlan Hamilton, the CPR's land commissioner, made a motion supporting Ross's suggestion and a petition was dispatched. As Sean Kheraj points out in his history of the park, the CPR had already tried to purchase some or all of the peninsula.[60] When the federal government refused to give any of it up, the CPR promoted Plan B, expecting that the creation of a public park would enhance the value of the properties that it owned in the West End, next door to the reserve. As well, it would keep the peninsula out of the hands of any rival property speculators should Ottawa change its mind.[61] The federal government approved the city's request and Stanley Park, named for Governor General Lord Stanley, opened in September 1888. Even before the park officially opened, crews installed a bridge across Coal Harbour to improve public access and built a road skirting the edge of the peninsula. The road was surfaced with crushed shells obtained by excavating the midden at Xway'xway; its route cut through the properties occupied by Indigenous residents.[62] Skeletal remains were taken by the Squamish and relocated to other burial grounds.

THE NEWLY ACCLAIMED MAYOR, David Oppenheimer, declared at the end of 1887: "At no time in the history of the world has there been a city whose prosperity has been so marked or its future promises so bright as the City of Vancouver."[63] No doubt a burst of growth followed its incorporation, but Oppenheimer was allowing his enthusiasm to get the better of him by claiming world-class status for his city. In the short term at least, the arrival of the CPR did not alter the basic orientation of the local economy. As historian Robert McDonald has pointed out, Vancouver in the 1880s remained isolated from the eastern half of the continent and even from the interior of the province. The economy remained oriented to the Pacific Coast and the Pacific Rim. Most of its trade was with California, Great Britain and Pacific ports. The sawmills exported to Chile, Peru, Australia and China, along with Great Britain, and the canneries at the mouth of the Fraser fed an enormous hunger for canned salmon among the British working class. Most of the investment capital came from Britain and from California. Vancouver was, in McDonald's words, "an enclave of self-perpetuating growth during its early years."[64] Much of the city's initial growth was based on faith in the future, and the future took a bit longer to arrive than many had hoped. The initial years of rapid growth were followed by fallow years of recession during the mid-1890s, as schemes collapsed and dreams were delayed. This would change, and change quickly, but the first decade of Vancouver's existence was more about laying the groundwork than reaping the whirlwind. It was in the following decade that an expanding Vancouver became an integral part of a continental economy.

The BC Electric observation car, hosted
for all but the first two years by Teddy Lyons,
toured the city's streets from 1909 to 1950.
Harry Bullen photo, City of Vancouver Archives,
AM336-S3-2-: CVA 677-40

• • •

CHAPTER TWO

Railtown

PROBABLY THE MOST RECOGNIZABLE PERSON in Vancouver in the years before World War I was a streetcar conductor named Teddy Lyons. He was born in Manitoba but came out to the coast as a boy and went to work for the BC Electric in 1910. The following summer a fluke landed him the job that made him a household name. Asked to fill in on one of the company's observation cars, Lyons turned out to be a born showman, and the job was his for the next thirty-nine years. The observation cars—also known as the "rubber-neck wagons"—were open-air tram cars with row seating, which toured the city showing visitors the sights. But Teddy, and his fellow conductor Dick Gardiner, added a whole extra level of entertainment. The less voluble Gardiner, who was a magician in his spare time, performed a set of magic tricks while Lyons was the stand-up comic, throwing off corny one-liners that kept his riders in stitches. His gags were so popular that the company published them in a book and began advertising the tour not as a chance to see Vancouver but to enjoy "2 hours of fun with Teddy Lyons."

At a pre-arranged spot along the run, Lyons asked his passengers to direct their attention to the brickwork on a building they were passing. Concealed behind a curtain in a second-floor window, photographer Harry Bullen snapped a picture of the wagon and its occupants. Bullen hurriedly developed prints, which he handed to a young assistant, who hopped on his bicycle and set off to catch up with the rubberneckers. Pedalling along-side, the assistant dropped the photos into a special box where Lyons, with feigned surprise, would find them at the end of the tour, and offer them for sale at a dollar apiece. Thousands of these candid snapshots ended up in photo albums around the world.

Part of the reason that streetcar conductors like Lyons and Gardiner were elevated to the status of celebrities was that during the years around World War I, Vancouver was Railtown. It is hard to exaggerate the influence of the railways on the city's streetscapes, soundscapes, economy and politics. To begin with, the "Terminal City" owed its very existence to the Canadian Pacific. If the CPR had not located its terminus in Burrard Inlet, the history of the city would be completely different. As well, two other transcontinental rail lines—the Great Northern and the Canadian Northern—terminated there. The bustling stations were temples of modernity, symbolizing the importance of railways in everyday life. The most opulent was the new station opened by the CPR on the waterfront at the foot of Seymour Street in 1914, next door to the previous station, which was demolished. The other lines had their stations on the False Creek flats, which would be filled in to accommodate the needs of the railways, transforming the natural geography of the city.

Then there was the railway of Lyons and Gardiner, the urban streetcar, spreading its network of tracks along the city streets and out to the suburbs. It was a vast circulatory system carrying the lifeblood of the community. People rode the trolleys downtown for work or shopping, to the cemetery to mourn a lost relative, to Stanley Park for a stroll around Lost Lagoon, to the Exhibition Grounds at Hastings Park, and all the way to Marpole and the banks of the Fraser River. "Owl cars" operated well past midnight. There were still few automobiles; the street railway was the rapid transit system of its time. On a single day in 1910 it carried 122,455 paying customers in a city whose population, including South Vancouver and Point Grey, was 120,000. The streetcar focused settlement along its lines and encouraged the expansion of population beyond the downtown core to new suburbs like Fairview, Kitsilano and Mount Pleasant. Even walking through the city, residents could not ignore the presence of the railways. A symphony of clanking railcars and puffing steam locomotives filled their ears, and office windows vibrated to the rumble of the trolleys as they passed.

THE ORIGINS OF THE STREET RAILWAY dated back to June 26, 1890, when hundreds of Vancouverites crowded the wooden sidewalks of

Westminster Avenue (Main Street) to get a look at the city's newest example of the latest thing. For the past year crews had been laying track; finally the street railway was lurching into operation. With the usual collection of dignitaries packed on board, conductor Dugald Carmichael manoeuvred Car 14 out of the barn on Barnard Street (later Union Street) and set off on the inaugural run. Once these formalities were completed, all four cars were launched into service and everyone rode free for the rest of the day. The trams were small four-wheelers with bench seating running lengthwise down the car. Trolley poles conveyed electrical power to the vehicles from overhead wires strung above the tracks. There were also two unpowered tow cars. Stoves kept the interior of each car warm while coal oil headlamps lit the way at night. Conductor and motorman stood out on open platforms front and rear. When the system, all 5.6 kilometres of it, was thrown open to regular service the next day, passengers paid a nickel for a ride.

Around the world, street railways were in their infancy. Horse-drawn cars were introduced to eastern Canada in the 1860s and it had first been assumed that the Vancouver system would utilize horsepower. But electricity was fast proving its efficiency. In 1886, Windsor, Ontario, installed the first electric street railway line in Canada, and Victoria had pioneered the technology in BC when it launched its own line earlier in 1890. The investors who were financing the Vancouver system decided to scrap their initial plans and convert to electricity, merging with the local light company to form the Vancouver Electric Railway and Light Company (VERLC). With the system up and running, the VERLC expanded rapidly, running its Granville Street line south across False Creek on a trestle to Broadway, then east to Westminster Avenue. A surveyor had named these slopes "Fairview." They were sparsely populated, but the CPR, which owned the land, was planning a posh residential development and wanted a transit connection to the downtown. As it turned out, Fairview did not flourish, at least not right away. The line was so expensive to build—seven bridges had to be built across the seven streams that flowed down the slope into False Creek—that not even the gift of sixty-eight lots from the CPR could make it a paying proposition, and early in 1893 the VERLC went bankrupt.

The street railway had fallen victim to an economic downturn that lasted until the end of the decade. The real estate boom collapsed, and unemployment was widespread. Another group of local capitalists, including Mayor David Oppenheimer, had built an electric rail line between Vancouver and New Westminster, the first interurban railway of its kind

The imposing headquarters of the
BC Electric Railway Company, shown
in 1928, still stands at the corner of
Hastings and Carrall.
Dominion Photo Co. photograph, Vancouver
Public Library 22735

in North America. The Westminster and Vancouver Tramway Company also failed to survive the slump. Expected settlement along the line did not develop, and in the middle of 1894 the WVTC followed the Vancouver operation into bankruptcy. In the dismal economic climate, local financiers did not have the resources to keep the companies going, and in the end it was British capital that came to the rescue. Creditors reorganized the systems—including Victoria's street railway—into a new company, the Consolidated Railway and Light Company. The future of the new operation was looking bright when a horrific accident occurred in Victoria. An overloaded streetcar was crossing the Point Ellice Bridge to Esquimalt when the span collapsed under the weight, dropping the car into the harbour. Fifty-five people died, many of them small children—it is still the worst accident in Canadian transit history—and the CRLC tumbled into insolvency. In 1897, after a series of financial manoeuvres, a new company emerged: the British Columbia Electric Railway Company, once again financed by British capital. The BCER had the good fortune to take over the transit system, and the electrical utilities, just as the province was pulling out of recession. It would run the system for the next six decades.

Better economic times arrived with the discovery of gold in the Klondike in 1898. Thousands of would-be prospectors heading north to the goldfields paused in Vancouver to buy their supplies. Every one of them had to purchase a grubstake: food, tools, durable clothing, coffee pots, tents and blankets—the list of necessary items was endless. No wonder Vancouver outfitters prospered, along with the hotels and bars that overflowed with patrons passing the time while they waited for their ship to sail. One local success story belonged to William Malkin, an immigrant from England who turned from farming to the wholesale grocery business based in a vast warehouse on Water Street in Gastown. W.H. Malkin & Co.—William was joined in the business by his brothers James and John—specialized in a wide variety of imported foodstuffs, notably coffee, tea and British tinned goods. In 1912 William built a new home for his family, Southlands, on Southwest Marine Drive in what was then South Vancouver.

At the same time as the Klondike strike, and more importantly for the local economy in the longer term, immigrant farmers were streaming onto the Canadian prairies, creating a heavy demand for all kinds of goods, especially wood for building farms and houses. The manufacture of lumber and wood products soared following the turn of the century. Robert McDonald calculated that "the quantity of lumber cut in British Columbia rose by 374 percent between 1901 and 1910."[65] Along with sawmilling and sash and door factories, the production of cedar shingles skyrocketed. Wood shingles were still the main roofing material in North America, and the best shingles were made from the red cedar that was so abundant locally. The number of shingle mills in the province rose dramatically from only nine in 1891 to ninety-three by the middle of World War I, most of them located in the Lower Mainland. Among the leading manufacturers were the McNair brothers—James, Robert and William. The McNairs, who came to BC from New Brunswick in 1892, established their first mill on the water in the Hastings Townsite near the south side of the Second Narrows. They did so well specializing in the manufacture of cedar shingles that the elder brother, James, became known as "the shingle king of the Northwest."

Shingles were just one product that profited from the continental boom. The rising tide floated all boats, including the mining sector, salmon canning and railway construction. And Vancouver manufacturers supplied all these industries. One metric for measuring the economic boom was the number of businesses needing electrical power; this number rose from 246 in 1906 to 2,555 six years later.[66] These were "the golden years," wrote Alan Morley in his history of the city.[67] The population almost quadrupled between 1900 and 1910, fulfilling the optimistic slogan: "By 1910, Vancouver then, will have 100,000 men." Allowing for the sexism, the actual population figure for the 1911 census was 100,401, which did not include South Vancouver or Point Grey, still separate municipalities. During the 1890s, Vancouver had surpassed Victoria as BC's largest city; by the outbreak of World War I it was challenging Winnipeg to be the third largest city in the country.

All of these newcomers required places to live, and during the pre-war years the city experienced a building boom, which peaked in 1912 when the annual value of building permits exceeded $19 million. "The forests vanished, and up went the city," wrote Ethel Wilson in her novel about early days in the West End.[68] Despite all the construction, housing supply could barely keep up with the demand. In mid-1907 the *Province* worried that a shortage of housing might yet thwart the city's ambitions. "Unless the housing problem, already a grave one, is speedily solved," the newspaper warned, "Vancouver will lose thousands of strangers who are only too anxious to make this their abiding place."[69] Major building projects from this era included a new provincial courthouse (1911, now the Vancouver Art Gallery); a main post office (1910, now the Sinclair Centre); the Vancouver General Hospital (1905) and an expanded, two-hundred-bed St. Paul's Hospital (1912); the Woodward's Department Store (1903); and a new fire hall (1905). Office towers included the Dominion Trust Building (1909), the tallest building in the British Empire until it was surpassed by the sixteen-storey World Building four years later; the Vancouver Block (1912), with its soaring clock tower; the elegant Rogers Building (1912), financed by the contractor and alderman Jonathan Rogers, with its extravagant basement barbershop; and the Credit Foncier Building (1914), where many members of the commercial elite had their offices. Not to omit the BC Electric's head office at Hastings and Carrall (1912), a five-storey brick edifice housing 300 employees and a drive-through depot for the interurban trams coming and going from the Fraser Valley.

No one embodied the zeitgeist of this period as flamboyantly as Alvo von Alvensleben. When he arrived in the city from his native Germany in 1904, von Alvensleben had hardly a penny to his name. What he did have was energy to burn, an immense charm and wealthy contacts back in Europe. Using all three he made a substantial fortune by investing in BC's booming industries and Vancouver's exuberant property market. He and his wife Edith, a schoolteacher from Ladner, lived with their three children in a handsome Kerrisdale mansion (later Crofton House School for Girls), where they entertained lavishly. Von Alvensleben, who was said to be a friend of the Kaiser, was responsible for funnelling millions of dollars of German investment into the province. And then it all ended. The 1913 crash took him down with it. The outbreak of war found him returning from Europe, where he had been trying to rustle up some money to meet his debts. He was rumoured to be a German agent and could not return to Canada. The government seized what remained of his assets and von Alvensleben was left stranded in the US, where eventually he was interned as an enemy alien. After his release he lived the rest of his life south of the border.

THE STREET RAILWAY doubled its trackage in the five years leading up to the war, scrambling to service the burgeoning residential neighbourhoods spreading away from the central business core. "While the fine business section is steadily improving and building up," reported Frank Yeigh, a prewar visitor to the city, "the excellent streetcar system is assisting in a rapid suburban expansion . . . More room, more homes for more people is the cry of Vancouver."[70]

The first of these "suburbs" was Mount Pleasant, creeping up the slope south of False Creek on either side of Westminster Avenue. The first landholder in the area was H.V. Edmonds, a speculator from New Westminster with extensive holdings in the Lower Mainland, who named the neighbourhood after the Irish birthplace of his wife Jane. By the time the street railway arrived in the early 1890s, crossing the trestle bridge that spanned

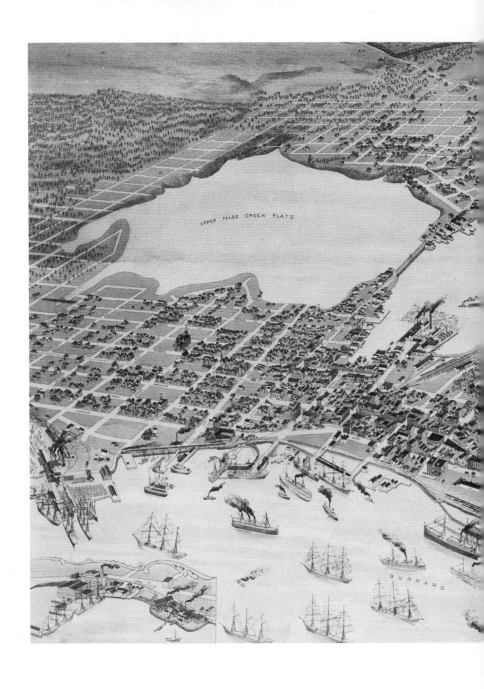

This bird's-eye view shows the city in
1898, the same year that the discovery
of gold in the Klondike kickstarted a
local economic recovery.
Vancouver World Printing and Publishing Co.
map, City of Vancouver Archives,
AM1594-: MAP 547

False Creek at a place the Squamish called Ki-wah-usks ("two points exactly opposite"[71]), there was a community developing at the intersection of Kingsway and Westminster. Farther east was China Creek—named for the Chinese farmers who raised vegetables and pigs nearby—where Charles Maddams established a 2-hectare farm in 1888. But for the most part the neighbourhood attracted working people employed at the mills, slaughterhouses, shipyards, foundries and machine shops that had been established on the south side of False Creek, an area that was fast turning into one of the young city's industrial centres. Mount Pleasant was also home to many employees of the street railway, which in 1905 was extended out to Westminster (by then renamed Main Street) as far south as 33rd Avenue in South Vancouver. Subsequently the company opened a large car barn at Fourteenth Avenue, a facility that remained in operation until the streetcars disappeared in 1955. (The site is now a shopping centre.)

Just to the east of Main Street, a creek flowed north out of what had been a large swamp, known as the Tea Swamp, around Sixteenth Avenue. Water from the creek had once travelled by flume to the Hastings Mill, where it filled the boilers in the steam plant. It earned the name Brewery Creek during the 1890s, when breweries began to settle on its banks to take advantage of the supply of fresh water. The largest of these was Vancouver Breweries, owned by Charles Doering and his partner Otto Marstrand. Maker of the popular Cascade Ale, "the beer without peer," Vancouver Breweries absorbed several other operations to eventually become a large conglomerate, BC Breweries Ltd., with Doering as president.

To the west of Mount Pleasant, Fairview began to fill with residents during the first decade of the new century. A creation of the street railway, this neighbourhood commanded a panoramic view across False Creek and downtown to the North Shore mountains. The streetcar line that had opened in 1891—and helped to bankrupt the original transportation company—circled the slope in a "beltline" that crossed the Granville Bridge from downtown, swung east down Broadway to Main Street, then circled back down Main to the city, making the neighbourhood just minutes from shops and offices. If it was not as upscale as the West End, it was more posh than the crowded streets adjacent to the business district. As an example of its rising popularity, when the newspaper executive and future mayor Louis Taylor bought a house in Fairview in 1899, his was the only home on the block; the surrounding lots were filled with stumps. Five years later there were ten homes on the block, and by 1907 the *Province* newspaper was calling Fairview "one of the better-class suburbs of the Terminal City."[72]

Still, the swankiest pre-war residential district was the West End. Located between the commercial core and Stanley Park, it was cleared completely for development during the 1890s and linked to the downtown by a trolley line down Robson Street to Denman. Once water service reached the entire neighbourhood, by 1909, building proceeded steadily. The West End was the centre of Vancouver's pre-war "high society," such as it was. Wealthy members of the commercial elite—bankers, CPR executives, professionals and industrialists—inhabited rambling Victorian mansions with soaring turrets, wide verandahs, Chinese servants and expansive lawns perfect for weekend croquet parties. The Vancouver Lawn Tennis Club installed itself on a set of courts at Denman and Barclay, with a membership list that read like a Who's Who, while Miss Gordon's School for Girls (the original Crofton House) and Queen's School for boys offered a proper British education to the sons and daughters of the elite. There was also a healthy sprinkling of more modest, though still substantial, homes for the middle class, characterized by the Mole Hill neighbourhood.

At the southern end of Denman Street was a short stretch of sandy beach known to the Squamish as Ay-yul-shun ("soft under foot").[73] This beachfront, much extended over the years and known to residents as English Bay, became a favourite recreational resort, especially once the streetcar arrived in 1895. The city took over several privately owned properties and developed a public bathing beach, complete with a three-storey waterfront pavilion. Next door to the pavilion a concrete bathhouse offered changing rooms, and perched at the end of a long pier extending out into the bay was a glassed-in conservatory for dinner and dancing. For a few years the Imperial Roller Rink stood across from the beach at the foot of Denman.

The informal "mayor" of this waterfront playground was Seraphim "Joe" Fortes, a former Gastown bartender originally from Barbados, whom the city named official swim instructor and special constable for the beach. There was hardly a resident of the city who did not claim to have been taught to swim by Fortes, "the dusky professor of the natatorial art" as one guidebook called him.[74] He lived in a small cottage near the water and watched over English Bay as if it were a personal fiefdom. When he died in 1922, his funeral attracted an outpouring of public respect and affection.

In 1899 Fortes was the inadvertent centre of a scandal that rocked polite society. "The 'Great English Bay Scandal' was a shocking thing," recalled Major Matthews several years after it happened. "It shocked all Vancouver."[75] There are at least two versions of what happened. In the early days the beach was divided into sections where men and women bathed separately. According to Matthews, one day a woman, "an impertinent hussy, bolder than the rest," strayed into the men's half wearing a revealing bathing costume, which at that time meant showing bare legs up to her knee. This breach of beach etiquette caused the local Women's Christian Temperance Union to write a letter of complaint to the newspaper, and in response the woman sued the WCTU for libel. The case went to court, where it dragged on for two years. The novelist Ethel Wilson presented another version. According to Wilson, the woman at the centre of the controversy was the president of the WCTU, Mrs. Gleason, and her perceived indiscretion was that she was seen "more than once in a public place, bathing in the arms of a black man"; in other words, taking swimming lessons from Joe Fortes.[76] When a zealous member of the union lodged a complaint against such indecorous behaviour, the complainant was expelled, at which point she sued, successfully, for libel.[77] Whatever the exact details of the incident, it suggests the straitlaced morality that characterized some elements of the city's social elite. (It also suggests that the colour-blind affection for Joe Fortes that modern Vancouverites tell themselves was universal may not have been shared by everyone at the time.)

Across English Bay from the beach, another new suburb was taking shape, also thanks to the streetcar. From his logging camps on the waterfront, Jerry Rogers had logged off most of the area that now comprises Kitsilano. When the CPR took possession as part of its generous grant from the province it tolerated the few squatters who had taken up residence but did not recognize their title, as Sam Greer discovered. Greer, an Irishman attracted to BC by the gold rush, claimed to have pre-empted a large piece of property behind Kitsilano Beach in 1882, before the CPR arrived. He lived in a cabin at the foot of Yew Street with his wife and daughter, but when the CPR subsequently took possession of its grant, the company sought authority through the courts to evict him. In September 1891 a party of police deputies arrived at the beach and tried to force their way into the cabin.[78] Greer responded by firing his shotgun through the door, wounding one of the officers. The men retreated but returned later in the day and arrested Greer for attempted murder.[79] He was found guilty on a lesser charge of assault and sent to the penitentiary, but was eventually pardoned and released from jail. Despite the fact that Judge Matthew Begbie called him "one of the worst men I ever met," Greer became something of a local hero for standing up to the rail company, and his property was known as Greer's Beach for several years.[80] (To the Squamish it was known as Skwa-yoos, and as an excellent place to catch smelt.)

Joe Fortes, the "mayor" of English Bay,
taught two generations of city youngsters
how to swim.
Photographer Unknown, Vancouver Public
Library 83598

The CPR did not immediately develop the property, which became a popular campground and swimming area, especially after the BC Electric extended a streetcar line across the False Creek trestle bridge and out to the beach in July 1905. A small community of tenters emerged, but after a few years the city felt obliged to ban tenting for sanitary reasons, instead building a pavilion and bringing in sand to create an expanded Kitsilano Beach. (The name, chosen by the CPR, refers to August Jack Khahtsahlano's grandfather Chief Khahtsahlanogh.) Residential development spread up the slope to the south as a second streetcar line opened out Fourth Avenue as far as Alma, the western limits of the city, in 1909. Another pocket of settlement was associated with the Rat Portage Sawmill on the south shore of False Creek beside Granville Island. The mill employed many Japanese and South Asian workers, some of whom settled nearby with their families. The first Sikh temple, or gurdwara, in the city opened in 1908 on Second Avenue just west of Burrard.

The character of these suburban neighbourhoods differed in ways both subtle and obvious. Some attracted more working-class residents, others appealed to the middle class. Most catered to both. Some featured large mansions with expansive lawns and gardens; others were characterized by humble cottages behind white picket fences. But one thing they all shared was a preference for the detached, single-family residence. Vancouver was a city of houses. The home ownership rate was much higher than older cities of eastern Canada and the US. The availability of land and the affordability of building in wood made home ownership possible for most working and middle-class families, whether they occupied a small cottage on the east side or a more substantial mansion in the West End. There were very few tenements; row housing was almost non-existent; most people owned their own homes. An expression of this phenomenon was the prefabricated wooden house manufactured locally by the BC Mills company at its Royal City Mills on False Creek. These homes were sold in pieces in a kit for ease of assembly and were offered in a range of sizes and designs. Initially intended for the settlers who were flooding into the West, they were adapted for a multiplicity of uses, including banks and schoolhouses. Quite a few were sold in Vancouver between 1904 and 1910 as convenient, inexpensive residences.[81]

Residential development did not spread uniformly like a shadow across the landscape. The pattern was more erratic. Like pieces of a half-done jigsaw puzzle, pockets of development interspersed with empty lots of ragged stumps. The artist Emily Carr lived in the pre-war city, painting and teaching art. She left this description: "Vancouver was then only a little town, but it was growing hard. Almost every day you saw more of her forest being pushed back, half-cleared, waiting to be drained and built upon—mile upon mile of charred stumps and boggy skunk-cabbage swamp, root-holes filled with brown stagnant water, reflecting blue sky by day, rasping with frog croaks by night, fireweed, rank of growth, springing from the dour soil to burst into loose-hung, lush pink blossoms, dangling from red stalks, their clusters of loveliness trying to hide the hideous transition from wild to tamed land."[82] Such was the pervasiveness of the real estate boom that even a struggling artist like Carr was able to invest in property during her time in the city, where she bought five lots in the Hastings Townsite.[83] "The extraordinary thing about Vancouver," observed Douglas Sladen, a British tourist who visited in 1894, "is that in the midst of all this wilderness it is so absolutely modern; no one would think to put up a house without a telephone and electricity."[84]

Vancouver was developing as a network of villages connected by the streetcar. No one lived very far from the bush. Take, for example, Talton Place, a small, upscale subdivision located just inside the city limits north of Sixteenth Avenue and east of Arbutus. It was developed in 1910 by the Prudential Builders Ltd. and named for the company's president, Thomas Talton Langlois. When building commenced, the surrounding area was largely undeveloped. "The actual site was chosen because of its commanding position, at a point high above the smoke of the city. . . at that time on the outskirts of the 'old' City of Vancouver," explained J.C. McPherson, an executive with Prudential Builders. "To the south and west there was practically no development at all, the land lay in clearing and in stumps."[85] The developer erected a set of California bungalows and put in paved streets and sidewalks with trees and shrubs planted. A vacant lot in the subdivision sold for $2,500; a complete home for as little as $6,000. According to McPherson, Talton Place was the first organized subdivision of its type in the city.[86]

Along with the urban street railway, the BC Electric also operated a network of interurban trains running between downtown Vancouver and New Westminster, Steveston and out the Fraser Valley as far as Chilliwack. Like the street railway, the interurban prompted the emergence of suburban neighbourhoods, specifically Grandview. The line entered Vancouver from the east, travelled down Commercial Drive (formerly a logging skid road) and where it swung west on Venables to head into downtown, there was a station, known as Largen's Corner after a blacksmith who had a shop there. Transit stations were nodes of development, just as they are today, and soon a scattering of houses spread up the slopes to the south and east

Mrs. Charles Burns and her husband were among the earliest residents.

The couple purchased a three-room cabin on Kitchener Street in 1892. "There was a water well, but no electric light, sewer, or sidewalk," Mrs. Burns later recalled, "and the road was a trail from the Vancouver-Westminster interurban." She continued: "we had chickens, hens, and later we had a cow, but not at first; when we did get the cow she rambled out in the clearing, and many a time they have stopped the interurban electric car to put her off the track."[87] Ten years later Grandview contained more than 1,700 houses, including several turreted mansions belonging to some of the city's leading businessmen, among them John J. Miller, creator of the Pacific National Exhibition, and Edward Odlum, alderman, respected scientist, land promoter and the individual usually credited with giving the neighbourhood its name.[88]

WHEN COMMUTERS disembarked from the streetcar or the interurban at the BC Electric Railway's main downtown depot on Hastings Street at Carrall, they emerged into a swirl of busyness. Hastings was the beating heart of the city, a bustling avenue of commerce and entertainment. During the daylight hours it was the place where Vancouverites went to shop, pouring into the neighbourhood from the outlying suburbs and aboard the ferry from the North Shore, which docked just an easy stroll away. The main attraction was Charles Woodward's giant emporium. Woodward was a storekeeper from Ontario who had prospered supplying the Klondike gold stampeders. He launched his original four-storey department store in 1903—it expanded steadily over the years—and if you couldn't buy it at Woodward's it wasn't worth having. At night, Hastings transformed into the city's entertainment district. The street featured eight theatres in a four-block stretch presenting vaudeville, live music and drama. There were cafés, coffee shops, hotels, restaurants and bars, ranging from the elegant—the Bismarck Café boasted an indoor fountain and music performed by a full orchestra—to the proletarian. On a Saturday night the downtown streets were crowded with bustling mobs of pedestrians. "The whole population of Greater Vancouver comes in to walk up and down Granville and Hastings Streets," reported one visitor. "It is a regular parade; immense crowds walk up and down, up and down, all the evening. The theatres, the picture shows, the billiard saloons, and the other kind of saloons, are all packed, and still the sidewalks are a dense mass of humanity, walking along."[89]

Until 1912, the Provincial Court House stood right where Hastings Street took a jog at Cambie, on the future site of Victory Square. Not surprisingly, given how much news was generated in the courts, the city's three daily newspapers congregated in offices close by. This was Vancouver's version of Fleet Street. Newspapers at the time were openly partisan, usually funded by political parties or business interests, and their owners/publishers were prominent participants in the political life of the city and the province. The oldest paper was the *Vancouver News-Advertiser,* founded by Francis Carter-Cotton in 1887. Carter-Cotton, who was born in London, England, in 1843, emigrated to the US, and then arrived in Vancouver on the lam from his American creditors. Remaking himself as a newspaperman, he used the *News-Advertiser* to support his political aspirations. He was elected to the provincial legislature for the first time in 1890 and held his seat until 1900, serving a stint as minister of finance. On one occasion he campaigned from a prison cell, where he was incarcerated briefly for contempt of court, stemming from a dispute with a business partner. He was defeated in 1900, then re-elected in 1903 and remained in the legislature until 1916. Carter-Cotton was a reformer and a supporter of working-class causes. He used his paper to oppose the influence of the corporate elite on government. The long-time mayor David Oppenheimer was a particular target of his editorial censure. Carter-Cotton sold the paper in 1910, then lost most of his personal fortune in the recession of 1913. He drowned in False Creek six years later, some said intentionally, though he may have taken ill and fallen.

The *News-Advertiser* was a reliable if staid purveyor of political news, resistant to the changes in journalism that were refashioning the daily press at the time. Newspapers were becoming less political, more commercial. They were adding photographs, printing cartoons and targeting new audiences with women's pages and sports departments. Political news was supplemented with human interest stories, coverage of the arts and social gossip. Both of Vancouver's other dailies—the *Province* and the *World*—embraced these changes and waged a spirited battle for readers in the pre-war era. Beginning life as a Victoria weekly, the *Province* moved to Vancouver in 1898 under the direction of its co-owner Walter Nichol, an Ontario-born journalist. Three years later, Nichol bought out his partner using money provided by the CPR and proceeded to make the *Province* into what one observer called "the supreme newspaper power on the coast."[90] His circulation manager was Louis Taylor, a middle-aged transplant from Chicago who in 1905 purchased his own paper, the *Vancouver Daily World.* Later he moved the business to a new home, the seventeen-storey World Tower at Pender and Beatty. (The previous owner of the paper was Sara McLagan, the first woman in Canada to manage a daily newspaper.) Nichol stood for everything Taylor despised—wealth and social privilege, elite business connections and Conservative Party allegiances that would eventually make him lieutenant governor of the province. Taylor, on the other hand, was a classic outsider, a self-styled socialist who saw himself as a thorn in the side of the establishment. Later he parlayed these sympathies into a career as the city's most successful local politician, serving eight terms as mayor. But Nichol and the *Province* opposed him all the way, taking delight in Taylor's business difficulties—he lost control of the newspaper to creditors in 1915—and belittling his every success. The animosity between the two men fuelled a bitter newspaper war that entertained Vancouver readers for almost a decade.[91]

The brawling between Walter Nichol and Louis Taylor suggests that for all its veneer of sophistication and the pride it took in its modern urban conveniences, Vancouver retained elements of an unruly resource town whose rough edges had yet to be worn smooth. The city's old downtown provided inexpensive accommodations for single men seeking work and loggers and miners in from the coastal camps and looking for some action. Bars, of which there were many, stayed open all hours, even on Sundays. In BC as a whole, liquor consumption was double the national average.[92] This was the world brought to life by Martin Allerdale Grainger in his 1908 novel/memoir, *Woodsmen of the West,* in which he describes men "drifting up the street to the Terminus and down the street to the Eureka, and having a drink with the crowd in the Columbia Bar, and standing drinks for the girls at number so-and-so Dupont Street." In 1908, with a population of about seventy thousand, Vancouver had forty-seven hotels, twelve saloons, seven liquor stores and several "blind pigs," which sold illegal liquor behind closed doors. "There are some shady characters in a town like Vancouver," warned Grainger, "and persons of the underworld."[93] Police corruption was commonplace. An 1899 investigation discovered that officers were extorting protection money from the brothels along Dupont Street, selling liquor confiscated from raids on illegal night spots, sharing the proceeds from fines and, for a fee, neglecting to register criminal convictions.

Vancouver was a city that faced in two directions. The railways connected the Pacific coast to the interior of the province and to the rest of the continent: to the farms of the Fraser Valley, the mines of the Kootenay and the Boundary, the grainfields of the western Prairies, the populated cities of the East. During the pre-war boom period, BC experienced a mania for railway building. In 1905 a second transcontinental rail line, the Great Northern, arrived at a downtown terminal on Pender Street at Columbia. It was followed by a third in 1919, the Canadian Northern Pacific (later Canadian National). All this rail construction created jobs and a steady demand for building materials, foodstuffs and camp supplies of all sorts. At the same time the city faced seaward. A stream of steamships flowed through the First Narrows to and from the waterfront docks night and day, connecting the city to the north coast and to ports across the Pacific. Canadian Pacific operated its fleet of elegant *Princess* ships on the triangle route between Vancouver, Victoria and Seattle and up the coast as far as Alaska. This in addition to CP's *Empress* liners, which provided passenger and freight service between Vancouver and the Far East. From its wharf at the foot of Carrall Street, the Union Steamship Company, created in 1889 by a group of local entrepreneurs, dispatched a fleet of smaller steamships to the camps, canneries and settlements between Vancouver and Prince Rupert. The Union boats were the supply line that kept the coastal economy humming, connecting the manufacturers and suppliers in Vancouver to their upcoast customers. They also provided a lifeline to the outside world for the thousands of people who lived and worked in the coastal hinterland.

Railway construction was a contentious issue in local politics during the first decade of the new century, especially as it affected the future of False Creek. At the time the waterway was about five times the size it is today, with the eastern portion consisting of a shallow tidal basin fringed with mudflats. Only smallish vessels could navigate the inner creek, so it did not attract the industrial development that characterized the western portion. In 1902 the province granted possession of the bed of the inner creek to the city, leaving it free to make plans for the basin.[94] Initially city engineers (in 1905) proposed reclaiming some of the flats close to shore and dredging the central basin to allow navigation. When the Westminster Avenue Bridge opened three years later it included a lift to allow medium-sized vessels to pass through into this envisaged inner harbour.

However, the city's plans were abandoned in favour of an ambitious proposal by the Great Northern Railway. The GNR, through its subsidiary the Vancouver, Westminster and Yukon, controlled by John Hendry, had extended its main line into Vancouver in 1905, entering the city from the east and crossing False Creek on a trestle just to the west of Westminster Avenue, terminating at its station on Pender Street next door to Hendry's Royal City Planing Mills. Desiring more space for its railyards and warehouses, the GNR proposed filling in the False Creek tidal flats adjacent to land it already owned along the northern shoreline, to build a new terminal. The initial agreement involved land around the rim of the inner creek, preserving for the city a central area where it could go ahead with its plans to dredge a basin.

During the 1910 election, voters were asked to approve the GNR plans, which they did. Then, in 1913, voters approved an agreement with a second railway, the Canadian Northern Pacific, to turn over the city's final holdings in the inner creek in return for the railway building its terminus on the flats as well. The way was now clear for the entire inner creek to be filled in, transforming it into a major rail terminus, a project that was more or less complete by the end of the war. The Great Northern moved in 1916 from its Chinatown terminal to a new building next door to the Canadian Northern—later Canadian National—station, which opened three years later. An associated project was the creation of Granville Island, a former mudflat that was expanded in 1916 with fill from dredging operations in the creek to create a venue for industrial tenants. With the creation of the railyards and Granville Island, False Creek was affirmed as Vancouver's industrial heartland.

IN PRE-WAR VANCOUVER the electric trolleys shared the streets with horse-drawn wagons, bicycles and a few automobiles. Dr. Robert Mathison, a dentist, owned the first bicycle in the city, which he had brought out from Ontario in March 1887. According to Major Matthews, by 1900 a bicycle "craze" had seized the city. "Almost every family had one," he wrote, "some had more." They were so popular that racks were installed in the vestibules of office buildings and in public places. "The 'machines' were so numerous," continued Matthews, "that the City Council ordered special bicycle paths constructed on those streets which were most frequently used."[95] While cycling continued to be a popular leisure activity, it was replaced after the turn of the century by the streetcar and then the automobile as the main mode of urban transportation.

The first automobile, looking very much like a buggy on bedsprings, had appeared in Vancouver in 1899. It was a Stanley Steamer, a two-seater powered by a boiler concealed beneath the front seat. Steam proved an impractical technology and the internal combustion engine using gasoline for fuel soon became the industry standard. Vancouver's first gas car was a primitive Oldsmobile, purchased by James Stark, owner of the Glasgow House hotel on Cordova Street, as well as a dry goods business, to use as a delivery van.[96] According to his son Billy, the vehicle had no fenders, no lights and no horn, but it proved to be the harbinger of car culture in the city. By 1908 the province as a whole still had just 263 automobiles, but in Vancouver the number was growing fast enough for Imperial Oil to have decided, a year earlier, to open the country's first gas station, a gravity-fed tank perched atop a concrete pillar filling cars through a length of garden hose. Motorized trucks and vans appeared in growing numbers as well, replacing the horse-drawn wagon as a means of hauling freight. In 1907 Vancouver was the first city in Canada to have motorized firefighting equipment when the city purchased three trucks for the fire department. Two years later it bought a new gas-powered ambulance, which ironically enough knocked down and killed an American tourist on Granville Street during its trial run. At first automobiles were toys for the rich; it was said that the financier Alvo von Alvensleben used to tool around town in a chauffeured Packard—he drove, the chauffeur sat in the back. But soon the family car had become a middle-class necessity, competing with the street railway for road space.

The rivalry between car and streetcar came to a head in 1914 with the appearance of the jitney. A jitney was a private automobile offering taxi service to all parts of the city for a nickel a ride ("jitney" was a slang term for a five-cent piece). Drivers cruised the main thoroughfares, picking up passengers and taking them directly to their destinations. Customers appreciated the speed and convenience of the jitney and as many as 250 of these freelancers appeared on the streets during the daily rush hour, stealing business from the transit company.[97] With ridership and revenues falling, BC Electric fought back by reducing fares and improving service on downtown routes. The company also used its considerable political clout to lobby the city and the province to regulate and then to ban the jitneys as unfair competition. Eventually in 1917 the province passed legislation allowing the city to outlaw the "jits," which it did the following year.

ONE OF THE MOST CONTENTIOUS ISSUES in the city during the pre-war period was the future of Stanley Park. A rapidly growing population was using the park more than ever and demanding that it be "improved" with all manner of public attractions: zoos, playing fields, museums, beaches. Twice voters were asked to make it more accessible by approving the construction of a tram line through the heart of the park, and twice they refused. But other developments enjoyed more support. There were fundamental disagreements in the city between those who wanted to keep the park as pristine as possible, those who wished to open it to as many people as possible, and those who sought a middle ground.[98] At the centre of the controversy was a Parks Board proposal to replace the entrance to the park, a decaying wooden bridge across Coal Harbour, with a causeway. At low tide water drained from the western inner portion of Coal Harbour, leaving behind a vast swampy quagmire, a "lost lagoon" as the poet Pauline Johnson described it ("It is dusk on the Lost

Lagoon / and we two dreaming the dusk away").[99] A causeway, or land bridge, would create an artificial lake that could be landscaped into a more pleasing entrance to the park.

In 1912 the Parks Board invited the renowned British planner and landscape architect Thomas Mawson to visit Vancouver and consult on the project.[100] Mawson came up with far more than a causeway; he concocted a grandiose plan to transform Georgia Street into a broad pedestrian corridor worthy of a European capital. A lavish promenade would lead from a central square in the downtown business district down the slope to a large circular pond at the entrance to Stanley Park. The boulevard would circle the pond, providing access to three monumental neoclassical buildings: a natural history museum, a sports stadium and a lavish restaurant. When it was finished Vancouver would have its very own Champs-Élysées.

Though he was a stranger to the city, Mawson put his finger on an essential element of its character: the abiding tension between location and ambition. Speaking to a meeting of the local Canadian Club, he told his audience that during his visit he had had many conversations that led him to conclude that residents belonged to one of two camps. Either they loved "Nature" or they were "interested only in commercial pursuits" and "would do anything to destroy Nature."[101] This dichotomy, he said, was reflected in the layout of the city: on the one side was Stanley Park, the city's greatest asset; on the other, a downtown marked by the tawdry signs of material growth. Vancouver, he seemed to suggest, was squandering its location in pursuit of the almighty dollar. The intention of his ambitious concept was to rescue the "overgrown village" by imposing on it his dramatic vision of an integrated city where culture and nature were artfully combined.

If Mawson was a visionary he was also practical enough to recognize that his spectacular plans for Vancouver to become the Paris of the Pacific Northwest would not appeal to every resident, or even most of them. So he also submitted alternative plans. One proposed a straightforward causeway with minimal changes to the park entrance; another proposed filling in the lagoon area and converting it to playing fields and recreational spaces. The first appealed to representatives of the city's socio-economic elite, most of whom lived in the West End and wanted the park preserved as a natural wilderness—the "Stanley Forest" as they called it—while the second appealed to working people who favoured a much more democratic approach to park development. The Parks Board chose to approve Mawson's grandiose vision, which almost certainly would have changed the park and the whole city profoundly, had the 1913 recession not interceded to drain away the enthusiasm for megaprojects. In the end a simple causeway was constructed, dividing Coal Harbour and transforming the inner tidal flats into a permanent lake, the Lost Lagoon.

THOMAS MAWSON'S "Champs-Élysées on the Pacific" illustrates the confident, boosterish mentality pervading Vancouver from the turn of the century, particularly after 1906. The city's future as one of the leading urban centres on the continent seemed assured. Opportunity, Mayor Louis Taylor told one magazine writer, was "knocking every day on the door of every man who is alert enough to hear her call and energetic enough to answer it."[102] But in 1913 opportunity stopped knocking. The provincial economy went into a tailspin. Concerned about the political situation in Europe, British investors, who had financed much of the boom, began withdrawing their money. Building construction slowed. The value of real estate tumbled. Businesses of all kinds failed, throwing thousands of people out of work. On the eve of World War I, unemployment in the city reached fifteen thousand.

Emblematic of the downturn was the demise of the Dominion Trust Company. From its founding in 1903, Dominion Trust had become one of the largest investors in the local real estate market. In 1910 it completed a new, thirteen-storey headquarters at the corner of Hastings and Cambie Streets, opposite the present site of Victory Square. Flamboyant and colourful, built in the Beaux-Arts style, the Dominion Building was the city's first skyscraper, and for a few years was the tallest building in the British Empire— until the World Building around the corner went four stories higher in 1912. While the building remains a civic landmark, the company did not survive the downturn. As property values fell, so did the fortunes of Dominion Trust. On October 12, 1914, the company's general manager, William Arnold, shot and killed himself in his garage. The *Province* reported that the gun had gone off while Arnold was "testing" it.[103] It turned out that he had been making unauthorized loans that had become worthless. Before the end of the month, Dominion Trust collapsed. It marked the end of a prosperous, energetic, optimistic time in the city's history.

These Chinese mill hands worked at
the Royal City Planing Mills at the foot
of Carrall Street on False Creek.
Philip Timms photograph, Vancouver Public
Library 78362

CHAPTER THREE

Intolerance

JOHN MCDOUGALL was public enemy number one during Vancouver's earliest days. McDougall was a contractor who specialized in land clearance. People in town called him "Chinese" McDougall because he insisted on employing Asian labourers (at half the wages he paid anyone else), despite the fact that the white majority wanted the "Celestials" gone from the community. Following the completion of the construction of the transcontinental railway, Chinese navvies who had worked on the line had settled in the Lower Mainland. In 1885 the federal government, in order to discourage immigration from China, placed a head tax of $50 on Chinese newcomers, but Vancouver residents worried about the Chinese people who were already in the country. They believed these men stole jobs from white workers, and they harboured xenophobic fears that the Chinese residents were going to impose their cultural norms on British Columbia. Organized labour asked employers not to hire Chinese workers. Crosses were painted on the doors of businesses that dared to deal with them. City government agreed to refuse them jobs on public projects, and some were harassed and intimidated into leaving town.

"Chinese" McDougall did not go along with these exclusionary efforts. When he won a contract to clear 140 hectares of forest in the West End, he brought in a crew of Chinese men to do the job. His first attempt to install his workers at the site was met by an angry mob, which forced the Chinese workers onto a boat bound for Victoria. Undaunted, McDougall returned a few weeks later with another crew, determined to carry out his contract. On the evening of February 24, 1887, about three hundred residents (William Gallagher described them as "tough characters, hotheaded, thoughtless, strong and rough"[104]) attacked the Chinese camp above Coal Harbour, pulling down their shelters and burning their possessions. "Those who were caught were in some instances badly kicked by some of the crowd," reported the *News-Advertiser*, "and then ordered to pack up and leave, in which they were assisted in no gentle manner."[105] Later that evening a smaller mob attacked Chinese homes and stores downtown on Carrall Street. The next day, authorities bundled about a hundred Chinese men onto horse-drawn wagons and transported them to New Westminster, where again they were put on a steamboat bound for Victoria. In no uncertain terms the message was sent: Chinese people were not welcome in Vancouver.

The provincial government reacted immediately to the violence. Attorney General A.E.B. Davie called what had happened "a reign of terrorism" and accused municipal authorities of being "in sympathy with the agitation."[106] No friend of the Chinese, provincial legislators disliked anarchy even more, and this, they thought, was anarchy. "This was not a Chinese question," Colonel James Baker assured his colleagues, "but a question of law and order."[107] The attorney general introduced legislation that quickly passed, suspending the city's policing powers—in effect declaring martial law. A force of armed constables travelled from Victoria to the city to keep the peace. The Specials, as they were called, arrested three men suspected of being the ringleaders of the attack, but when no one came forward to testify against them they were released.

Under protection of the province, some of the Chinese workers filtered back into the city. A number of families lived on a large lot on Westminster Avenue (Main Street), where they established market gardens. Another group built homes and gardens and kept livestock at Anderson Point in Stanley Park, overlooking the site of what is now the Royal Vancouver Yacht Club. (Remote as this tiny settlement was, the persecution did not abate. Under the pretext that it presented a threat to public health, the Parks Board ordered the ranger to evict the residents and burn down their houses, which he did in the summer of 1890.) But most Chinese settled around the intersection of Dupont (Pender) and Carrall Streets, which emerged as the city's original Chinatown.[108] Here, in the face of white hostility and discrimination, Chinese residents created a haven where they could live and carry on their businesses. Many of the men, most of whom were single because they could not afford to pay the head tax to bring their families from China, found work at the nearby Royal City Planing Mills at the foot of Carrall on False Creek. Others cleared land, worked in laundries, hotels, brickyards and fish canneries, as pedlars and household servants, and on the coastal steamers. A handful of prominent merchants engaged in importing/exporting, real estate, opium manufacture and other businesses. By 1901 this bustling district numbered 2,100 residents, about 7 per cent of the city's population.[109] From this core, Chinatown spread westward during the next few years to include Shanghai and Canton Alleys and eastward down Dupont toward Main.

Antipathy toward the Chinese was motivated by a combination of racial prejudice and economic rivalry. The population of Vancouver was overwhelmingly Anglo-Saxon. Newcomers arrived mainly from Great Britain and its white colonies—Australia, New Zealand and South Africa. By 1911 one Vancouverite out of three came from the British Isles.[110] Migrants from eastern Canada were also mainly British stock, supplemented by a liberal number of Americans and western Europeans. This white majority considered "Celestials" to be disease-ridden, physically inferior and morally corrupt. Their homes were considered to be squalid, their neighbourhood a cesspool of whorehouses, gambling parlours and opium dens. The 1902 Royal Commission on Chinese Immigration called the Chinese "a people that cannot assimilate." The commissioners went on: "With their habits of overcrowding, and an utter disregard for all sanitary laws, they are a continual menace to health."[111] As a result they had to be segregated so as not to debase mainstream society. The Chinese were not allowed to vote, to hold professional jobs, to own property or to operate businesses outside of Chinatown. Chinese Vancouverites tended to congregate together to be close to relatives and certain cultural services, but segregation was not wholly a choice; it was enforced by law. At the same time, employers paid Chinese workers lower wages than white employees, and the labour movement, which was vehemently anti-Chinese, feared that they would drive down white incomes and monopolize the labour market.

The Chinese were not the only victims of racial animosity in early Vancouver. The British/American majority targeted anyone who it believed threatened its hegemony and the mores of what it considered *its* community. This included Japanese, South Asian and Indigenous people as well as the Chinese. On Powell Street east of Westminster Avenue, a neighbourhood of Japanese businesses and rooming houses took shape after 1900. The proximity of this "Little Tokyo" to Hastings Mill meant access to jobs for

1

2

1 When this photograph was taken, in 1904, Dupont Street was the centre of Chinatown. Three years later the street's name changed to Pender.
Philip Timms photograph, Vancouver Public Library 6729

2 A certificate for the head tax paid by Don Lee in 1918. By that time the tax amounted to $500. The tax was collected by the federal government until 1923, by which time it had been levied on about 82,000 Chinese immigrants.
Photographer Unknown, Vancouver Public Library 30625

the men who settled there. Japanese newcomers fell victim to the same restrictive laws as the Chinese, making it impossible for them to vote or to follow certain occupations. In 1903 the federal government raised the head tax on Chinese immigrants to $500, expecting that this would end immigration from China. The Japanese were not included in the head tax because Japan had agreed to limit the number of emigrants it allowed to leave for North America each year. Yet Asian newcomers continued to arrive, and racial panic continued to spread through White Vancouver.

Matters came to a head in 1907, when Vancouver experienced the worst racial turbulence in its history. The previous summer a large number of South Asian immigrants from India had arrived in the city. "Horde of Hungry Hindoos Invades Vancouver City," read a headline in the *World* newspaper, and "Starving Coolies Roam the Streets."[112] According to the paper, white women and children feared for their lives, while medical authorities warned that the newcomers posed a threat to public health. When none of these dire predictions came true the panic subsided, but it turned out to be only a prelude to the events of the following year, when the arrival of several thousand Asian immigrants set off alarm bells in white neighbourhoods. During the first six months of 1907, several hundred South Asians arrived in the city, but this number was dwarfed by the more than 3,200 Japanese arriving in port, followed by 2,300 more in July alone.[113] R.G. Macpherson, a druggist and local Liberal Member of Parliament, was one of the leading fear-mongers. "I can see without any difficulty the Province of British Columbia slipping into the hands of the Asiatics," he warned.[114] Macpherson lobbied the federal government to ban further immigration from Asia. "I regard the influx of Japanese as a menace to this country," he thundered. "This thing has got to be stopped."[115] Many in the city agreed, and on August 12 a local branch of the Asiatic Exclusion League (AEL) held its inaugural meeting. Founded in San Francisco two years earlier, the league had spread to cities all along the Pacific coast. In Vancouver its organization was spearheaded by the Trades and Labour Council and a variety of anti-Asian zealots. Rhetoric at the gathering reached a fever pitch; former mayor James Garden warned of a coming war between whites and "all other colours." The meeting endorsed the familiar call to ban all immigration from Asia and made plans for a rally to focus public indignation against the Japanese.

On the evening of Saturday, September 7, a large crowd gathered at the Cambie Street Grounds, an athletic field at Cambie and Dunsmuir that the Parks Board had purchased from the CPR. Forming a procession, the protestors marched to Hastings Street, then down Hastings to city hall on Main Street. This ornate building just south of the Carnegie Library at Hastings and Main had been built in 1889 as a market; in 1898 city council had taken over the second floor. Marchers waved small flags that read "A White Canada for Us" and held banners entreating onlookers to "Stand for a White Canada." A brass band played patriotic songs. The atmosphere was part festive, part threatening. One estimate put the size of the crowd massed outside city hall at ten thousand people. Inside the hall a capacity audience of about two thousand listened to a series of inflammatory speeches, and from time to time some of the same speakers—clergymen, politicians, visiting agitators from Seattle—went outside to address the milling throng, which had stirred itself up by burning an effigy of Lieutenant Governor James Dunsmuir, unpopular for his refusal to sign anti-immigration legislation.

At about nine o'clock a group of rowdies moved around the corner into Dupont Street and down into Chinatown, where they began heaving stones and bricks through store windows and smashing property. Terrified Chinese residents took shelter. After a few minutes the mob swung north and headed over to Little Tokyo on Powell Street. Here they encountered resistance for the first time. Knowing what was coming, residents had had time to arm themselves with clubs, bricks and bottles, which they used to hold off the aggressors until the police arrived. It was dawn before peace returned to the streets. On Sunday, white agitators who returned to Chinatown threatening violence found police guarding the neighbourhood, and the residents themselves stood ready to repulse any attacks. When stores

The anti-Asian riots of 1907 began at the Market Building on Main Street, the second floor of which was then serving as city hall. W.J. Moore photo, City of Vancouver Archives, AM54-S4-: City N12

opened on Monday morning many Chinese residents rushed to buy guns to protect their homes and businesses. Chinese employees held a three-day general strike to protest the attacks. Millhands, domestic servants, and laundry and restaurant workers all stayed out. On the Monday evening, rowdies tried to set fire to the Japanese Language School on Alexander Street, but locals chased them away.

Tensions remained high in the city for several days. No one was seriously injured during the violence, though twenty-four people were arrested, five of whom were convicted and jailed. The local press tried to make light of the episode. The *World*, for example, characterized the riot as "the mad frolic of a drunken mob" and played down its seriousness.[116] (Future mayor Louis Taylor, who owned the paper, was a member of the AEL.) If anti-Asian activists saw nothing to apologize for, the federal government was seriously embarrassed. Five weeks after the riot it announced the formation of a commission, headed by deputy minister of labour and future prime minister William Lyon Mackenzie King, to assess damages suffered by Japanese property owners during the violence. King arrived in the city on October 20 and for two weeks met daily in the Pender Hall with individuals who submitted damage claims. In the end the government disbursed about $9,000 in payments. (A further $26,000 in damages was paid to Chinese claimants the following spring.) Once King had completed his adjudications Prime Minister Laurier commissioned him to undertake a more wide-ranging inquiry into the issue of Japanese immigration. King concluded in a report presented in July 1908 that the Vancouver riots were directly linked to the sudden influx of Asian newcomers that preceded them, and he counselled that government should consider limiting the amount of Japanese immigration. This was a policy that had already been initiated by the so-called Gentlemen's Agreement between Japan and Canada, whereby Japan agreed to allow no more than four hundred Japanese citizens to migrate to Canada annually. Meantime the AEL continued to agitate for a total end to Asian immigration, though the league's importance faded.[117]

The influence of the AEL may have ebbed, but anti-Asian feeling continued to fester in the city. South Asians from India (or "Hindoos" as they were commonly called, a reference to the region of Hindustan in British India) began arriving in the province in 1903; by 1906 there were about 2,500 in BC. The following year the province stripped them of the right to vote—as it had the Chinese and Japanese years earlier—and then in 1908, federal legislation required new immigrants to Canada to travel non-stop from their country of origin, a measure that effectively cut off migration from India, where no direct passage was available. The government also required each newcomer to be carrying $200, another regulation aimed particularly at South Asians. With all these restrictions, the flow of South Asian immigrants slowed to a trickle, and by 1911 only 730 lived in Greater Vancouver.[118] Nonetheless the white majority was sensitive to any attempt by "Hindoos" to get around the regulations and stood ready to defend the "white man's country" with force if necessary.

In May 1914, the tramp steamer *Komagata Maru* arrived in the harbour carrying 376 passengers, mostly Sikhs from the Punjab who wished to enter Canada. Having originated in Hong Kong, the *Maru* was in violation of the direct passage regulation and officials in Vancouver refused to allow the vessel to dock or anyone to disembark. The standoff that followed lasted for several weeks. Authorities dragged out the usual landing procedures while allowing only the minimum amounts of food and water to reach the stranded passengers. An armed launch kept the anchored vessel under guard. In the city the local South Asian community raised money to buy food and to hire a lawyer, J. Edward Bird, to challenge the ban. Finally, immigration officials agreed to allow a test case, and a passenger named Munshi Singh was chosen to appear before the BC Court of Appeal. On July 6 the court ruled that Munshi Singh, and by implication all the other passengers, were forbidden to land. The judges decided that the passengers were in violation of the continuous journey provision, and that Canada had the authority to bar British subjects from entry anyway. The *Maru*, and everyone on board, would have to go.

But the ship lingered on as Gurdit Singh, who had chartered the vessel in the first place, negotiated how provisions for the journey back to India would be paid for and delivered. As the passengers became more desperate, they seized control of the ship so it could not leave. On July 19, in the middle of the night, a local immigration agent named Malcolm Reid led an armed force of police and ex-army volunteers out to the ship aboard the tug *Sea Lion*, intending to board and return control of the vessel to its crew. In response, passengers rained down lumps of coal, bricks and pieces of scrap metal onto the deck of the tug, forcing it to retreat to shore. By this time lawyer Bird was receiving death threats and had to go into hiding with his family. The militia was put on alert, armed troops massed on the waterfront and rioting was expected to break out in the streets at any moment. The authorities were prepared to storm the *Maru* but only as a last resort, fearing that an armed attack would bring casualties. Finally a federal cabinet minister, Martin Burrell, arrived from his Okanagan constituency and negotiated an end to the impasse by agreeing on behalf of the

Passengers pass the time stranded aboard the *Komagata Maru*, waiting in vain for the Canadian government to allow them to land. After two months the ship was forced to leave Burrard Inlet and return to India.

In 2016 Prime Minister Justin Trudeau formally apologized on behalf of Canada for the incident.
Leonard Frank photograph, Vancouver Public Library 6226

Two Indigenous women on West Hastings
Street in 1905, perhaps selling their wares
door to door.
Philip Timms photograph, Vancouver Public
Library 67507

government to provision the ship. The naval vessel HMCS *Rainbow* arrived from Esquimalt to escort the *Maru*, and on July 23 it hauled anchor and left the harbour.

When the *Maru* arrived in Calcutta, British colonial officials tried to herd the passengers onto a waiting train, sparking a riot in which soldiers killed eighteen people. In Vancouver the aftermath was violent as well. The South Asian community was enraged at the treatment of the would-be immigrants and retaliated against suspected police informants in its midst. Two informants were murdered and then a third, Bela Singh, was cornered in the Sikh temple and killed two people trying to escape. Bela Singh was captured, and his trial began in Vancouver on October 21. As the immigration agent and spymaster William Hopkinson waited outside the courtroom, he was assassinated by another activist, Mewa Singh, who gave himself up and was hanged for the murder early in the new year.[119]

Mewa Singh's execution, and the beginning of the world war, brought an end to this period of racial violence in the city's history. The combination of restrictive measures put in place to halt, or at least moderate, immigration from Asian countries succeeded in keeping Vancouver predominantly "white." The census of 1911 revealed that just 6 per cent of the population was Asian, down from 10 per cent a decade earlier.[120] Nonetheless, the fear of an Asian influx exceeded the objective "threat" and an incipient racism, periodically boiling to the surface, characterized mainstream society in Vancouver for many years to come.

IN JULY 1887—six months after the anti-Chinese violence in the West End—police descended on a ramshackle collection of buildings next door to the Hastings Mill, known as the "Indian rancheria," and evicted all its residents. The evictees were squatters, mostly Indigenous millworkers and stevedores and their families who had settled close to their place of employment at the mill and its docks. According to churchmen and city officials, the rancheria was a shameful centre of depravity and they wanted it removed, if for no other reason than the CPR main line ran right through the shanty town and the railway did not want its passengers exposed to such squalid sights. Some of the squatters must have returned, however, because five years later a reporter from the *Vancouver World* visited the site, consisting of "two straggling rows of huts or shacks that line the foreshore of Burrard Inlet." The reporter continued: "These huts contain a few white and colored men of the lower class, several Japs, and during certain seasons a large number of Indians." The rancheria, he claimed, was a gathering spot for "the lowest of the low."[121] Bootleggers came to sell their liquor.

According to the press, drunken brawls were common, as was sex work among the Indigenous women. STDs were rampant. Finally, in 1896, the city's medical officer supervised the final destruction of the shacks under the pretext of protecting the public health.

The fate of the rancheria and the thuggery against the Chinese were linked events, part of the same desire on the part of the city's white majority to ghettoize ethnic minorities. Just as Chinese, Japanese and South Asian immigrants were unwelcome and forced to live in their own segregated neighbourhoods, the Indigenous inhabitants who had lived on the shores of Burrard Inlet for centuries were gradually expelled from their homes and erased from the cultural fabric of the city in the years before World War I.

When Stanley Park was created in 1887, there was a significant settlement of Squamish people living on the beach at Xway'xway (Lumberman's Arch), which had been home to them and their ancestors for millennia. "Untold ages past men lived on this clearing," reported August Jack Khahtsahlano.[122] Residents of Xway'xway had greeted Captain Vancouver and his men as they passed through the First Narrows in June 1792. The people dug clams, fished, killed waterfowl and utilized the cedar forest to build houses, canoes, utensils, baskets and ceremonial items. As well, the Squamish and Musqueam lived at least seasonally at several other sites around the park.[123] The population was depleted by early smallpox epidemics but still occupied dwellings along the foreshore.

In 1876 the federal and provincial governments appointed the Joint Indian Reserve Commission to resolve the issue of Aboriginal land rights. The three-person commission arrived at Xway'xway on November 16, 1876. Though fifty people inhabited the site, the commissioners mistakenly believed that Xway'xway was a recent village with "no old associations with the spot," in the words of commissioner Gilbert Sproat. In other words, the Indigenous inhabitants were thought to be squatters. They received no reserve, and in 1888, when the construction of the park road passed right through their settlement, the people were forced to relocate to Squamish and Musqueam reserves on the North Shore and in South Vancouver. A few years later the Parks Board burned the remaining buildings.[124] Only one person remained, a Squamish woman known as Aunt Sally, who continued to live in the park until she died in 1923. Her daughter Mariah then sold the property to the Parks Board, which burned the house down.[125] (At Brockton Point, another so-called squatter community consisting of families of mixed European and Indigenous heritage persisted until the Parks Board evicted them in the 1930s.)

Unlike the inhabitants of Xway'xway, residents of Vancouver's other main Indigenous village, Sen ákw, located at the entrance to False Creek, had been granted a small reserve by the Reserve Commission. Commissioner A.C. Anderson described the village site during his 1876 visit: "This Reserve is heavily wooded, as a whole, but with partially cleared patches," he wrote in his diary. "Adjoining the house of the Chief is a well-fenced garden, of about an acre or more, in which were growing thirty apple trees, Rasp-berries, Strawberries & other fruit, with cabbages and other vegetables—the whole in very good order."[126]

However, as the city expanded southward, the white majority came to agree that the 32-hectare site was far too valuable to leave in the hands of the sixty or seventy people who lived there. After initially refusing to leave, the Squamish acceded to pressure from the provincial government and in 1913 agreed to sell their land, for fear that they would have it taken from them. On April 9 a scow arrived to carry away the twenty or so families along with their belongings. Once again the remaining buildings were torched. The people went to live at other local reserves. Afterward the attorney general actually boasted how he had obtained the land for far less than it was worth.[127] The last Indigenous village within the city limits was gone.

Curiously, just a month earlier, Vancouver had witnessed an unprecedented outpouring of grief and respect when the renowned "Mohawk Princess," poet and stage performer Pauline Johnson, died at a private hospital on Bute Street. Johnson, who was from the Six Nations Reserve in Ontario, had been living in the city since her retirement from touring in 1909 and had been ill with breast cancer for some time. She died on March 7. The following day the *Province* called her "a great daughter of the flag" and noted her "generous charity towards everything and everybody with whom she came in contact."[128]

Her funeral at Christ Church Cathedral was attended by many city notables. Flags were lowered to half mast and civic offices closed. Onlookers lined the sidewalks to pay their respects. "It was as if the rush and noise of the city had been stayed in respect to this gifted Indian woman," reported the *Sun* on its front page.[129] It is doubtful that any of the mourners paused to consider that they were venerating the life of an Indigenous celebrity at the same time as their government was driving a group of Indigenous people from their homes at Sen-ákw.

ETHNICITY WAS ONE CRITERION that early Vancouverites used to decide who could live where. Another was morality. In her autobiographical novel *The Innocent Traveller*, Ethel Wilson describes her life as a young girl living in the pre-war city. On Saturday mornings her young alter ego Rose would leave her privileged residential enclave in the West End to go downtown shopping with her aunt. Walking along Cordova Street, writes Wilson, Rose "sometimes saw glorious ladies in fashionable black, who sauntered, often in pairs. These ladies were beautiful. They did not shop. They sauntered lazily with a swaying of opulent hips and bosom, looking softly yet alertly from lustrous eyes set in masks of rose and white. 'Aunt Rachel, Aunt Rachel, *look* at those pretty ladies, who are they, just look!' Rose had sometimes whispered. But Aunt Rachel did not look. She behaved as if she were blind and deaf. It appeared that she did not know the pretty ladies at all."[130] Cordova Street was just around the corner from Dupont Street, which at the turn of the century was the city's Red Light district inhabited by the "pretty ladies" who respectable society did not want to know. During the daylight hours it was a bustle of Chinese vegetable vendors; by night the three or four blocks filled with mobs of men in search of drink and female companionship at one of the clapboard buildings in which the sex trade flourished.

Sex work had been part of the city's lifeblood from the beginning. It always existed in an uneasy relationship with the mainstream, both geographically and morally. During the 1870s, when Vancouver was still Granville, Birdie Stewart operated the first brothel on Water Street, next door to the Methodist Church and just a few steps from the jail. She was burned out by the fire, but like everything else the sex trade rebounded, and by 1892 there were reported to be eighteen or nineteen brothels primarily serving the floating population of millworkers, loggers, sailors and other transients. Authorities dealt discreetly with the brothel-keepers, who were allowed to continue in business in return for making regular "contributions" to the city's finances.

William Gallagher explained that in the first weeks following the election of the inaugural city council, there was no money available to pay the salaries of civic officials. "The situation was pressing and desperate, but not forlorn," said Gallagher. "It was clearly a case for the Chief of Police and he was told to 'get busy' and started to 'clean up the town.'" The police rounded up about twenty "vagrants," a category that included sex workers, and each was fined $20 by Mayor Malcolm MacLean, who in the absence of the magistrate was filling in on the bench. (A reluctant MacLean had to be generously plied with "invigorating stimulant" at the Bodega saloon, Gallagher recalled, before he agreed to the plan.) "The money from their fines was very convenient at the moment to solve the more pressing needs of our civic finance," reported Gallagher.[131] Later it was customary for the police to take bribes to turn a blind eye to the activities of the women.

There was a limit to the public tolerance of the sex trade. Madams were expected to confine their operations to the margins of settlement, which Dupont Street was in the early years. But as the downtown expanded south toward False Creek, civic officials served notice that the brothels would have to move. Moral zealots wanted the prostitutes run out of town completely, but the more practical-minded recognized that they would only return. As police chief C.A. Chisholm told a reporter in 1906: "I make no concealment of my view that ultimately one place, one district remote from respectable streets and centres, will have to be set aside for these dames."[132]

For a while that destination appeared to be Shanghai Alley and Canton Alley at the western edge of Chinatown. Within a year it was reported that 105 brothels were operating in these two laneways; most were single rooms in the crowded tenements that lined the alleys, not full-fledged houses. A delegation of reformers visited Shanghai Alley in the company of a reporter who left a lurid description of the scene: "A long string of red lights told all too plainly the nature of the resorts," he wrote; "from behind the curtains and through the half-opened doors the women of the street could plainly be seen inviting passersby to enter. As quickly as visitors to the place left, the occupants of the room attired in the briefest of skirts, and with décolleté apparel to the limit, took their choice from the waiting crowd about the door."[133]

Local merchants were unhappy with the proliferation of the sex trade in Chinatown and in nearby neighbourhoods closer to Main Street, and in 1912, encouraged by authorities, many brothel keepers relocated to Alexander Street, closer to the waterfront and to the Hastings Mill. For the next few years this was the city's new red light district, tolerated by police and civic government, excoriated by hardline abolitionists who desired the complete suppression of "the social evil." In November 1912 the newspaper *The Truth* published a sensational account of the goings-on in Alexander Street. Its reporter discovered perfumed women in gaudy dresses parading brazenly in the street while lights blazed all night from every window and the sounds of raucous music spilled from the doorways. At the House of All Nations, the reporter discovered, "you can get everything from a chocolate coloured damsel up to a Swede girl." Alexander Street, he concluded, "was never as open as it is now."[134] No matter what they said in public, in practice civic officials were happy enough to leave the sex trade alone so long as it remained confined to a "segregated district" in the east end and did not spread into the business district and the west of the city.

LATE IN THE EVENING of April 13, 1903, a well-known socialist and labour activist named Frank Rogers was standing with two companions near the CPR tracks at the north end of Abbott Street. A strike by railway workers against the CPR had been raging for several weeks and Rogers may have gone down to the tracks to investigate reports that some union men were in a fight with a pair of "substitutes," scabs whom the railway brought in to break the strike. Suddenly what one newspaper called "a fusillade of shots" rang out of the darkness.[135] Rogers went down in a heap with a bullet wound to his stomach. No one saw the gunman, and once the echoes died away silence returned to the street. His companions carried Rogers to a nearby hotel and then to the hospital, where he died hours later. A young policeman named Alfred Allan had been seen near the shooting and was taken into custody. When his revolver failed to match the fatal bullet, Allan was released, and a substitute who had been at the scene, James McGregor, was arrested and charged with murder.[136]

Rogers, a longshoreman by trade, was a leading figure in Vancouver's fractious world of left-wing politics, a co-founder of one of the socialist parties that kept relations between capital and labour on a high boil. He was the leader of the bitter fishermen's strikes on the Fraser River in 1900 and 1901 and twice ended up in jail for his militant activities. Union men, therefore, did not believe his shooting was an accident. To them it was a targeted assassination orchestrated by a company, the CPR, well known for resisting the influence of unions among its employees. Hundreds of unionists turned out on the Saturday following Rogers's death to walk in a long procession behind his coffin. "Work in the city was practically stopped," reported the *Daily Colonist;* it was "the largest number of people on foot of any funeral which ever took place in Vancouver."[137] But Rogers's killer was never found. In early May a jury acquitted McGregor—the CPR provided his lawyer—and no one else was ever charged.[138]

Rogers's death was the low point in the bitter dispute between the CPR and the United Brotherhood of Railway Employees (UBRE), which was trying to organize the freight handlers and clerks who worked for the rail company. The CPR had arrangements with several craft unions but it hoped to limit unionization among its less skilled workforce. At the beginning of the year the company decided to take on the UBRE, launching a campaign of intimidation and coercion against workers that led to the walkout at the end of February. When the company summarily fired all the strikers, sympathy walkouts spread to CPR freight handlers, and then to longshoremen on the Vancouver waterfront and to miners in Nanaimo. While support for the strike was wide spread, it was far from unanimous, with conservative unionists in the city refusing to endorse it. The railway brought in strike-breakers and eventually the strike collapsed. The UBRE was smashed, at least in Vancouver, as the power of the CPR over its workforce was confirmed. "Never before had [the CPR] fought a union with such resolute determination," writes Hugh Tuck, the main historian of the conflict. A federal Royal Commission on Industrial Disputes was tasked with investigating the causes of the unrest in BC—there had also been strikes in local coal mines—and reported that in its opinion the problem was not wages or working conditions but rather radical American unions, which were leading local workers astray and threatening the economy of western Canada.[139]

The UBRE strike was one of the most dramatic work stoppages in pre-war Vancouver, but hardly the only one. The return to good times initiated by the Klondike gold strike created a strong demand for labour and put workers in a position to insist on better terms. The refusal by employers to grant these demands, at least not without a fight, resulted in an increase in the number of strikes—twenty-two in 1902–3 alone—and an increased militancy on the part of labour.[140] In 1903 employers came together to form the Employers' Association of Vancouver to take joint action against the unions. Like the Royal Commission on Industrial Disputes, the association blamed the militant upsurge on outside socialist agitators. "Nowhere else in Canada is the labour question so prominent," observed the English social critic J.A. Hobson after he visited the city in 1905; "nowhere else is the class sentiment of employer and employed so much embittered."[141] Marches, protests and strikes were facts of everyday life in the city. Harry Archibald, an engineer, wrote home to his family in Nova Scotia in 1910: "This Vancouver is full of Socialists. They have meetings nearly every evening and on Sundays."[142]

The historian Robert McDonald identified several unique characteristics of the pre-war Vancouver working class.[143] Most important, the city lacked a large factory-based workforce. By comparison, in 1911 Toronto had 35 per cent of its workers employed in manufacturing, Montreal just over 33 per cent and Hamilton about half; but in Vancouver, manufacturing employed just 18.5 per cent of the workforce.[144] Wood products plants were the main industrial employers. The Hastings Mill was the city's largest single industrial enterprise, but there were many other shingle mills, sawmills and sash and door factories. Indeed, McDonald called wood manufacturing "Vancouver's only really large industry," employing as it did more than 60 per cent of the industrial workforce.[145] Construction was another significant employer, given how quickly the city was growing. In 1911, 17.6 per cent of the workforce were involved in the building trades—

carpenters, bricklayers, stonemasons, electricians and so on—compared to just over 12 per cent in Toronto.

With a labour force so dependent on resource industries and construction, seasonal changes had a deep impact on the local working class. For many workers, winter was a time of forced unemployment as building projects shut down and logging camps and fish canneries closed. When jobs were in short supply the unemployed congregated in Vancouver, placing a strain on civic charities and alarming local government officials who feared the potential for social unrest. Another characteristic of the local work force was the large component of Asian workers, who destabilized the labour market because of their willingness to work for lower wages than the norm. And lastly, Vancouver had a relatively small number of females in the work force, chiefly because of the scarcity of factory jobs. In 1911 women accounted for just 12.7 per cent of the city's workforce—mainly domestics, office workers, teachers and nurses—about one half the rate of Toronto, where factory jobs for women were more plentiful.

Workers in Vancouver were not unanimous in their approach to the "class question." The moderate mainstream adhered to a version of labourism, a mild reformism that emphasized the achievement of better wages and working conditions through the democratic political process. Labourists wished to improve capitalism, not overthrow it. To this end they endorsed candidates for public office and fought for reforms that bettered the situation of working people. A typical labourist issue was the eight-hour working day. In 1909, voters in the city overwhelmingly supported a plebiscite in favour of the eight-hour day for civic employees. Charles Douglas, the wealthy realtor who had been elected mayor in that year's election, failed to introduce the reform, and it was again a major issue in the 1910 election when Douglas sought a second term. He was challenged by the newspaperman Louis Taylor, who made the issue his own. Taylor's opponents called him a demagogue and a socialist who was stirring up class warfare by pitching his appeal to the working class, but the voters did not agree, electing Taylor to the first of eight non-consecutive terms as the city's mayor. (He remains the longest-serving mayor in Vancouver's history.) At its first meeting, the new council introduced the eight-hour day with no reduction in pay. This was the sort of incremental reform that labourism thought was the purpose of working-class political involvement.

More radical socialists advocated not reform but revolution. They were divided between the so-called "impossibilists," who advocated uncompromising class struggle while rejecting unions as a panacea, and the more conciliatory approach represented by members of the Socialist Party of

Canada, who thought that parliamentary democracy could be used to make the revolution. The most militant activists were the Industrial Workers of the World, the "Wobblies." Founded in Chicago in 1905, the IWW spread across the border into BC, preaching direct action and industrial unionism; that is, the organization of workers across an entire industry, regardless of skill level, ethnicity or gender. Wobblies thought that workers should overturn the capitalist state, not participate in its elections. They supported the general strike as a legitimate weapon in the struggle with capital. The Wobblies, who scorned middle-class reformers and intellectuals, were not popular with mainstream labour but found a sympathetic audience among the unskilled and seasonal workers who gathered in Vancouver in the winter or when jobs were in short supply.

Civic authorities were leery of this floating population of transients, the cost they might impose on the relief system and the threat they posed to civic peace. For certain the authorities, supported by major employers, did not want IWW activists using city streets to foment their brand of radicalism. On April 4, 1909, soapbox orators from the IWW and the Socialist Party of Canada were declaiming to a crowd at the corner of Carrall and Hastings when police, acting on instructions from civic officials, broke up the meeting and arrested six of the speakers, one of whom went to jail.[146] (Another speaker was arrested in a separate incident and fined $100.) Outraged at what they took to be the suppression of their freedom of speech, members of the labour movement responded with rallies and protests, and after several weeks of agitation in the streets, the police backed off.

The "free speech" fight broke out again early in 1912. The previous summer there had been a general strike in the building trades over the issue of the closed shop. Carpenters and other trades were determined to make their job sites union-only, while contractors were equally determined to retain their freedom to hire non-union labour. Other trades joined the carpenters until by mid-June there were some four thousand construction workers on strike. Ultimately the strikers failed—they could not stop employers from bringing in non-union workers, and by the end of the summer they had returned to work. Still, it was the largest sympathy strike in the city to that time and served to heighten class tensions, as did the high levels of unemployment that winter.[147]

During the civic election in January 1912, the issue of transiency and crime was in the spotlight. The successful candidate for mayor, James Findlay, railed against the crime wave that he said was sweeping Vancouver. Findlay blamed transients for the problem and at one point even suggested they be tied to the whipping post and flogged as a way of discouraging their presence in the city.[148] Following the election, the *Province* newspaper pointed its finger at "the gang of thugs and thieves who have made life a burden here for weeks" and urged the mayor to run them out of town "without delay."[149] Agreeing, the new city council passed a bylaw banning outdoor meetings, which the IWW promptly defied. Protest gatherings attracted as many as ten thousand people. On January 28, police on foot and horseback wielding clubs and whips waded into a large meeting at the Powell Street Grounds and arrested more than two dozen people. But activists were undeterred, and the police continued to arrest "vagrants" and break up rallies. Finally, labour leaders and politicians brokered an agreement that ended the violent confrontations. Speakers were allowed to operate without fear of arrest, and by mid-February peace had returned to the streets.

ONE CONTROVERSIAL IDEA that became associated with Vancouver during the pre-war period was the single tax, a notion made famous by the American social reformer Henry George. In his 1879 best-seller *Progress and Poverty*, George argued that private ownership of land was the root cause of economic inequality. He believed that wealth resulted from the co-operation of capital and labour, but through no efforts of their own, landlords profited from escalating property values, draining away the economic surplus and creating poverty and misery. A tax on land—the so-called single tax—would control speculation and confiscate excess rents for the good of the community. Georgeites believed that taxes on improvements and incomes, being taxes on labour, stifled economic development. A tax on unimproved land value, on the other hand, transferred wealth from the speculator to the community as a whole.

The single tax gained a wide following, usually within progressive circles, but in Vancouver the idea achieved mainstream political respectability less as a social justice measure than as a strategy for encouraging economic growth. A Single Tax Club formed in the city in 1889, and two years later alderman J.T. Carroll ran for mayor, albeit unsuccessfully, on a single tax platform. In 1897 the municipality of South Vancouver decided not to assess improvements as a way of keeping taxes low, but by this time, as A.H. Lewis, the chronicler of South Vancouver's history, pointed out, the single tax was not to be confused with Henry George's idea. While George advocated public ownership of land, wrote Lewis, the BC version of his idea "is a tax designed entirely with the object of encouraging building."[150]

The main local proponent of what might be called "single tax lite" was Louis Taylor. Taylor became so associated with the idea that he was known across North America as "Single Tax Taylor" and Vancouver gained a reputation as "the Single Tax City." In the spring of 1910, during Taylor's first term as mayor, council approved the complete abolition of the tax on property improvements. Taylor credited this change for sparking the building boom that preceded World War I. According to him, the single tax had put Vancouver on the map. "As Macaulay said of Byron," he boasted in his own newspaper, the *World*, "the city awoke one morning and found itself famous." Queries about Vancouver's application of the tax were pouring into city hall from across North America, he reported.[151] Locally, however, the tax was not universally approved. The *Province* worried that a heavy tax on property would drive capital away from the city and all the land eventually would end up publicly owned. "Surely the affairs of Vancouver can be conducted without giving way to every form of Socialistic fad and scatterbrained folly," the paper editorialized.[152]

As local lawyer and prominent Liberal F.C. Wade argued in a letter to the editor of the *Province*, it is doubtful that the single tax had much to do with the pre-war prosperity. Taylor's claims for the benefits of the tax were, he said, "humbug." In Wade's view, the single tax as implemented in Vancouver was a pale shadow of what Henry George had proposed, and more a detriment to economic prosperity than a boost. In the end it is difficult to say how much the abolition of the tax on property improvements contributed to the boom, but it is useful to note that when times turned bad following the war, the city once again began assessing improvements and the single tax was quickly forgotten—even by Mayor Taylor himself, who, many years later, when interviewed about his career, did not even mention the single tax among his many accomplishments.[153]

AS THE EUROPEAN WAR APPROACHED, Vancouver was a house divided. Economic boom times had not brought industrial peace. Capital and labour staged bitter fights over who would control the workplace, and quite regularly their struggles bubbled over into strikes and street protest. At the same time the city's white majority betrayed deep anxiety about losing control of the community. Out of all proportion to their actual numbers, the influx of Asian newcomers—Chinese, Japanese and South Asian— threw a scare into the local elite, for its impact on the labour market as well as its threat to white hegemony. Just three months before the war began, the streets had almost erupted in racial violence as the case of the *Komagata Maru* made its way through the courts. With the outbreak of war, however, the attention of Vancouverites turned to other, more distant enemies, and for a while, at least, domestic differences took a back seat to the crisis in Europe.

Two young girls at Strathcona School in 1930.
The Strathcona neighbourhood east of
Chinatown was a melting pot of immigrant
families from all over the world.
Stuart Thomson photo, City of Vancouver
Archives, AM1535-: CVA 99-2186

CHAPTER FOUR

• • •

War,
and Postwar

ON AUGUST 4, 1914, World War I began. "We stand shoulder to shoulder with Britain and the other British dominions in this quarrel," Prime Minister Robert Borden told the House of Commons, promising to send Canadian troops overseas to join the conflict. In Vancouver, as across the country, young men responded with enthusiasm. About 30 per cent of the city's population was British-born with strong emotional and family ties to the homeland. Most believed, along with their prime minister, that when Britain was attacked, so were they.

In his war memoir, *Maple Leaves in Flanders Fields*, Dr. George Gibson (writing as Herbert Rae, his middle names), an Edinburgh-born physician who had established a practice in Vancouver in 1911, captured the excitement that greeted the outbreak of war. The city was abuzz with rumour and expectation. "The newspapers seized the opportunity and gleaned a golden harvest," wrote Gibson. "Special editions appeared by the half-hour, and were as rapidly bought up . . . The clubs were crowded with anxious business men, too excited to talk business, and the bars conducted a feverish trade."[154] Everywhere the talk was of war, and how to join up: "Day by day the recruits swarmed in. Such recruits were surely never seen before. The woods disgorged them; the mountains shook them clear; they deserted from the ships and the harbour; they hit the ties from across the great divide. The mines, the camps, the canneries and the orchards, all sent their share."[155] After a few days of initial training the new enlistees marched to the station and boarded the trains that would bear them eastward to the assembly camp at Valcartier, Quebec, before embarkation for Europe. "All through the Empire these same scenes were being enacted, troops marching to tuck of drum, men cheering, women crying, and all with eyes turned on the common objective, Berlin."[156] Gibson himself joined the parade. He served overseas for the entire war as a medical officer and was present at many of the major engagements involving the Canadian Corps.

The initial euphoria of war quickly gave way to anxiety. Europe was a long way from British Columbia, but Germany had naval vessels in the Pacific that were rumoured to be steaming toward the West Coast. "How will this defenceless province protect herself from raids by hostile cruisers?" asked the *Province*.[157] Soon after the declaration of war, the German battleship *Leipzig* was spotted patrolling the coast of California. They needed coal for their fleet, so it made sense that the Germans might have the Vancouver Island mines, perhaps even Vancouver itself, in their sights. In this atmosphere of heightened alert Premier Richard McBride's purchase of two submarines from a Seattle shipyard was less quixotic than it seems in hindsight. The subs were being built for the Chilean navy, which was slow to pay for them, and McBride was able to pick up the pair for a little over $1 million. For three days BC had its own navy, the only province ever to do so, before turning ownership of the vessels over to the federal government. For the next three years they patrolled the Strait of Juan de Fuca and the west coast from their base in Esquimalt and may have played a part in discouraging a German attack. For whatever reason the *Leipzig* turned south, where it took part in the defeat of a British squadron off the coast of South America. It was not really until the end of the year, when British destroyers defeated the Germans in a naval engagement at the Falkland Islands, sinking the *Leipzig* in the process, that fears of an immediate attack on the coast abated. Meanwhile the military installed two guns overlooking the First Narrows, joined by another couple of guns at the tip of Point Grey.

Anxiety mixed with gloom over the economic situation. The recession that had begun in 1913 persisted. There were 15,000 jobless people in the city when the war began, and unemployment was running at twice the national rate.[158] A reporter for the *Labour Gazette* wrote that it was not unusual to be accosted by panhandlers in the street.[159] The value of building permits in 1915 amounted to less than a tenth of what it had been three years earlier, with the obvious impact on lumber producers and construction workers. Shipping was interrupted by the war. In 1913 the port's first grain elevator opened but so little grain was moving through it that it became known as "Stevens' Folly," after H.H. Stevens, the local MP who had lobbied for its construction. Similarly, the promise of the Panama Canal, which opened just days before the outbreak of war, did not materialize for several years. With the outlook for work so grim, many people left to seek opportunity elsewhere. Combined with the number of men who enlisted for overseas combat, the city's population fell by 20 per cent by the middle of the war.

NOT SURPRISINGLY, given the deteriorating economic situation, civic voters chose to toss out the incumbent mayor, Truman Baxter, when they went to the polls at the beginning of 1915. The campaign, which began on January 2, was one of the liveliest in the city's history. Four candidates declared themselves. Along with Baxter there were two other former mayors, the wealthy realtor Charles Douglas and the newspaper publisher Louis Taylor. The wild-card candidate was Joseph Martin, a transplanted Manitoban who had made a fortune in real estate, which he used to finance his political ambitions. Elected to the provincial legislature in 1898, he had served a brief term as premier, largely because the lieutenant governor couldn't find anyone else to appoint. Martin was a champion talker, brash and combative. He earned his nickname, "Fighting Joe," for the time he came to blows with Richard McBride on the floor of the legislature. By the time of the 1915 civic election, Martin was living part-time in London, where he had managed to get himself elected to the House of Commons.

Both Taylor and Martin presented themselves on the campaign trail as friends of labour and enemies of the elites, and they saved their heaviest vitriol for each other. Taylor accused his opponent of being a land speculator— Martin owned a great deal of property in the east end—who favoured higher taxes for working people and lower taxes for property owners such as himself. "I have worked consistently for the masses and don't care a hang for the bankers and the classes," thundered Taylor.[160] For his part, Martin promised to reduce extravagant spending at city hall and abolish the single tax, one of Taylor's signature policies.

On election day, Taylor emerged the victor with 33 per cent of the popular vote. It was a narrow victory and it turned out only to be round one in a more protracted battle. Sensing that he was vulnerable, Taylor's opponents petitioned the provincial Supreme Court to overturn the election based on a technicality to do with whether or not the property he owned in the city was debt-free. The court ruled against Taylor, and ordered another election. This time the opposition ran a single candidate, alderman Walter Hepburn, and Taylor suspected a trap. According to the rules, if Taylor won the second election and was disqualified again, then the other candidate would be declared the winner. To foil this ploy, he convinced his good friend, the architect William Tuff Whiteway, to join the race. Now if the results of the second round did not stand up in court, at least there would have to be a third.

The most remarkable moment of the campaign belonged to "Fighting Joe" Martin, who this time was not even a candidate. Appearing at a meeting in the Dominion Hall in support of Hepburn, Martin spewed charges of personal dishonesty and corruption against Taylor, claiming that the publisher was broke and dependent on support from "Chinese gamblers" and owners of the brothels on Alexander Street. "L.D. can go to the courts of law about these statements and I'll prove them," Martin shouted. But actually he couldn't prove anything; four days later he retracted his remarks and apologized.[161] Even by the free-wheeling standards of civic politics at the time it was a stunning performance, and may have propelled Taylor to victory, which he claimed by a comfortable margin. (His friend Whiteway received just 85 votes, which was perhaps 84 more than he expected.)

POLITICS PROVIDED A BIT OF COMIC RELIEF from the recession and the relentless gloom of the casualty reports that had begun to flood in from overseas, and so did sport. Two weeks after the second election confirmed Louis Taylor as mayor, on the night of March 26, 1915, the Vancouver Millionaires hockey club defeated the Ottawa Senators 12 to 3 in the third and final game of their Stanley Cup championship series. It was the first time that a team from western Canada had captured the symbol of hockey supremacy and it remains the only time that a Vancouver team has brought home the cup. The local press broke out its purplest prose. "The victory last night of the Vancouver hockey team in annexing the world's title is historic in the annals of that whirlwind winter pastime," the *Vancouver World* editorialized, "as it means that for the first time since the trophy was donated by Lord Stanley, Governor General of Canada, 22 years ago, this vice-regal emblem of mundane superiority in the Canadian national winter sport will sojourn in the sunset doorway of the Dominion for a year at least."[162]

The Millionaires were the creation of the Patrick brothers, Lester and Frank. Both outstanding hockey players—Frank once scored six goals in one game, a remarkable feat for a defenceman—the brothers moved west from Ottawa in 1910 to work in their father Joe's sawmill in Nelson.

The Vancouver Millionaires hockey club in 1914. Cyclone Taylor is second from right, back row. Frank Patrick is seated in the middle of the front row. A year later the team won the Stanley Cup.
Stuart Thomson photo, City of Vancouver Archives, AM1535-: CVA 99-126

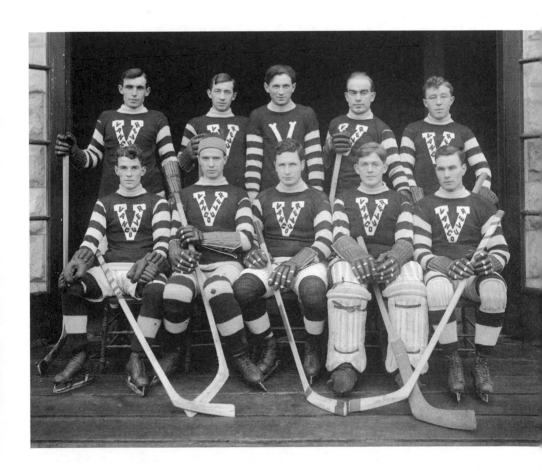

When Joe sold the mill, the family used the proceeds to build hockey arenas in Victoria and Vancouver, and to launch the three-team Pacific Coast Hockey Association. (The third franchise was in New Westminster.) Vancouver's Denman Arena, located on Denman Street at Georgia, not far from the entrance to Stanley Park, was emblematic of the optimism that pervaded the city during the pre-war boom. Despite the fact that professional hockey was not well established, the arena, which opened at the end of 1911, had seating for 10,500 spectators and the largest artificial ice surface in the world (28 x 67 metres). It rivalled ice palaces such as Madison Square Garden in New York and Duquesne Gardens in Pittsburgh, cities many times the size of Vancouver. Described by one architectural historian as "a monotonous and massive pile," the Denman Arena was basically a box of concrete and brick, but it was only the second hockey rink in Canada to feature artificial ice (the first was the Patricks' rink in Victoria, opened a few weeks earlier), and the first to have an upper tier of seating.[163] By the 1915 season the Patrick brothers assembled a powerhouse of a team, bringing star players the calibre of Fred "Cyclone" Taylor to Vancouver. On a ten-man roster the Millionaires had seven players who eventually ended up in the Hockey Hall of Fame. The PCHA folded in 1926; the arena remained a West End landmark until it burned to the ground in 1936. It was survived by the Denman Auditorium, which the Patricks built next door in 1927. Later renamed the Georgia Auditorium, it was a popular venue for concerts, political rallies and live performances of all types until it was torn down in 1959.

The success of the Millionaires offered the public a brief reprieve from what was a steady diet of bad economic news, not to mention the war. The city was spending $16,000 a month on relief for the unemployed, some of whom were set to work on public improvements at a dollar a day. Skimpy as this assistance was, in early April city council felt forced to refuse it to non-residents. The decision touched off a riot. On April 6 a parade of two thousand men who did not qualify for relief under the new order—most of whom were "Austrians and Russians," according to the *Province*—marched down Hastings Street smashing windows, demanding free food in restaurants and pelting the police with fruit and tobacco tins.[164] At a public meeting in Strathcona, organizers threatened more violence if council did not lift the new regulations. Council refused to back down, but by the end of the week the provincial government had responded to the city's plight with an emergency bailout of $10,000, which allowed the issuance of some meal tickets. But this was no long-term solution to the fiscal crisis. The mayor and aldermen voted themselves a pay cut, began to lay off civic employees and cancelled a number of expensive capital projects. Mayor Taylor personally felt the effects of the recession. In March he was forced to sell his newspaper to pay off his creditors.

Finally, in 1916, the local economy and the city's finances began to rally, thanks largely to the war. A number of manufacturers converted to the production of munitions, chiefly artillery shells. More important, shipyards in False Creek and on the North Shore received commissions to build large wooden and steel vessels to replace the many merchant ships that were falling victim to enemy U-boats. By dollar value, these commissions amounted to more than those received by any other province in Canada.[165] One of the firms involved, John Coughlan and Sons, a steel assembler before the war, added shipbuilding facilities in False Creek—becoming the city's largest single employer—and produced nine steel steamships, more than any other shipyard in Canada. With the demand for minerals and timber growing among allied countries, BC's mines and mills were working overtime. Jobs were suddenly plentiful as war industries and the armed forces absorbed most of the unemployed; many positions were filled by women, replacing men who had gone overseas.

The improving economy brought its own conflicts. While the cost of living rose dramatically during the war, wages did not keep pace. Working people experienced a decline in their standard of living and began to feel that they were making a disproportionate contribution to the war effort. When conscription was introduced in 1917, working-class resentment increased. Tensions between labour and employers that had flared earlier in the century rose to the surface once again. One measure of this alienation was an unprecedented increase in the number of workers who joined labour unions. When the war began there were 5,165 unionists in the city, a number that fell to just 3,788 two years later. Yet by 1918, more than fifteen thousand workers belonged to a union. Another metric was the number of times workers grew frustrated enough to walk out on strike. In 1914 there were just two work stoppages in the Lower Mainland; in 1918 that number had increased to forty, involving more than eighteen thousand workers.[166]

The summer of 1918 was particularly strife-filled. At the end of May, five thousand shipyard workers struck for higher wages. So important was it to keep the yards working while the war still raged that Prime Minister Borden dispatched one of his cabinet ministers, Senator Gideon Robertson, to the west coast to broker a deal. Within two weeks Robertson managed to facilitate an agreement that ended the strike. Next it was the turn of the street railway workers, who went on strike in mid-July for the second time in two years, once again demanding better wages. The BCER agreed to an

A group of local women celebrate the launch
of a vessel at Coughlan's shipyard on False
Creek in 1918. Coughlan's was the city's
largest employer during the war.
Dominion Photo Co. photograph, Vancouver
Public Library 20544

increase when the city agreed first, to allow streetcar fares to rise to six cents; and second, to pass a bylaw banning the jitneys from city streets.

But the real fireworks came early in August, when Vancouver was convulsed by a sympathetic strike. A week before, police had shot and killed Albert "Ginger" Goodwin, a well-known labour activist and draft resister, in the hills near Cumberland on Vancouver Island. Despite the poor state of his health, Goodwin had been classified fit for combat and most of his friends believed that the government was railroading him into the army as a way of silencing his union activity. A grand jury exonerated the officer who shot Goodwin, believing his claim that it was self-defence, but the labour movement thought it was cold-blooded murder. In Vancouver the Trades and Labour Council, along with the Metal Trades Council, called a one-day protest strike to begin at noon on August 2, the day that Goodwin was buried in Cumberland. Streetcar drivers, stevedores, shipyard and garment workers, and the building trades all walked off the job. The city stuttered to a halt. Many returned veterans opposed the action; they considered draft resisters like Goodwin to be Hun sympathizers and Bolsheviks. A mob of anti-strike soldiers stormed into the Labor Temple on Dunsmuir Street and ransacked it, breaking windows and heaving furniture and files into the street. Victor Midgley, the VTLC secretary, was only saved from being tossed out of a second-floor window by Frances Foxcroft, an office secretary, who grappled with the intruders. Instead the veterans roughed up Midgley and forced him to kiss the British flag.

Mayor Harry Gale and the Chamber of Commerce supported the veterans. Gale said that he considered the strike to be "most un-British and most unfair to the citizens of Vancouver."[167] Together they drew up a blacklist of labour leaders who they demanded leave the city. The next day brawling resumed, this time at the Longshoremen's Hall, where a group of determined stevedores held off a crowd of veterans who tried to invade the building. Mayor Gale sped to the scene in his car and managed to persuade most of the veterans to take their protest to the Cambie Street Grounds.[168] Eventually calm returned to the streets. Demonstrations like the Vancouver strike, and similar violence in Toronto, convinced the federal government that it was facing a revolutionary situation, and at the end of September it passed a series of draconian laws aimed at repressing labour unrest.[169]

Even as the war drew to a close that November, the fear of civil unrest remained strong. Early in the new year the first general strike in US history began in Seattle. Several tens of thousands of workers eventually joined in and federal troops were dispatched to keep the peace. According to employers and the city's mayor, Ole Hanson, it was Red revolution. There was no violence during the strike, which ended after just a few days, and despite the bellicose rhetoric of the mayor, there was never any evidence that strike leaders plotted to overthrow the government. Still, anti-Red anxiety was at an unprecedented level and some of this paranoia leaked across the border to Vancouver.

That spring a general strike in Winnipeg seemed to confirm fears that the country was on the verge of mass social upheaval. A wave of sympathy strikes swept the country, from Nova Scotia to Vancouver Island. In Vancouver the Trades and Labour Council called out its members on June 3. Some ten thousand workers walked off the job, including street railwaymen, telephone operators, shipyard workers and civic employees. With the support of city hall, a Citizen's Committee organized to fight the strike, its volunteers providing essential services. The city allowed the jitneys back on the streets to replace the street railway. Still, support for the strike was far from unanimous, and Vancouver's version of Red revolution ended in an anticlimax with workers dribbling back to the job as squabbles divided their leadership.

THE PROVINCIAL GOVERNMENT introduced two major progressive reforms during the war years: women's suffrage and prohibition. In both cases the measures followed years of debate, but it was the war that gave the final incentive to bring about their achievement. In Vancouver, women had possessed a limited right to vote in civic elections since 1886 when the charter granted suffrage to widows and single women who owned property. In 1911, thanks in part to the support of Mayor Louis Taylor, city council extended the franchise to married women as well. Still, women were not allowed to cast ballots in federal or provincial elections. The *Province* expressed the view of most men when it wrote: "The cry raised here for woman suffrage is, of course, an echo of the hysterical scream which for the past two years has pierced the ears of the people of Great Britain."[170] Premier Richard McBride opposed female suffrage and his government repeatedly refused to endorse it. When McBride resigned at the end of 1915, his successor as premier was the former attorney general William Bowser. Also opposed to female suffrage, Bowser agreed to put the question to a referendum because he expected it to lose. Many suffragists opposed the idea of a referendum; after all, only men would vote in it. But once the campaign got underway in the summer of 1916 they threw themselves into the fight. Pressed to take a stand, organized labour came out against the women. Union leaders worried that if they received political power women would not give back the jobs they had been filling while men were at war. Suffragists argued that with women contributing so much to the war effort, they deserved to enjoy equal political rights. Despite the odds against it, and thanks to the spirited campaign mounted by the suffrage organizations, 70 per cent of voters approved the referendum—in Vancouver 67 per cent voted in favour—and on April 5, 1917, BC women achieved the right to vote in provincial elections. The federal franchise followed a year later.

The vote was a great victory for the many women activists who had led the fight for electoral equality, none more so than Helena Gutteridge. When she arrived in Vancouver from her native England in 1911, Gutteridge was already a veteran of the suffrage movement and a vocal labour leader. A worker in the needle trades since she was fourteen years old, she had marched in the streets of London with Emmeline Pankhurst. In Vancouver she took a leading role in organizing working women. Finding the leadership of the suffrage movement too timid and middle class for her liking, she took the struggle to the streets, organizing street-corner rallies and stirring up support among working women. After the vote was achieved, Gutteridge retired from politics for several years. She married and moved to a chicken farm in the Fraser Valley. But she returned to the city during

Helena Gutteridge, a young tailor from England, was a leading activist in the fight for women's suffrage. Later she served as the first woman elected to city council.
City of Vancouver Archives,
AM54-S4-2-: CVA371-2693

the 1930s, became active in the socialist Co-operative Commonwealth Federation, the forerunner of the NDP, and in 1937 became the first woman elected to Vancouver City Council.[171]

The war also breathed life into the campaign for prohibition. Retrospectively prohibition has come to seem a disastrous public policy, but at the time, its supporters viewed it as a progressive reform addressing the negative impact of alcohol on personal health and family stability. Its introduction followed decades of debate right across the country, but without the war it probably would not have gained sufficient support to become law. The war added a sense of urgency. All the resources of the country had to be dedicated to supporting the armed forces overseas. Every step had to be taken to strengthen the home front for the great struggle. Valuable items such as grain and sugar could not be wasted producing liquor. Sobriety and self-restraint were required to carry on the fight.

In August 1915, thousands of supporters filled the Georgia Arena—it was the "largest prohibition gathering ever held in Vancouver," according to the *World*—to listen to suffragist Nellie McClung and Anglican educator and missionary George Exton Lloyd give rousing speeches condemning the "liquorites" and demanding an end to the destructive liquor traffic. Speaking about the closure of the hotel tavern, Reverend Lloyd compared it to the removal of an appendix, "somewhat painful while it lasts, but after it is over the patient will feel fine, for we are going to remove that nasty dirty appendix from the sick man, the hotel proprietor, after which the hotel traffic will be all right again."[172] Again Premier McBride was unsupportive, but after he retired at the end of the year, the legislature passed a prohibition act banning the sale of liquor and consumption of alcoholic beverages anywhere except in the privacy of one's home. Before it was enacted, the act needed to be endorsed by voters in a referendum, which it was during the provincial election of September 1916. On October 1, 1917, British Columbia became the final province, aside from Quebec, to introduce prohibition.

Almost from the start the policy was a failure. It was simple enough to ban drinking, another thing altogether to enforce the ban. Bootlegging flourished, both for personal use and for sale to others. It remained legal to import booze from out of province for personal consumption. Police could be bribed to turn a blind eye to infractions. Bars and blind pigs operated with little fear of interference. "Medicinal spirits" were exempt from the law, so doctors and pharmacists did a steady business selling prescriptions for alcohol-based "medicines." At Christmas 1919, one eyewitness reported customers lined up for a mile outside a Vancouver liquor store waiting to fill their prescriptions. Hotels were allowed to sell "near beer," a mildly alcoholic beverage about one fifth the strength of regular beer. Some hotels got around the law by establishing themselves as private clubs where patrons could legally consume liquor if they brought their own. Aside from the arbitrariness of enforcement, prohibition stirred up class resentment because it seemed to favour the wealthy. While working people could no longer obtain a glass of decent beer at their local tavern, the well-to-do could import as much liquor as they wanted to drink in their own homes.

Once the war ended, support for prohibition lost much of its urgency. Respect for the law was not helped by an embarrassing scandal in December 1918. The press reported that the prohibition commissioner, Walter Findlay, the top official responsible for enforcing the liquor ban, had been arrested for bootlegging. Findlay was accused of importing a train-car load of rye whiskey from a distillery in Toronto for sale in Vancouver. The cargo was estimated to be worth more than a million dollars at today's value. This was the same Walter Findlay who routinely gave interviews criticizing the police for not enforcing the anti-liquor laws strongly enough. He ended up serving two years in prison. The incident seemed to sum up all that was wrong with prohibition: its hypocrisy, its corruption, its unfairness. By the fall of 1920 the government was convinced that an alternative had to be found. In a second referendum, voters opted to replace all-out prohibition with a system of government-regulated liquor sales, and on June 15, 1921, the first public liquor stores opened in the city.

WORLD WAR I ended at 11:00 a.m. on Monday, November 11, 1918. Word reached Vancouver early that morning local time, and as people heard of it they dashed into the streets in nightshirts and nightgowns, eager to celebrate. In the harbour, ships sounded their horns. Factory whistles blew. Celebrants gathered on corners, banging pots and pans and blowing on whatever musical instruments they could improvise. "Towards noon, self-appointed marshals organized a great impromptu procession of citizens and soldiers," Major Matthews wrote, "with motor cars, pedestrians, bands, bugles and flags all mingled promiscuously together to parade the streets in one vast throng of exultation."[173] Bonfires on the beaches blazed well into the night. It was the end of a nightmare in which 1,400 of the city's young men had lost their lives, a greater death toll per capita than any other city in Canada.

And the dying was not over yet. As Vancouver celebrated the armistice, it was also a city under siege. A devastating influenza pandemic was sweeping the world and Canada would not be spared. Demobilized soldiers returning from Europe brought with them the deadly infection, known as the Spanish flu (so named because the first outbreaks to be publicized occurred in Spain, though the flu may have originated in the United States). It appeared first in Quebec in August 1918, then spread relentlessly across the country, carried on the troop trains heading home. On October 5, Dr. Fred Underhill, Vancouver's medical health officer, confirmed the city's first case. By the middle of the month there were two hundred more. Seven people were dead and dozens were falling ill every day. On October 18, Dr. Underhill gave in to mounting public alarm and declared the city "closed," meaning that a ban was placed on public gatherings and most businesses locked their doors. Schools, movie theatres, poolrooms, playing fields, union halls, libraries, churches, shops, dance pavilions—everywhere people congregated was closed as a possible zone of infection. By this time there were well over a thousand patients in hospital, and thirty-two people had died. Nine days later, on October 27, two dozen people died, the worst single-day death toll of the epidemic.[174]

The flu appeared suddenly in the form of cold-like symptoms—sore throat, cough, stuffy nose, mild fever—then worsened into achiness, extreme lassitude, head pains, even delirium. In the worst cases, pneumonia set in. Often as death approached, the body turned blue and patients began coughing up blood. It was sudden: a victim could be healthy in the afternoon and dead by the next morning. Doctors were powerless. Nothing they tried had any effect. Infected homes were quarantined, marked by a bright yellow placard in the window. Anyone venturing out was urged to wear a mask over their mouth. The BC Electric Railway Company fumigated the trolley cars daily. Hospitals were taxed to the breaking point. Staff were so overworked that a call went out for volunteers to help on the wards. Dr. Underhill himself fell sick but he was among the lucky ones— in a few days he was back at work. Funerals were so numerous that fresh flowers became hard to find in the shops.

On November 19, the worst appeared to be over, and the city reopened. Once again people could go to a show, attend a ball game, go to church or hold a dance. But it was the following April before medical officials believed the epidemic had truly burned out, by which time nine hundred people had died in the city.[175] At least 30 per cent of the province's population had come down with the flu. Canada-wide it claimed as many as fifty thousand lives; worldwide the death toll may have exceeded fifty million. It was a tragic end to a war in which so many had already died.

With the war's end it seemed necessary to honour the many men who had served and died with a monument. Government Square offered the best location, situated as it was in the heart of the downtown between the original townsite and the new "uptown" business district. The square had been vacant since the provincial courthouse came down in 1912. During the war a recruiting tent had occupied the site, along with a large wooden building, the Evangelistic Tabernacle, used for religious revivals. In the summer of 1918, returned veterans had installed a replica of the front lines, complete with barbed wire, trenches and underground dugouts. After several years of discussion, the city moved ahead with plans to improve the site and, on April 27, 1924, unveiled a memorial cenotaph. At about the same time the Southam family, owners of the *Province*, provided money to landscape the square, now known as Victory Square, which became the focus of many public gatherings over the coming decades.

IN 1920, VANCOUVER was embarking on a decade of significant growth: in geographic area, in population, in economic productivity. At the start of the decade it was the fourth-largest city in Canada with a population of 117,000 occupying borders that had not changed significantly since 1886. At the end of the decade it had a population of 246,590, and was the third largest city in the country behind Toronto and Montreal, sprawling across the entire peninsula from Burrard Inlet to the Fraser River. The harbour underwent phenomenal growth, based in large part on the burgeoning grain trade. Utilizing the Panama Canal route, Canada could now ship grain from the Prairies to markets in Europe, as well as to Asia through Vancouver. By 1930, seven grain elevators were handling a hundred million bushels of grain per season, and Burrard Inlet had become the largest export terminal by tonnage in the country.[176] The CPR built a new passenger terminal for its trans-Pacific liners, and in 1923 the Harbour Board opened Ballantyne Pier as an alternative to the CPR. Other piers, docks and freight terminals crowded the waterfront, and away from the harbour, several buildings appeared that have since become emblematic of the city: the Orpheum Theatre (1927), at the time the largest theatre in Canada; the new Point Grey campus of the University of British Columbia (1925); the Marine Building (1929), an art deco masterpiece; and the Commodore Ballroom (1929) with its sprung dance floor.

Another indicator of growth was the rapid expansion of car culture. During the postwar era the motor vehicle became a commonplace possession for the middle class. In 1920 there were only 6,500 automobiles in the city; by 1929 that number had grown to 36,500.[177] On the first day of 1922 the city broke with one reminder of its British heritage by switching traffic from the left to the right-hand side of the road. The newspapers predicted mayhem. "It was supposed and prophesied by croakers that there would be a scene of wild confusion," reported the *Province*.[178] But the change went off without a hitch. Access to the North Shore arrived in 1925 with the opening of a combined rail and automobile bridge at the Second Narrows. One popular destination for drivers was Lookout Point on Southwest Marine Drive, where Nat Bailey, who got his start hustling bags of peanuts on downtown street corners, converted a Model T truck into a mobile lunch counter. Hot dogs sold for ten cents, ice cream for a nickel. So successful was the operation that in June 1928, Bailey opened his inaugural White Spot drive-in restaurant in an imitation log cabin on Granville Street at Sixty-seventh Avenue, the first drive-in in Canada. Popping up in locations across the city, White Spots became the favourite hangout for generations of city teenagers.

Perhaps it was the optimistic spirit of the times that encouraged Vancouver voters to experiment with the electoral system they had been using since the city was created. Beginning with the election in January 1921, they abolished the wards and the first-past-the-post method for electing aldermen. Instead the city introduced a preferential ballot. Voters marked their choices for aldermen—not mayor—in order of preference, choosing councillors for the city as a whole, not individual wards. The candidate receiving the fewest votes was eliminated and his or her second choices were distributed among the remaining candidates, a process that was repeated until it determined a winner. After three elections the experiment was deemed a failure. In most cases the candidate who led on the first count ended up winning the election. The whole process turned out to be confusing for voters and a headache for the officials who had to count the ballots. For the 1924 election (actually December 12, 1923) the city re-established the wards and returned to the single-choice ballot.

For many people the 1920s were an era of prosperity and mobility, but for many others it was a time of strife and struggle. British Columbians enjoyed rising per capita incomes (about $1,100 a year for a male worker in 1921 and $675 for a female), but wage gains were more than eaten up by increases in the postwar cost of living. And the unemployed, of course, had no wages at all. At the end of the war, veterans returned home to flood the job market at the same time as war industries such as shipbuilding and munitions slowed down. Unemployment in BC ran consistently ahead of the national average until 1924,[179] posing an intractable problem for civic officials. In the summer of 1921 there were reported to be 5,600 jobless people in Vancouver, and the situation only got worse in the winter when single men tended to migrate to the city from coastal work camps and other parts

Following the war, car culture exploded as the motor vehicle quickly became a common possession. Gas stations like this one on Hornby Street downtown opened to service the thousands of vehicles that suddenly crowded the city's streets.

of the country.[180] The unemployed received direct relief as well as work on public projects such as building roads and clearing land. At the end of 1921 the city opened a camp for 620 single jobless men at Hastings Park, where they received 20 cents a day for chopping firewood and landscaping a golf course.[181] Assistance from senior levels of government was intermittent. Arthur Meighen's Conservative government in Ottawa agreed to pay a portion of civic relief costs, at least during the winter months, but following their victory in the December 1921 federal election, the Liberals, led by new prime minister William Lyon Mackenzie King, ended this support, claiming it was unconstitutional. The provincial government was also reluctant to extend help beyond the winter season, so the city was left pretty much on its own to deal with the needs of the unemployed until the economic situation improved in the middle of the decade.

Attitudes about race had changed little since the anti-Oriental riots of 1907. The city was even more British than it had been before pre-war immigration restrictions were imposed. According to the 1921 census, the population of Vancouver was 80 per cent British origin; that is, from

Britain or born in Canada to British parents. The two largest racial minorities were Japanese, concentrated along Powell Street in "Japantown," and the Chinese in Chinatown. Together these two groups numbered 10,700 residents, or just 9 per cent of the population,[182] but to the white majority they represented a threat out of all proportion to their number. In 1921 the *Vancouver Sun* published a novel, *The Writing on the Wall*, which forecast an eventual war for domination in British Columbia between Chinese and Japanese while the whites die off in a typhoid epidemic spread by Asian immigrants. The book was written by Hilda Glynn-Ward, a pseudonym for Hilda Howard, a freelance journalist originally from Wales, who turned to writing when her husband was invalided by the war. The majority of her readers may not have shared Howard's apocalyptic vision, but there was nonetheless a widespread suspicion of Asian influence, and pervasive measures were taken to counter it. George Nitta, a Japanese Canadian who lived in Vancouver at this time, explained in an interview that Asian customers did not receive service at certain restaurants, nor were they allowed to use local swimming pools. "In the movie theatres," Nitta said, "upstairs was for coloured people, including us."[183] White retailers urged consumers to boycott Asian-owned businesses. White farmers wanted the government to prevent Asians from owning land. A re-energized Asiatic Exclusion League lobbied against Asian immigration. The civic government continued its policy of banning Asian workers from civic construction projects and charged hefty licence fees in an attempt to drive Chinese vegetable pedlars out of business.[184] All of this activism bore results on July 1, 1923, when a new federal law came into effect banning almost all Chinese immigration into the country.

Symptomatic of the virulent racism that pervaded Vancouver society was the infamous Janet Smith murder. Smith was a twenty-two-year-old Scottish nanny who worked for a prominent family at its Shaughnessy mansion. On the morning of July 26, 1924, an unknown assailant shot and killed her while she was ironing clothes in the basement of the home. Suspicion fell on the family's Chinese houseboy Wong Foon Sing, and when the police had to release him for lack of actual evidence, vigilantes took matters into their own hands. They kidnapped Wong and held him for six weeks while they tried to torture a confession out of him. Eventually Wong's abductors released him, whereupon he was arrested and formally charged with the murder. That fall a jury ruled there was insufficient evidence to proceed to trial. Released again, Wong returned to China; the people responsible for his ill-treatment, including members of the police and prominent politicians, were never punished. Nor was anyone ever apprehended for the murder of Janet Smith. The case continues to intrigue not just because it was never solved but also because it reveals the depth of animosity and fear that white Vancouverites felt toward Asian residents of the city.[185]

For the white majority, Chinatown (or "Celestialland" as it was sometimes called) was a place apart, synonymous with vice, disease, crime and squalor. This prejudice heightened during the 1920s with the war on drugs. Prior to 1908 drug use was perfectly legal in Canada. Consumers had access to a variety of opiates in patent medicines available from pharmacies and doctors, and authorities took no steps to control their use. This laissez-faire attitude changed in the aftermath of the anti-Asian riots of 1907. When William Lyon Mackenzie King arrived in Vancouver as a federal government emissary to assess the property damage inflicted by the riots, he became convinced that the widespread use of opium that he witnessed in Chinatown should be curtailed. In July 1908, not long after his return to Ottawa, Parliament passed a law prohibiting the importation, manufacture and sale of the drug. This was the beginning of the criminalization of psycho-active drugs in Canada; it was followed by the prohibition of cocaine and morphine in 1911, and codeine and marijuana in 1923.[186]

Despite these laws, drug use was widespread in Vancouver. As a port city, it was one of the main entrance points for illicit drugs making their way into the country. By the early 1920s the Chinese were blamed for the spreading problem of drug abuse and for corrupting young white men and women by seducing them into Chinatown drug dens. At the beginning of 1920, the *Vancouver Sun* led a crusade against the drug traffic, in one instance calling for the eradication of Chinatown. "If the only way to save our children is to abolish Chinatown," wrote the *Sun*'s editorialist, "then Chinatown must and will go, and go quickly."[187] Early in 1922 it was the turn of the *World* newspaper to launch its own front page war on drugs, publishing a series of stories about the perils of drug abuse and the allegedly key role played by Chinatown in the criminal drug traffic and the corruption of the city's youth.[188] A variety of service groups, along with the mayor and city council, came out in support of the *World*'s campaign demanding tougher prison sentences for drug dealers and the deportation of Chinese traffickers.

At the height of the drug panic, a letter appeared in the pages of the *Sun*. Written by Won Alexander Cumyow on behalf of the Chinese Benevolent Association, of which he was president, the letter pointed out that "it is too obvious to state that habit-forming drugs do not of their own sweet accord drop from the blue heavens into 'Chinatown' and it is needless for us to state that all means of ingress and egress by which this illegal drug traffic can be carried on is neither directly nor indirectly controlled by the Chinese."[189] In other words, the traffic in illicit drugs that the paper and the public were bemoaning was controlled by whites, not by the Chinese, who were its victims as much as anyone else.

Won Alexander Cumyow would have been well known to readers of the *Sun*. His parents migrated north from California to the BC goldfields in 1860, settling in the tiny hamlet of Port Douglas at the top of Harrison Lake. When Won Alexander was born the following year, he was the first Chinese person born in Canada. Trained as a lawyer, though unable to practise because of the prejudice of the time, Cumyow spoke several languages and served as interpreter for almost five decades in the Vancouver police court. He also owned several businesses and a fair amount of real estate, and raised money for a variety of worthy causes in the Chinese community. But no matter how distinguished his resumé, Cumyow's argument fell on deaf ears. White Vancouver continued to believe in the connection between Chinatown and the drug traffic.

During the early 1920s the alarmist-in-chief was Judge Emily Murphy, a well-known writer under the pen name "Janey Canuck." Murphy was an Edmonton police magistrate, the first woman in the British Empire to be appointed to the bench. She began publishing a series of articles in *Maclean's* magazine alerting the Canadian public to the dangers of "narcotic drugs." Her work in the court alerted her to the prevalence of drug abuse and sparked her crusade against the illicit trade. In 1922 she expanded her articles into a book, *The Black Candle*, a lurid exposé that highlighted the supposed corruption of Canada's youth by "the drug evil," centred in places like Vancouver's Chinatown, "that queer district where men seem to glide from nowhere to nothing."[190] In Murphy's view, the drug trade was part of a conspiracy by "the yellow race" to bring about "the downfall of the white race" and achieve world domination.[191] Concern about drug use played a major role in the government's decision to ban Chinese immigration in 1923.

Drug abuse was not the only crime in the city, and Chinatown, no matter how much it haunted the white imagination, was not the only place where vice crimes flourished. Moral crusaders considered the East End generally to be home to a flourishing criminal underworld. From the brothels on Alexander Street to the gambling dens on Hastings, from the blind pigs on Powell Street to the bootleg joints in Hogan's Alley, the East End was, in the popular imagination, "the square mile of crime." During the war, one incident in particular had confirmed this reputation. In March 1917, a pimp named Robert Tait barricaded himself inside an apartment above a grocery store on East Georgia Street that he shared with his girl-friend Frankie Russell. When police tried to enter the apartment, Tait fired on them with a shotgun. Aside from wounding the police officers, Tait's gunfire killed a young boy who was passing in the street. When police chief Malcolm MacLennan arrived and tried to enter the apartment Tait shot him as well, then killed himself. MacLennan died of his wounds. Tait was a Black man from Detroit who used drugs; Russell a white woman who was a sex worker. Such a sensational mixture of race, drugs, sex and murder con-firmed for the general public that the east side of the city was a place into which respectable people ventured at their peril.

During the 1920s, public concern that criminal influence had spread out of the speakeasys and brothels and into the upper echelons of civic gov-ernment grew. The police force was corrupt, and notable gangsters such as Joe Celona, the reputed "King of the Bawdyhouses," and Shue Moy, "King of the Gamblers," enjoyed unusual access to city hall. These were among the incendiary charges made by alderman T.W. Fletcher, a member of the police commission, in April 1928. Fletcher demanded a provincial inquiry. Instead city council appointed local lawyer R.S. Lennie to hold hearings. The Lennie inquiry lasted a little over two months, heard 180 hours of testi-mony from ninety-eight witnesses and monopolized the front pages of the local newspapers. Informants testified that the police routinely received bribes in return for protecting gamblers and brothel keepers from pros-ecution. Police officers revealed that their superiors told them to ignore the activities of known gangsters who were under the informal protection of city hall; i.e., they were friends and/or supporters of the mayor, Louis Taylor. Fletcher hired his own lawyer, Gerry McGeer, who made himself the centre of attention with his charges that organized crime ran the city and his demand that Taylor be removed from office.

Far from backing down, Taylor defended his lenient approach to poli-cing. He was not elected, he said, to make Vancouver "a Sunday school town." An understaffed police force had more important things to do than chase down every gambling den and house of prostitution. Officers should focus their attention on murder and property crimes while confining vice crimes to certain sections of the city. Taylor's approach, which advocated an accommodation with vice, did not win favour with the moralists who wanted an all-out war on sinfulness and crime. The inquiry did not succeed in prov-ing that Taylor was in the pay of the criminal underworld, but neither did it leave him blameless. Lennie felt that Taylor's "open policy" had left the police force demoralized and ineffective, as well as understaffed and under-paid. It was clear that the city's police force was corrupt, largely because of incompetent leadership. Taylor avoided formal censure but the inquiry left him unelectable in the next civic vote.

IN POSTWAR VANCOUVER, popular entertainment flourished in the vaudeville palaces, cinemas, music halls and hotel bars along Hastings and Granville Streets. Neon arrived and the theatre marquees twinkled with liquid light. One of the most anticipated shows in the city's history was an appearance in 1923 by the forty-eight-year-old magician and escapologist Harry Houdini. It was the only time that Houdini visited Vancouver. Appearing twice daily at the Orpheum Theatre—on a bill that also featured "a Spanish gypsy revue" and a few minutes of "wit, music and patter" by Jack Benny—Houdini arranged with the *Vancouver Sun* to publicize his show by performing an outdoor stunt at the newspaper's offices on West Pender. At noon on March 1, as a huge crowd gathered in the street, Houdini allowed himself to be trussed up in a straitjacket and hung upside down by his ankles from a crane three stories above the sidewalk. It took him three minutes and thirty-nine seconds to work himself loose and drop the strait-jacket to the ground, at which point, reported the *Sun*, "a cheer arose and swelled into a roar."[192] Film footage of the event was quickly developed and used as part of his act that very evening at the Orpheum.

During the war, jazz had made its way across the border from the United States and found a ready audience, especially among the city's small African-American population in Strathcona. The most popular joint was the Patricia Hotel on East Hastings, where Will Bowman managed the Patricia Café. In the early 1920s his house band, led by Oscar Holden, featured an itinerant pianist named Jelly Roll Morton and a singer named Ada "Brick-top" Smith, both on their way to achieving fame in the night clubs of Chicago and Paris.

However, there was limited interest in the fine arts. When Emily Carr lived in the city (1906–1910), she was dismissive of the society ladies and Sunday painters with middlebrow tastes and no serious commit-ment to their art.[193] Vancouver was an unsophisticated city when it came to the modernist movements of the early twentieth century. Local artists mainly painted conventional landscapes or society portraits. Things began to change following the war, when outside influences infiltrated the city. In 1921 a small group of enthusiasts created the British Columbia Art League to promote the arts generally and, more specifically, to open an art school and establish a civic gallery. The first objective was achieved in 1925, when the Vancouver School of Decorative and Applied Arts opened its doors. Principal Charles Scott hired significant artists such as Fred Varley from Toronto and Jock Macdonald and Grace Melvin from Scotland to teach at the school. Together they brought a sense of cosmopolitanism and innovation to the art scene. Scott was also instrumental, along with Henry Stone, a businessman, in the creation of the Vancouver Art Gallery in 1931.

Another important catalyst for the changing arts environment was John Vanderpant, a Dutch photographer and writer who immigrated to Canada in 1911, first to Alberta, then to the Lower Mainland. Vanderpant struck up a friendship with Fred Varley and was a great advocate for the Group of Seven artists, whose work was beginning to be shown in the city. His Vanderpant Galleries on Robson Street, opened in collaboration with Harold Mortimer-Lamb, another local champion of the arts, was a cultural hub where the cognoscenti attended exhibitions, musical events and literary readings. Vanderpant was an accomplished pictorialist photographer (as was Mortimer-Lamb), advocating for the artistic, "painterly" merits of photography as opposed to its strictly reproductive virtues. There was hardly a cultural event in Vancouver in the 1920s and 1930s that didn't have his fingerprints on it. After Vanderpant died in 1939, Jock Macdonald lamented: "The city seems different without Vanderpant around."[194]

The art of the First Nations people had yet to be appreciated in the city. Squamish women from the North Shore reserves wove baskets and trays from spruce root and cedar bark and brought them to the city to sell door-to-door. Chief Simon Baker recalled that his grandmother, Mary Agnes Capilano, "used to go in her dugout canoe from the Capilano reserve across the narrows into Vancouver . . . and pack her clams, berries, baskets and mats to the Hotel Vancouver and around the West End where all the rich people lived."[195] But the handmade items were considered more craft than art. In the early 1920s the Art, Historical and Scientific Association came up with a plan to install an "Indian village" in Stanley Park, not far from where the Indigenous inhabitants had been evicted several decades earlier. Initially, members wanted to relocate the Kwakwaka'wakw community of Alert Bay to the park holus-bolus. When this proved unfeasible, they purchased two totem poles and two houseposts from the Kwakwaka'wakw and erected them near the site of Xway-xway (Lumberman's Arch) in 1923. Further plans angered the local Squamish, who objected to the importation of upcoast artifacts when their own culture was not reflected in plans for the site, which was after all located on their traditional lands. The AHSA turned over the pieces they had already installed to the Parks Board, and over the years more poles were erected. Today the display at Brockton Point is one of the most popular tourist attractions in the city.

WHILE THE INTELLIGENTSIA gathered at Vanderpant's gallery, and the press fretted about police corruption, and xenophobes fulminated about the dangers posed by an Asiatic invasion, civic officials had a new preoccupation: town planning. Planning had its origins in the pre-war "City Beautiful" movement, of which Thomas Mawson's ambitious plans for the Stanley Park entrance are one example. City Beautiful advocated the use of planned green spaces—parks, boulevards, gardens—to make urban places more aesthetically pleasing and, hopefully, more liveable. For the most part, however, early Vancouver grew without much thought given to how to direct that growth. Following the war, beautification grew teeth with the introduction of more rigorous planning strategies such as zoning to create a harmonious urban unit.

There had always been "informal zoning."[196] Racial prejudice confined Asian residents and their businesses to specific areas of the city. Moral squeamishness did the same for the sex trade and other illicit activities. Shopping and warehouse districts developed out of convenience. Neighbourhood hubs emerged around street railway stops. But formal zoning began with the Town Planning Commission, which city council appointed early in 1926 under the terms of the Town Planning Act, passed by the provincial government the previous year. Among the commission's earliest initiatives was to hire the American consultant Harland Bartholomew to come up with a comprehensive plan for the city. Bartholomew's report, submitted in 1929, covered everything from the design of specific streets to the landscaping of residential gardens. It proposed ways of improving traffic flow; it identified neighbourhoods where industrial and residential areas needed to be separated; it evaluated the streetcar system and suggested the creation of new parks and scenic drives.

In many ways Bartholomew endorsed the directions in which Vancouver had been developing for decades. He opposed any further filling in of False Creek and recommended it be preserved as an "industrial entity." He took for granted that all of the Burrard Inlet shoreline should be preserved "for harbour purposes": i.e., industry. He extolled the virtues of Stanley Park—"Stanley Park . . . is Vancouver and Vancouver is Stanley Park"—while urging the creation of other large parks in different parts of the city. He suggested that the English Bay beachfront be acquired and preserved for recreation, a process that was already underway. In 1929 the city expropriated fourteen properties with the intention of expanding the beach area to the east. The Depression, followed by the war, followed by a housing shortage, delayed the removal of the houses, but finally, in 1950, that process began.[197] It concluded in 1981, when fire destroyed the Englesea Lodge at the entrance to Stanley Park, the sole remaining building along the English Bay beachfront. This commitment to making the waterfront accessible for public use is one of the defining characteristics of the city, reflected most dramatically in the seawall pathway, begun in 1917 and now extending 28 kilometres along the waterfront.

The Bartholomew Report's most ambitious proposal, the creation of a six-square-block civic centre overlooking the entrance to False Creek and including a new city hall, a courthouse, a library and an art gallery never came about, though another major recommendation, the construction of the Burrard Street Bridge, did. Overall the report was a landmark in the history of the city. Although it was never legally adopted, it remained an essential reference for subsequent councils and planners. Nonetheless, its immediate impact was limited, partly because the Depression intervened, partly because vested property interests frustrated some of its suggestions. An example of the latter was the controversy over zoning in the West End, where larger homes were being converted to boarding houses or demolished to make way for apartment blocks. When the Planning Commission tried to retain the single-family character of the neighbourhood by zoning against apartments, property owners and business interests successfully rebelled and a revised zoning bylaw, introduced in 1927, designated the West End an apartment district.[198] In the years ahead Vancouver continued to evolve as a negotiation between the planner and the real estate developer, with many critics frustrated that the developer always seemed to have the upper hand.

THE BARTHOLOMEW REPORT was submitted to council just as the city prepared for its long-debated amalgamation with South Vancouver and Point Grey. When the merger occurred on January 1, 1929, Vancouver doubled its population (to 228,193) and almost tripled its area (from 4,268 to 11,655 hectares). Much as the amalgamation had long been anticipated, it was not a simple change to bring about. The three municipalities were dissimilar in character, with different histories and interests. Several years of courtship were required before the marriage could be solemnized.

When Vancouver was created, its southern boundary ran along Sixteenth Avenue between Nanaimo and Alma Streets. Land to the south and west was at first unorganized and largely unoccupied, with the exception of the Musqueam people, who had lived along the banks of the Fraser River for thousands of years. In 1864 a reserve was established where some seventy families lived. The Musqueam economy relied on fishing, work at the Steveston fish canneries and seasonal hop picking in the Fraser Valley. As well, the people engaged in mixed farming, logging and cutting cordwood, and hired themselves out as farm labour to white settlers. Women worked as domestics and, like the Squamish on the North Shore, sold woven baskets door-to-door. Beginning in 1877, the Department of Indian Affairs allowed several Chinese farmers to lease land on the reserve. They grew mainly vegetables, which they sold to city grocery stores, and worked the holdings into the 1960s.

The earliest non-Indigenous settlers on the southern slope were farmers: Samuel Mole, Hugh McRoberts and brothers Fitzgerald and Samuel McCleary. In the 1860s they pre-empted land along the riverfront to the east of the Musqueam Reserve, where they grew a variety of crops and raised dairy cattle, selling their produce in New Westminster and to the logging camps in Burrard Inlet. As the peninsula was logged off, more settlers arrived, and on April 13, 1892, the area west of Boundary Road running all the way to the tip of Point Grey was organized into the district of South Vancouver with an elected reeve and council. The municipality had one employee, a clerk. The province paid his salary of $50 per month since the local government had no revenues. For several years the council met in the open air, until a municipal hall opened at Fraser and Forty-first Avenue in 1898.

South Vancouver's rural character gave way to rapid residential development during the pre–World War I boom; the 1911 census showed a population of 16,126. Many of these homes were distributed haphazardly across the district, interrupted by stretches of stump-infested vacant lots, but several nodes of settlement appeared, chiefly around streetcar and interurban stations. At the south end of Granville Street the community of Eburne grew up on the north arm of the Fraser. Eburne actually spanned the river. As of 1889, the North Arm Bridge crossed to Sea Island in Richmond, where for many years a general store initially owned by Harry Eburne and later by the Grauer family anchored a thriving, although small, business centre. On the Vancouver side there was a sawmill west of the bridge and an interurban station near the community's centre at Hudson and Marine Drive. One interurban line travelled east to New Westminster, servicing all the mills and lumberyards that lined the river. A second track crossed the river and headed south to Steveston. Farther west, at the foot of Blenheim Street, a fish cannery opened in 1897 and remained in operation until World War I. Associated with the cannery, a small community of Japanese-Canadian fishing families lived nearby until they were expelled in 1942. With the paving of Granville Street all the way to the river and the arrival of the streetcar down Oak Street, Eburne—soon to be renamed Marpole—flourished as a mini-metropolis.

Farther east, other small villages emerged around the interurban stations at Eighteenth and Commercial (Cedar Cottage) and Vanness and Joyce Street (Collingwood). Fraser Street was a major north-south thoroughfare, one of the first roads across South Vancouver. Originally the North Arm Road connecting Kingsway to the river, it was extended into Richmond via a new bridge in 1905, and thereafter shuttled a steady stream of farm produce into the city. The Village of South Vancouver emerged at the south end of Fraser and Main Streets. The street railway pushed inexorably south into South Vancouver. As one example, in 1904 the "cemetery line" travelled down Main Street as far as Thirty-third Avenue and the entrance to Mountain View Cemetery. The street grid also pushed south as the line of settlement spread steadily toward the river, creating neighbourhoods such as Killarney and Fraserview.

The exception to South Vancouver's working-class character was the very upscale neighbourhood of Shaughnessy. It was a subdivision for the super-rich laid out at a cost of $2 million by the CPR on its holdings south of Sixteenth Avenue. Named for company president Thomas Shaughnessy, Shaughnessy Heights featured winding tree-lined boulevards, large grounds and mansions designed by the city's leading architects. It was a requirement that no home cost less than $6,000, six times what a middling house cost elsewhere in the city. The average lot size, about 1,500 square metres, was four times the size of lots for single-family homes elsewhere.[199] The CPR made loans available but only as long as the applicant's home measured up to the company's design standards. A golf course and tennis courts were built close by. Work on the project began in 1907, and by the outbreak of war there were more than two hundred homes. Residents petitioned the provincial government for permission to create their own municipality so that they could ensure that only the right sort of people joined them in "CPR Heaven." Permission was denied, but Shaughnessy did receive one elected representative on the municipal council as well as control of its own tax revenues.[200] The success of "First Shaughnessy" encouraged the CPR to develop "Second Shaughnessy" (King Edward south to Thirty-seventh Avenue) and then "Third Shaughnessy" (between Thirty-seventh and Forty-first).

On January 1, 1908, Point Grey seceded from South Vancouver to create its own municipality west of Cambie. Two years earlier the province had begun selling off Crown lots in what would become Kerrisdale and West

Point Grey. At about the same time the CPR made more of its original grant available for purchase. As settlers moved on to these westside properties, they organized themselves into the Point Grey Improvement Association and began to consider secession. In the words of the Bartholomew Report, these people saw themselves as a "first-class residential district" and wanted to be free of the penny-pinching austerity of the South Vancouver administration. The initial voting population of Point Grey was only sixty-two, but the west side grew steadily and then, following World War I, rapidly. The centre of the community was Kerrisdale—the district hall was located at Forty-ninth and West Boulevard, where the tram line linking downtown

Members of Vancouver's business elite gather for a banquet at the Vancouver Club in 1920. The club, founded in 1893, constituted a Who's Who of the city's economic, social and political leaders.
City of Vancouver Archives, AM54-S4-: PORT P1187

Vancouver to Richmond had a station. The CPR opened this line in 1902 to service the canneries at Steveston and the farms on Lulu Island. (The company had its own market garden near Forty-first and East Boulevard to supply produce to its hotels and trains.) Known as the Sockeye Limited, the line did not prosper, and after three years the CPR turned it over to the BC Electric company, which absorbed it into its electric interurban network. According to Henry Ewert, a commuter could travel between downtown Vancouver and Marpole in just twenty-three minutes for a fare of 40 cents return, with a car departing every fifteen minutes.[201] One of Major Matthews's informants told him that the first resident of Kerrisdale was a Mr. Bell, who opened a grocery store and post office at the corner of Wilson Road (Forty-first Avenue) and West Boulevard. At the time, Wilson Road was "a trail of mud in winter and of dust in summer. All around was a wilderness of forest with an occasional bit of clearing with stumps and brush."[202]

Following the war, Dunbar and West Point Grey came into their own as residential suburbs, catering to "the settled suburbanite with a family," in the words of a *Province* reporter.[203] Dunbar Heights was initially developed by the real estate promoter Charles Trott Dunbar. In 1920 the BCER ran a streetcar line south down Dunbar Street to Forty-first, and with increased accessibility to downtown the neighbourhood grew rapidly, attracting young middle-class couples wanting homes to raise their children. West Point Grey was slightly more upscale; in 1928 the average house there cost $4,120 to build, compared to $2,524 in South Vancouver and $2,686 in Vancouver proper.[204]

While Point Grey flourished, South Vancouver fell on hard times. As the population grew so did the demand for services but tax revenues failed to keep pace. In January 1911 ratepayers voted overwhelmingly to join Vancouver. In a second plebiscite later that same month, residents of Vancouver also voted for amalgamation, though the extremely low turnout suggested that the issue was not a priority for many ratepayers. In the event the province, which had the final say, did not support amalgamation, so nothing happened.[205] "In the half decade between 1913 and 1918," read the Bartholomew Report, "South Vancouver passed through harrowing times indeed."[206] With the war, revenues fell even further, and by 1918 the municipality was facing bankruptcy. It had borrowed nearly a million dollars from an American lender and could not pay it back. At the municipal council's request the province stepped in, took over repayment of the loan and appointed a commissioner, F.J. Gillespie, to run the local government. It was 1923 before self-government was restored.

With its history of financial instability, it was no wonder that South Vancouver welcomed the opportunity to amalgamate with its neighbours. Point Grey and Vancouver were less enthusiastic. Ratepayers in the former worried about losing control of their own development, while in the latter they saw no reason why they should pay for infrastructure upgrades in the outer suburbs. As a result of these concerns, amalgamation of all three municipalities was defeated the first time it was put to a popular referendum. It took two more referendums and a lot of negotiations before a plan agreeable to the three communities could be worked out and approved.

VETERAN MAYOR LOUIS TAYLOR, who had supported amalgamation for years, must have been disappointed not to be in the mayor's chair when it finally came about at the beginning of 1929. Seriously wounded by the Lennie Commission's findings on police corruption, he had faced a tough opponent, the wealthy grocery wholesaler William Malkin, in the civic election the previous October. Malkin positioned himself as a crusader for "clean government." "You all read the report of the police enquiry," he told one campaign meeting. "You know what awful things are going on. We as parents want the streets of this city to be safe for our children."[207] Everyone seemed to agree that the city was in the hands of "a vicious professional vice ring," in the words of the *Sun*, and a new broom was needed to sweep city hall clean of criminals. Taylor managed to hang on to much of his east-side support, but Malkin swept the west side on his way to a decisive victory.[208]

As things turned out, the new mayor had picked up a poisoned chalice. Within a year of his taking office, world stock markets collapsed. Thousands of jobless men camped along the waterfront and in the city's parks, and protest marchers filled the streets. The Great Depression had arrived.

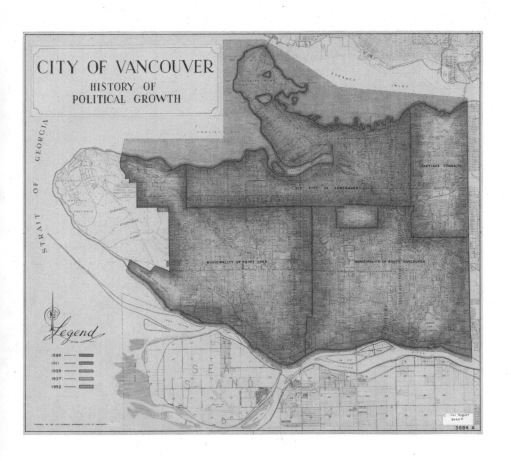

This map, dated 1952, illustrates the geographical growth of the city. The original "old city" (i.e., 1886) included the downtown peninsula and the south side of False Creek as far as Sixteenth Avenue. The Hastings Townsite and a small rectangle south of Sixteenth joined in 1911. The amalgamation of 1929 added the municipalities of Point Grey and South Vancouver.

Vancouver (B.C.) Planning Department map, City of Vancouver Archives, COV-S445-3-: LEG1201.1

Three jobless men at one of the "jungles" in 1931. Because of its mild climate, Vancouver was a magnet for the unemployed during the Depression.
W.J. Moore photo, City of Vancouver Archives, AM54-S4-: Re N8.2

7406

CHAPTER FIVE

Protest

As **HARD ECONOMIC TIMES** descended on the city, several thousand homeless men congregated in makeshift shantytowns scattered around the East End—on the old Hastings Mill site, in the railyards of the False Creek Flats, at the former city dump between Heatley and Campbell Avenues and under the Georgia Viaduct. The men threw together shelters from scavenged boards, boxes, bricks and crates, or holed up inside the rusting frames of abandoned cars. They drank from stagnant ponds, foraged for food and roamed the streets of the city asking for handouts. And Reverend Andrew Roddan, radio preacher and minister at First United Church on East Hastings, was their advocate.

Roddan belonged to the social gospel wing of the Presbyterian (later United) Church. He arrived in Canada from his native Scotland in 1910, working first in Winnipeg and Thunder Bay before relocating to Vancouver at the start of the Depression. As a social gospeller he believed that the church should play an active role in ameliorating social conditions in the city. With the numbers of jobless and destitute mounting, he organized a soup kitchen at the church, managed by his tireless lieutenant Jeannie MacDuff, and ventured into the hobo communities to minister to the men. His book *God in the Jungles* introduced many city residents to the desperate conditions of the "boxcar tourists" living in their midst.[209]

By the middle of the summer of 1931, more than a thousand men were living in the "jungles." Hoping to publicize their plight, Roddan invited a friend, the photographer W.J. Moore, to accompany him to one of the False Creek camps to take some photographs. Moore, who trained with the mountain photographer Byron Harmon in Banff, had set up shop in Vancouver just before World War I and developed a reputation for his striking panoramic photographs of urban settings. He worked closely with Major Matthews at the civic archives, to which he donated many of his negatives. "If there ever was a man to whom Vancouver and its posterity is deeply indebted," Matthews once remarked, "it is to William J. Moore."

A light drizzle was falling on the evening that Moore and Roddan arrived at the shantytown. Moore characterized the inhabitants as "men from everywhere, all sorts of ages, education, characters, attainments, and which a common want and some misery had banded together in larger or smaller groups for mutual help." As he was taking his pictures, an ardent young woman preaching Communism began to harangue the itinerants. "You call yourselves men?" she shouted at them. "You stand for this and do nothing! Why don't you fight?" According to Moore, the men ignored her, no doubt because they did not want to put at risk their opportunity for a hot meal.[210]

Roddan's attempts to rouse sympathy for the homeless men failed. Authorities saw the shantytowns as breeding grounds for crime, disease and, worst of all, revolution. On September 3, after a meeting of the civic relief committee, alderman W.C. Atherton sent a telegram to the federal government pleading for assistance. In his message to Ottawa, Atherton reported that more than sixteen thousand individuals were registered for relief, along with 2,500 families needing clothing and rent. Atherton recorded the number of single homeless men as two thousand, with an additional seventy arriving in the city every day. "Immediate Action is Imperative," wired Atherton.[211] But rather than wait on the federal government, local officials took matters into their own hands. Using the medical officer's report of three cases of typhoid in one of the shantytowns as an excuse, city crews moved in and razed the camps, burning some shacks and smashing others into pieces. Most of the men were relocated to temporary shelters before moving to the government work camps that opened later that fall in the interior of the province.

THE ECONOMIC CRISIS that followed the stock market crash of October 1929 was global in its scope but local in its implications. British Columbia was particularly vulnerable, given its reliance on the export of natural resources: wood products, minerals, fish, fruit. As exports of prairie grain slowed as well, so did activity in the port. Businesses failed, wages fell, construction ceased, jobs disappeared. As the number of local unemployed multiplied, they were joined by a steady flow of transients from east of the Rockies and the customary congregation of seasonal workers who descended on the city in the winter. Together they made a combustible mixture that did not take long to ignite.

At first, for people at the time, the meaning of the crash took a while to sink in. Just before Christmas 1929, showing a combination of confidence and blind complacency, the *Sun* published a glowing report on its front pages under the headline "New Prosperity Era Here." After recording several examples of buoyant economic growth, the paper concluded that "Vancouver has cause to face the new year and the immediate future with the keenest of optimism."[212] Yet the armies of unemployed were already marching in the streets of the city.

Vancouver was no stranger to public protest. From the earliest anti-Chinese violence in 1885 through the 1907 anti-Asian riot to the free speech fights of 1912 and the jobless protest marches of the 1920s, the city's divisions, both ethnic and socio-economic, regularly played out in the streets. But the unrest seldom reached the pitch it did during the troubled years of the Depression. It began modestly in mid-December, 1929, when a crowd of jobless men occupied the civic relief office on Cambie Street demanding "Work, Not Sympathy," as one of their placards read. Street protests picked up steam in the new year, becoming almost a daily occurrence and culminating in a large demonstration at the Powell Street Grounds at the end of January. When several hundred protestors began a march downtown, mounted police rode in among them with whips and truncheons flailing. Police Chief W.J. Bingham refused to apologize for police actions. The fault lay with Communist rabble rousers who were bent on violence, he said; he would not "stand by like a puppy" while disorder filled the streets.[213]

At the centre of the protests was the issue of civic relief. Constitutionally, it was the provinces that were responsible for unemployment relief, but as the numbers of jobless grew, the provinces passed that responsibility on to the municipalities. In 1930, for example, the city had to pick up 78 per cent of total relief costs, and it was 1932 before the provincial share exceeded 50 per cent for the first time.[214] Vancouver's relief office dispensed assistance in the form of meal tickets, which could be redeemed at any of a number of approved cafés, and bed tickets, which were worth a night in a local rooming house or charitable mission. Men also received one to two dollars a day for menial labour on public works projects.

By the middle of 1930 it was obvious that the cost of relief was going to be well over what the city could handle. Authorities halted payments to transients and single men, trying to force the province or Ottawa to pick up the slack. (Of course it didn't help that the relief officer, George Ireland, and one of his clerks were discovered to be taking kickbacks from cafés in return for sending relief cases to them.) But even when R.B. Bennett's new Conservative government in Ottawa finally agreed to spend $20 million on a new works program, the city continued to be overwhelmed. By October the new senior relief officer, Colonel H.W. Cooper, reported that there had to be at least ten thousand unemployed in the city. As the months wore on, more single men were removed from the relief rolls and the value of meal and bed tickets were slashed (for meal tickets, from 50 cents per person per day down to 22 cents). Many of these desperate men migrated to the "jungles," which began to take shape the next spring.

Sympathetic as many Vancouverites were to the plight of the jobless, they were also anxious at the turmoil in the streets and the apparent increase in crime and political unrest. The press reported that the city was experiencing a "crime wave" and blamed it on the presence of so many jobless, home-less men, and the Communist agitators who were taking advantage of the situation to recruit followers. "The great majority of these unemployed,"

Reverend Andrew Roddan supervises the distribution of food to the unemployed in one of the "jungles" on False Creek, summer 1931.
W.J. Moore photograph, Vancouver Public Library 12748

editorialized the *Province*, "are, we believe, decent and law-abiding folk, in unfortunate circumstances and eager only to find a job. But there are others, agitators and propagandists, who are exploiting the miseries of the unemployed for their own ends. It is these who are the trouble-makers."[215] It was part of a crackdown on "trouble-makers" that the police moved in on the jungles that September, and that the province began opening the first of some two hundred work camps in the interior to siphon off the urban unemployed.

With the opening of the camps, and the destruction of the so-called jungles, an enforced calm returned to the city's streets. But nothing had been resolved. Homeless men still arrived at suburban back doors looking for handouts; women still combed the garbage in search of waste food; transients still slept under the bridges and in the parks. The years "1932 and 1933 were the blackest years for Vancouver," theatre manager Ivan Ackery recalled in his memoirs. "The streets were filled with people just wandering around in despair, many past even trying to help themselves."[216] During 1931 the unemployment rate in BC reached 28 per cent, the worst in the country. The Chinese Benevolent Association calculated that in the Chinese community, which organized its own relief efforts, that figure reached 40 per cent.[217] Early the next March, thousands of protestors marched from the Cambie Street Grounds down Hastings Street to city hall (then located in the Holden Building near Hastings and Carrall), objecting to conditions in the provincial work camps. When a delegation tried to gain access to the building, a phalanx of mounted police, both city and RCMP, waded in with nightsticks flailing. Protestors fought back with whatever came to hand. The *Sun* called it "Vancouver's most serious jobless demonstration."[218] City authorities used the melee as an excuse to ban all further marches. Instead of bringing people together, the economic crisis had exposed the gulf between the haves and have-nots, which was getting harder and harder to cross.

THROUGHOUT THE DECADE, a dramatic symbol of hard times in the city was the British Columbia Hotel, better known today as the third Hotel Vancouver. The origins of this iconic landmark date back to World War I, when the Canadian Northern Railway was negotiating the deal with the city that allowed it to build its terminus on land reclaimed from the False Creek flats. As part of the deal, Canadian Northern agreed to open a large hotel in the downtown. For several years the project stalled until finally the city took the railway to court, demanding compensation if the hotel was not built. In 1928, the railway, by then Canadian National, broke ground at the corner of Burrard and Georgia. Less than a year later the Depression struck, work halted and the bare skeleton of the unfinished building loomed as a sad reminder that the life had gone out of the local construction industry. Still, the decade was not all doom and gloom, not even in the building trades. Despite the dire economic situation, construction of several major infrastructure projects proceeded. In July 1931, a new airport opened with much fanfare on land owned by the city on Sea Island in Richmond. The project had been a favourite of Mayor Louis Taylor—back in office after defeating William Malkin the previous December—ever since he had met the American aviator Charles Lindbergh at a lunch in Seattle. Lindbergh told the mayor he could not fly into Vancouver because the city did not have a decent airfield, prompting Taylor to launch his campaign to find a site and get an airport built. The city operated the facility until the federal Department of Transport purchased it in 1962.

Another project with its roots in the previous decade was the Burrard Street Bridge. The Bartholomew Report recommended a new automobile crossing of False Creek to connect downtown with the burgeoning west side neighbourhoods of Kitsilano and Point Grey. In order to build the bridge, the city needed 3.25 hectares of land at the south end that belonged to the former Kitsilano Reserve. Ever since the Squamish residents

The skeleton of the third Hotel Vancouver, stalled in mid-construction, loomed over Burrard Street for several years. The building project came to symbolize the state of the local economy during the Depression.
Leonard Frank photograph, Vancouver Public Library 5695

had been forced off the reserve in 1913, its ownership had been in dispute between the province, the federal government and the Squamish themselves. In the case of the bridge, a three-person arbitration board decided that the city should pay $44,988 to the Squamish, less expenses of almost $29,000. It was almost literally a steal, given that white property owners at the north end of the bridge received anywhere up to $125,000 for their properties.[219] The new bridge opened on July 1, 1932, when Mayor Taylor snipped a ribbon with a pair of golden scissors.

On the other side of the downtown peninsula, the construction of another bridge, this one crossing the First Narrows to the North Shore, turned out to be much more of a challenge. The municipality of West Vancouver initially promoted the bridge and tried to persuade private developers to take on the project.[220] But a bridge depended on the construction of a roadway through Stanley Park, linking it to the city. Would the Vancouver public stand for such a blatant infringement of their park? In a 1927 plebiscite, voters answered no. But then two events took place to change their minds. First of all, in mid-September 1930, a log barge struck the Second Narrows Bridge, putting it out of commission. For four years the North Shore was cut off from all automobile traffic, indicating how precarious a reliance on just one crossing truly was. Second, the unemployment crisis hit the city, and any project promising well-paying jobs suddenly took precedence over the preservation of parkland. In a second plebiscite at the end of 1933, ratepayers voted strongly for the causeway, and by extension, the bridge. It was a victory, said Mayor Taylor, for "work, not relief."[221] There was still the necessity to get federal government approval, but by the spring of 1937 all hurdles had been cleared and construction began on the project. The Lions Gate Bridge—financed in part by the Guinness brewing interests, who also owned land for development in what would become the British Properties—opened to car traffic in November 1938. Initially it was a toll bridge; car and driver cost 25 cents to cross. In 1955 the province took ownership, maintaining tolls for another eight years, by which time it calculated it had recouped the $6 million it had paid for the magnificent span.

The last of the major Depression-era construction projects was a new city hall. For many years local politicians had been wanting to relocate their offices from the Holden Building (now the Tellier Tower) on Hastings Street, where they had moved following amalgamation. These quarters were always meant to be temporary, but settling on a permanent location proved difficult. The Bartholomew Report recommended a new civic centre west of Burrard Street on the slope looking south over False Creek, but ratepayers preferred a site closer to the business district. In 1934 during the civic election, a plan to build near Victory Square was approved by pleb-iscite.[222] However, the same election returned Gerry McGeer as the new mayor, and he favoured building on Strathcona Park, a site south of False Creek at Cambie Street and Twelfth Avenue, a site never considered in the many discussions up to that time.

According to one analysis, McGeer wanted the new building to be insu-lated by distance from the political turmoil of downtown streets. Of course it was not McGeer's decision alone. But the new mayor, ignoring the results of previous plebiscites, appointed his own commission to get the result he desired. Of the three commissioners, one was a personal friend of the mayor and another was an architect who expected to receive the commission to design the new building. McGeer also issued "baby bonds" to raise money to pay for the project. Unsurprisingly the commission recommended Strathcona Park, council endorsed the choice and, despite loud public opposition, the decision was made. As was so often the case in the city, the CPR played an influential role behind the scenes. The company favoured the Strathcona Park location as a stimulus to the development of its land holdings in South Vancouver. To encourage council to make the "right" decision, the company donated a parcel of its own property to replace the loss of Strathcona Park to construction; this parcel became Hillcrest Park.[223] Canadian Pacific also lobbied for the site; Louis Taylor claimed that when he was still mayor, the company had tried to persuade him to use his influence in favour of the Strathcona Park site.[224] In the event Vancouver became the only major city in North America not to have its city hall located in the downtown core.

The official opening of the new city hall on December 4, 1936, was the highlight, and the conclusion, of the city's fiftieth birthday celebrations. Mayor McGeer and the Golden Jubilee Society planned a full slate of festive events including fireworks, bonfires, parades, a Chinese "carnival," displays of Aboriginal culture, concerts and banquets: eight hundred hours of partying in total. The Jubilee Fountain unveiled in Lost Lagoon was a birthday commemoration, as was the statue of Captain George Vancouver at city hall. Both the Lord Mayor of London and Lord Tweedsmuir, the Gov-ernor General of Canada, were honoured guests during the jubilee. It was an early example of how civic leaders deployed boosterism and spectacle to divert public attention from pressing economic and political problems. Expo 86 and the 2010 Winter Olympics would provide later examples.

MUCH AS GERRY McGEER was able to use the jubilee to burnish his own and the city's reputation, his tenure as mayor was a stormy one. He had swept into office in December 1934 on a reformist wave, winning almost 80 per cent of the popular vote and bringing to a stunning end the long career of Louis Taylor. McGeer, a lawyer by profession, came to prominence during the 1920s as an advocate for BC's interests in the freight-rate negotiations that brought so much development to the port. He had inserted himself into the Lennie Commission hearings in 1928, which is when he and Taylor had first gone head to head over the influence of criminal figures in the civic government. In the 1933 provincial election he was elected to the legislature as a Liberal. Given his prominence (according to *Maclean's* magazine, "he knows everyone in Vancouver and everyone knows him"[225]), and his own self-importance, McGeer was surprised that Premier Duff Pattullo did not invite him to join the cabinet. Looking for new fields to conquer, he welcomed an invitation from the Better Vancouver League, an anti-Communist group founded by a local timber exporter, Nelson Spencer, to run against Taylor.[226] As mayor, he hoped to put into practice some of the eccentric economic ideas he would articulate in his 1935 book *The Conquest of Poverty*, in which he argued that the government should manipulate the money supply to give people more spending power. At age forty-seven, McGeer was more than thirty years younger than Taylor and bristling with energy and ideas, while the elderly incumbent had proven powerless to do anything about the Depression.

Not only was McGeer an authority on finance, albeit self-proclaimed, he was promising to purge the city of its criminal elements, which he claimed were terrorizing the streets. The most prominent gangster in the city was Joe Celona, Vancouver's very own Al Capone. Celona, who had arrived from his native Italy shortly after World War I, owned a tobacco shop on Main Street, but his more profitable businesses were brothels and the illegal booze traffic. He used to boast of his connections to city hall, his friendship with Mayor Taylor and his influence with successive police chiefs. Celona was very much in the news during the 1934 election, having just been arrested for keeping a "disorderly house" on the top floor of the Maple Hotel on East Hastings. McGeer was at his most bombastic describing the activities of the "gamblers, racketeers and vice-mongers who are making our city a rendezvous for the criminal class."[227] Unlike Taylor, who made no secret of his tolerance of vice crimes, McGeer promised an all-out war on the underworld. "We're going to Bar Celona," he promised.[228] He was also the anointed candidate of the business establishment, which expected him to support efforts to quash the emerging forces of radical change.

Once in office the new mayor made a show of cleaning up the police force. Chief Cameron resigned, replaced by Colonel W.W. Foster, a former Conservative member of the provincial legislature, a decorated veteran of World War I and an experienced mountaineer, but not previously a police officer. Foster, who represented the new blood that McGeer had promised, set about purging the force of crooked cops. In February a report by the force's new legal advisor alleged that under Cameron's administration "commercialized vice and organized crime" had flourished under the protection of senior officers. In the end, the alcoholic, completely discredited Cameron was arrested, though charges against him were dismissed at trial, suggesting that the VPD was perhaps not as corrupt as McGeer's campaign alleged. Several gangsters did receive prison sentences, including Joe Celona, and the VPD received a thorough reorganization.

Fighting crime was one thing; doing something about the Depression was another. On January 6, 1935, Mayor McGeer declared a civic day of prayer, but it had no noticeable impact on the state of the economy. The dilemma facing the city was straightforward: the high cost of relief, and the inability of so many ratepayers to remit their property taxes, meant that the city had to borrow more and more money to make up the shortfall. It did so by issuing bonds and by borrowing from the banks. The city fell deeper into debt. Each year hundreds, sometimes thousands, of properties were claimed for nonpayment of taxes, and there was no one with any money to buy them. Even in an elite neighbourhood like Shaughnessy Heights, more than 250 properties were repossessed during the decade. One prominent mansion, valued at $75,000 in 1920, sold for just $7,500 in 1939. Many residents were reduced to taking in boarders or converting their large homes to rooming houses.[229] In the city at large the situation was so dire that homeowners were allowed to work on public relief projects as a way of paying off their taxes. It was the same desperate situation for neighbouring municipalities, three of which—Burnaby, North Vancouver City and North Vancouver District—went bankrupt, their governments taken over by provincial commissions. The possibility that the same fate might befall Vancouver—or even worse, that a Communist led insurgency might take over local government—was the nightmare scenario for the city's business and political leaders.

The fears of the business class were reflected in a particularly fanciful report presented to the provincial government at the end of the summer of 1932. Under pressure from his pro-business supporters, Premier Simon Fraser Tolmie had agreed to appoint an outside commission to evaluate how the government was handling the Depression. Led by George Kidd, a former president of the BC Electric, commissioners included W.L. Macken, a Chilliwack dairy executive; Victoria industrialist R.W. Mayhew; and two Vancouver members, mine owner Austin Taylor and lawyer A.H. Douglas. It turned out that what these men had in mind was close to a coup d'etat. Believing that any additional taxation was like getting blood from a stone, the commissioners instead recommended deep cuts to public expenditures. Their report's many proposals included reducing the size of the provincial legislature by half; slashing the salaries of provincial employees, including reducing teachers' salaries by one quarter; closing the university if it could not continue without its provincial grant; eliminating mothers' allowance; ceasing all public works except road maintenance; and so on. Impatient with the messiness of party politics, the businessmen recommended greater power for the lieutenant governor and the creation of a "non-partisan" coalition government. The historian Robin Fisher has called the commissioners "Robin Hoods in reverse; they wanted to steal from the poor and give to the rich."[230] In the end the commission was roundly condemned by public opinion and its report shelved. But the whole episode illustrated how unnerved the business community was by the economic crisis and the threat of social unrest.

In 1932 the federal government had assumed responsibility for the unemployed relief camps. Increasingly the men in the camps grew disenchanted with the military discipline that ruled their lives. The work was pointless; the living conditions were spartan. It did not take long for the Communist-backed Relief Camp Workers' Union to organize the men in protest. During 1934 there were a hundred disturbances of one kind or another in the BC camps alone. Throughout the winter of 1934–35, "relief stiffs" from the camps drifted back into the city, where they subsisted on public relief and private charity. The men held tag days to raise donations and snake dances through the streets to raise public awareness. Sympathetic homemakers invited the men for home-cooked meals, but McGeer and his council were less supportive. To the mayor this was "Red revolution." On April 23, a large crowd of men from the camps and their sympathizers marched through downtown and into the Hudson's Bay Company store, where attempts to evict them resulted in nineteen arrests. The protestors next gathered peaceably in Victory Square, from where they sent a delegation to city hall (then still down the street in the Holden Building) to meet with the mayor. McGeer told the men he could do nothing for them and as they left, ten delegates were arrested on charges of vagrancy.

McGeer hurried to the square where, on the advice of Chief Foster and worried that the gathering was a prelude to Communist insurgency, he mounted the cenotaph and read the Riot Act. It was the most memorable moment in McGeer's mayoralty and at first it seemed to work. Intimidated by police in riot gear, the crowd dispersed. But that evening, in response to police raids on their meeting rooms, angry protestors once again gathered in the streets. Chief Foster fired up his men by telling them that the time had come for "stern measures," then released them against the demonstrators—with the usual bloodshed and broken limbs resulting.[231] For another five weeks Vancouver was convulsed by marches and rallies. Business leaders responded by forming a "Citizen's League," which raised money to pay for hundreds of special police officers. The league warned in its newspaper advertisements that "decent and orderly institutions" were threatened "by the deliberate cunning of a small group of Communists."[232] The streets remained a battle zone until early in June, when many of the unemployed boarded CPR freight trains and headed east to take their grievances to the seat of government. It was the beginning of the famous "On-to-Ottawa Trek" that ended in tragic violence in Regina.

Any civic officials who breathed a sigh of relief with the departure of the camp strikers did not have long to enjoy the peace. On June 18, a two-week-old longshoremen's strike flared into violence on the waterfront. A crowd of about one thousand strikers and their sympathizers, objecting to the use of replacement workers, marched to the docks, led by Victoria Cross winner Mickey O'Rourke, who carried a large Union Jack. When the marchers ignored an order from Chief Foster to disperse, police set on them with truncheons and tear gas. "The Battle of Ballantyne Pier" was over in short order, though skirmishes continued in nearby streets for several hours. Police arrested twelve militants and banned waterfront picketing, while the city cut striking workers off the relief rolls. For Mayor McGeer, and for the business leaders who backed him, the strike was a Communist plot aiming at the heart of the established order and had to be put down ruthlessly, as it was. Later that year the strike ended in defeat for the longshoremen's union.

THE DIVISIONS OF THE 1930S led to two changes in the civic electoral system that have endured to the present day. With the exception of a brief period in the 1920s, wards, or electoral districts, had been part of local elections from the beginning. Initially the city was divided into five wards with two aldermen elected from each. (The mayor was chosen city-wide.) Over the years the number of wards grew to eight and then, with amalgamation, to twelve.[233] Which is where things stood in 1935, when Mayor McGeer unveiled a plan to abolish the ward system and return the number of aldermen to eight. McGeer, who had significant support from the provincial government, unions and the local press, framed the proposal as a way to streamline civic administration, reduce its costs and improve its efficiency. There was a growing consensus that the city was plagued by corruption, not just in the police force but in the relief department and elsewhere as well. Many people blamed the wards, which were thought to encourage aldermen to favour narrow neighbourhood interests over the interests of the city as a whole. "Ward politics tends inevitably to pettiness and section-alism," argued the *Province*. "The temptation is always to work for the ward rather than for the city, because it is in the ward, and not in the city, that the vote lies which will re-elect the alderman."[234] The *Sun* agreed, warn-ing its readers that "whatever is petty, small, obstructive and reactionary in civic politics is perpetuated and fostered by the ward system."[235] However, the aldermen themselves would not agree to put the matter of wards to a plebiscite. As a result, locally elected MLAS went over the head of council and asked the provincial legislature to organize a vote. (Under the terms of the Vancouver Charter, the city's founding document, a committee of the legislature regulated municipal affairs. The charter gives the city broader powers than those of other BC municipalities.) In the plebiscite that was held at the end of 1935, ratepayers voted two to one in favour of abolishing the wards and installing an at-large system, which was done in time for the 1936 civic election. While the issue has been debated many times since, the ward system has never been reinstated.

The other innovation was the onset of party politics in civic affairs. In 1932 a coalition of labour unions, academics, social gospellers and farm groups met in Calgary and formed a new leftist political party, the Co-operative Commonwealth Federation (CCF). In the turmoil of the Depres-sion, the new party met with astonishing success, at least in BC, where it captured almost a third of the popular vote in the provincial election of November 1933, sending seven members to the legislature—enough to become the Official Opposition. In Vancouver the CCF formed a civic wing and began running candidates. In the 1936 election it took advantage of the new at-large system to elect three aldermen with a little more than a quarter of the popular vote. Its opponents decried the arrival of "party politics" at city hall but acknowledged the need to fight fire with fire. In November 1937, a group of Conservative and Liberal Party supporters met to discuss what to do. The result was the formation of a new civic group, the Non-Partisan Association. Prominent members included Nelson Spencer, formerly of the anti-Communist Better Vancouver League, newspaper publisher Victor Odlum and an assortment of prominent lawyers and businessmen, all connected in some way to the two mainstream parties. Gerry McGeer himself joined the executive, as did former mayor W.H. Malkin and the wealthy retailer W.C. Woodward.[236] The new group might have been non-partisan in the sense that it drew from both Liberal and Conservative camps, had no formal platform of its own and generally favoured "good government," but it was decidedly partisan in its determined opposition to the CCF. And it worked. Candidates with NPA backing dominated civic politics for decades to come.

THE POLITICAL STRUGGLE for dominance in the city was mirrored in the world of art. Slowly but surely modernism was gaining traction and the forces of conservatism lashed back. "Modern art is a menace to any country whose citizens call themselves sane," bellowed the critic John Radford in the pages of the *Vancouver Star*.[237] The local representatives of this "dangerous" movement were teaching at the art school and lecturing at John Vanderpant's gallery on Robson Street. They included the landscape painter turned abstractionist Jock Macdonald, the volatile Fred Varley and the charismatic spiritualist Harry Tauber. These three, and the coterie of like-minded artists they attracted, outraged the local art establishment. For their part, the art school group disdained the conventionality of their critics, defenders of what Emily Carr called "the dead photographic art of the last century."[238]

The Vancouver Art Gallery was often caught in the middle of this shouting match. The gallery opened its doors in October 1931, supported by a fundraising campaign led by Henry Stone, a wealthy wholesaler. Initially conservative in its acquisitions, the gallery held an all-Canadian exhibition in 1932, featuring works by the Group of Seven, which the traditionalists considered outlandish. Reviewing the exhibit in the *Sun*, Radford described the modern artists as "prolific producers of artificialities, grotesque fantasies, gruesome hallucinations, morbid conceits . . ." and so on.[239] None of this discouraged the gallery from purchasing three of the canvases, and the "culture war" between conservatives and modernists bubbled along throughout the decade. Another impact of the art school was that it seemed to offer young women a new pathway to careers in art and design. Maud Sherman, Lilias Farley, Beatrice Lennie and Irene Hoffar Reid all became professional artists after studying at the school.

Since arriving from eastern Canada to teach at the art school, Fred Varley had become a lightning rod for opponents of the new art. He did not help matters in the way he led his private life. He took up with the young, attractive Vera Weatherbie, a talented artist herself, and while the pair met in Varley's cabin on the North Shore, his wife and four children struggled to make ends meet in a series of homes in the city. The decade he spent in Vancouver was highly productive artistically, but Varley wore out the patience of even his supporters with his drinking and inability to earn an income. By the time he returned to live in the east in 1937, the forces of modernism were robust enough in the city to get along without him.

ONE LOCAL "BUSINESS" that thrived despite the bad times was rum-running.[240] BC's own unhappy experiment with alcohol prohibition ended in 1921, but in the US prohibition continued. Until 1933, while liquor was legally produced and consumed in Canada, it was illegal in the US. Quite naturally a traffic developed between the two countries. It began with a few small-time operators "jumping the line" with their boats laden with bottles, which they dropped off at secluded harbours in Puget Sound or the San Juan Islands. But it soon grew into an elaborate network of corporate suppliers and a fleet of ocean-going supply ships deployed along the length of the Pacific Coast. Vancouver, complained one clergyman, became "the city of refuge for all the whisky-soaks and booze artists of the whole hemisphere." Coal Harbour was home to an armada of speedy supply boats—the so-called "mosquito fleet"—and all the shipyards, machine shops and businesses associated with boat construction and repair. "Here in Vancouver," wrote a visiting journalist, "liquor and the liquor traffic is blatant. It laughs at the American law."

As time passed, control of the liquor traffic shifted into the hands of a small number of export cartels owned by prominent business people in the city. The largest operator was Consolidated Exporters, based in the warehouse district on Hamilton Street in Yaletown. Consolidated acquired much of its product from United Distillers, located at the foot of Oak Street on the Fraser River. One of the principal owners of United was George Norgan, a local philanthropist and sportsman. When Norgan died in 1964, his net worth in liquor interests and real estate was estimated by the *New York Times* to be $25 million, and he was said to own one of the finest stables of race horses in the country. Another name associated with rum-running in the city was the Reifel family. The Reifels were important brewers and distillers long before prohibition but Henry Reifel and his two sons, George and Harry, took advantage of the liquor ban to make large profits shipping booze to the US. Henry Reifel and his brother Jack had arrived from their native Germany in 1888 and began a small brewery on Main Street that grew into a major local industry. The two sons trained to be brewers and entered the family business. George Reifel built the mansion on Southwest Marine Drive known as Casa Mia, and he also built the Commodore Ballroom in 1929 for his wife Alma, who thought the city needed more places to go dancing. An avid outdoorsman, he had a hunting retreat on Westham Island at the mouth of the Fraser River, where the Reifel Bird Sanctuary is now established. In other words, very prominent members of the Vancouver business elite were involved in the liquor traffic during Prohibition.

These operators developed a complex system for moving hundreds of thousands of cases of liquor into the US at one time. First of all, large vessels, known as "mother ships," parked off the coast of California and Mexico just outside the territorial limit on what was called Rum Row, their holds crammed with whisky, rum, gin, wine and beer. Under cover of fog or darkness, smaller, speedier boats made their way out to the mother ships, took on their orders, then hurried back to shore to transfer the contraband to waiting trucks. The larger freighters might remain at sea for months, resupplied by other vessels that brought food, fuel, mail and more crates of liquor down from Vancouver. By the late 1920s this operation was under the command of Captain Charles Hudson, described by one writer as "the true master mind of Rum Row." Hudson was a decorated veteran of the Royal Navy who had come to Canada following World War I, tried his hand at farming in Manitoba, then migrated out to the west coast, where he used his naval experience to get into rum-running. As the general manager of Consolidated Exporters, he organized the orders, dispatched the boats, hired the crews and kept the fleet supplied. Hudson claimed that, during the early 1930s the rum-runners brought prosperity back to the port of Vancouver, given how much they spent on supplies, wages, fuel and boat repairs. Though he may have been exaggerating, Hudson had a point. The liquor traffic gave a significant boost to the local economy when it most needed it.

On the Canadian side of the border, the rum-runners and the big suppliers were not breaking any laws. "Cappy" Hudson insisted that what they did was not a crime but "public philanthropy," giving the American drinking public what it wanted but could not provide for itself. Unsurprisingly the US government did not see things in the same light. Following the end of Prohibition, the Vancouver liquor barons were forced to repay more than a million dollars to the American treasury in back taxes and fines, a small portion of the profits they had made in the glory days of rum-running.

A few years after the demise of Prohibition, it was the booze business that resurrected baseball in Vancouver. Professional ball had come to the city in 1905 with the construction of Recreation Park on land leased from the CPR at the corner of Homer and Smithe. A group of local businessmen acquired a franchise in the Northwestern League and fielded a team called the Vancouver Veterans. For the first few years the squad had its share of front-office difficulties, until in 1910 Bob Brown stepped in as new owner, manager and shortstop. Vancouver's "Mr. Baseball," Brown was an American from Pennsylvania with a long history of managing in the minor leagues. He bought the team, by then called the Beavers, for $500, and within a season the franchise had claimed the league championship. More important, Brown rounded up the capital to build a new facility, Athletic Park, at Sixth Avenue and Hemlock on the south side of False Creek, where the Beavers debuted in 1913 and played for almost a decade.

Organized pro ball fell on hard times in the 1920s, when the league folded and the team disbanded, but it reappeared thanks to the efforts of Con Jones, a tobacconist known for his "Don't Argue!" chain of pool halls and his enthusiasm for local sport, whether it was soccer, lacrosse or baseball. Prior to World War I he built the ten-thousand-seat Con Jones Park (later Callister Park) in East Vancouver, and it was there that he fielded

The Asahi ball club, shown here in 1929, was the pride of Japantown until it disbanded in 1942 with the wartime internment of Japanese Canadians. The team won ten city championships during the interwar period.
Stuart Thomson photograph, Vancouver Public Library 11750

the Vancouver Maple Leafs of the Western International League (WIL) in 1937. After fifteen years, professional baseball was back in Vancouver. The team only survived two seasons, but it was at this point that liquor and sport converged. Emil Sick, a Seattle brewer and owner of the Seattle Rainiers of the WIL, purchased the club, bringing on Bob Brown as a partner. The revamped team was named the Capilanos, after the brewery Sick owned in Vancouver. It was a name that would survive for almost two decades, during which time the franchise moved to a new home, Capilano Stadium at the base of Little Mountain (later named Nat Bailey Stadium after the founder of the White Spot restaurant chain), generally conceded to be one of the prettiest baseball venues in North America.

The Beavers/Maple Leafs/Capilanos were not the only baseball team in Vancouver, not even the most popular. That title belonged to the Asahi, an amateur club founded by a dry cleaner named Matsuhiro Miyasaki in Japantown, in 1914. The team was infamous for playing a style known as "brain ball," compensating for their relatively small stature by spraying hits all over the field and running the bases with flair and intelligence. The team won several championships, including the Pacific Northwest League five years in a row. In 1942, when the city's Japanese population was removed from the coast, the Asahi disbanded. The club was later inducted into the Canadian Baseball Hall of Fame.

WITH THE CELEBRATION of Vancouver's jubilee year in 1936, Mayor McGeer and his festival organizers tried to give the impression that the worst of the Depression was over. But it wasn't. Not for the unemployed men still putting in their days at the government relief camps, and not for the city. McGeer saw out his term, then retired to focus on his other job as a federal Member of Parliament. It was his successor, George Miller, a former alderman, who was in office in the spring of 1938 when the provincial forestry camps closed and once again Vancouver streets were flooded with the jobless and the desperate. Like McGeer, Miller was a law-and-order mayor who met the challenge of social unrest with a heavy hand, slashing relief rolls and banning panhandling. In response, on May 11, hundreds of unemployed occupied the lobby of the Hotel Georgia, the civic art gallery and the downtown post office in an act of audacious civil disobedience. After a week the protestors at the hotel agreed to accept a payment of $500 and left, but the others settled into a month-long siege.

A sympathetic public rallied in support with food and blankets and the police took a wait-and-see approach. Finally the patience of the authorities ran out. Early in the morning of June 19, a day that became infamous as

"Bloody Sunday," police commanded the sit-downers to leave. At the gallery city police cleared the building without incident, but at the post office the confrontation escalated into mayhem. At about 5:00 a.m., postmaster G.H. Clarke, flanked by senior police officers, entered the building from the Hastings Street side and addressed the men, telling them they had twenty minutes to pick up their belongings and exit by one of two main doors. The men voted to remain. As they waited nervously, police gathered outside and a great crowd of the curious assembled. When the deadline arrived, Clarke announced he would extend it by another ten minutes. At this point a dozen RCMP officers appeared in the lobby, each armed with tear gas bombs and a stout whip. While they sang in defiance, the men prepared themselves by soaking their shirts and handkerchiefs in water to hold over their mouths when the gas came. Finally, at 5:40 a.m. police released the first gas. In response, a deluge of objects—tin cans, boxes, clubs, whatever the men could lay their hands on—came flying through the windows of the building. Then the men came. "A wave of humanity, frantic, screaming, tears streaming from their eyes, milled in the entrances, jammed for a moment, then poured out in one mass into the street," reported the *Sun*.[241] As the escapees streamed through the doors, police beat them with whips and clubs, singling out the operation's leader, Steve Brodie, a veteran of the On-to-Ottawa Trek, for special treatment. Thirty-eight men ended up in hospital—including Brodie, who almost lost an eye—and another twenty-two in jail.

An angry mob stormed down the street "maddened by gas and galvanized by police truncheons," in the words of the *Province*, smashing hundreds of store windows.[242] That afternoon ten thousand people gathered at the Powell Street Grounds to protest police actions. A delegation left for Victoria carrying their demands for emergency relief and a public works program to the provincial legislature, but the protest petered out in the face of official intransigence. "You were very ill-advised to do what you did," Premier Pattullo lectured the men during a twenty-minute meeting. "There comes a time when too much sympathy can be shown the men. That time has now come in Vancouver."[243] Eventually the federal and provincial governments came up with a plan to disperse the jobless back across the country, but it was only the war that would provide a solution for the problem of unemployment.

ON THURSDAY, MAY 25, 1939, the new Hotel Vancouver, under construction for a decade, finally opened its doors. Hurried to completion in time for the arrival in the city of King George VI and his wife Elizabeth, the seventeen-storey, 556-room hotel, built in the chateau style at a cost of $12 million, opened under the joint management of Canadian National and the CPR. More than 650 guests celebrated the opening at a luncheon addressed by Lieutenant Governor Eric Hamber and several other political heavyweights. "The Great Golden Inn of the West," as the *Sun* dubbed it, featured the Panorama Roof Ballroom where band leader Dal Richards headlined for twenty-five years.

The king and queen arrived in the city on the royal train a few days later, as part of their six-week tour of the country. It was the first time a reigning British monarch had visited Canada. "Whole City Thunders Greetings" blared the main headline of that day's *Sun,* and it was no overstatement. Everywhere the royals went, people lined the sidewalks and filled every window and rooftop, brandishing small flags and cheering ecstatically; war veterans, factory workers, homemakers, school children, Boy Scouts and Girl Guides, even two hundred blind students. The hospital cancelled all operations so that patients could be wheeled outside to see "Their Majestics." After visiting city hall, the procession of limousines headed downtown for lunch at the new hotel, then departed on a circuit around Burrard Inlet, crossing the Second Narrows Bridge and driving westward across North Vancouver to the site of the British Properties development, where the motorcade paused briefly for tea before returning to the city via the newly completed Lions Gate Bridge. That evening the royal couple departed by steamer for Victoria, and things in Vancouver were allowed to get back to normal.

The royals were in the country to rally support for a war everyone knew was coming. It arrived just three months later, when Germany invaded Poland and Britain and France declared war. After a pause to maintain appearances, Canada entered the conflict on September 10. Once again the Dominion was asked to rally to the support of its allies overseas. Once again a world war rescued Vancouver from depression.

Just a few days into the conflict, the *Vancouver News-Herald* published a harrowing account that brought home the reality of war to Vancouverites. On September 3, less than a day after it left Liverpool for Montreal, the liner *Athenia* sank in the North Atlantic, torpedoed by a German U-boat in the first hostile naval action of World War II. Among the *Athenia*'s 1,103 passengers was a twenty-six-year-old Vancouver woman, Dorothy Dean, who, with her mother, was on her way back from a visit to see relatives in England. Dean and her mother survived the sinking. On September 12, as she approached the coast of Newfoundland on a rescue ship, Dorothy wrote a letter home, the first inkling her family had that she was alive. It was this letter, with its eyewitness account of the attack, that the *News-Herald* published under the banner headline "Vancouver Girl Tells Horrors of Athenia Disaster." When the torpedo struck their ship, Dorothy and her mother managed to get into a lifeboat. She saw parents separated from their children, watched a young woman who had jumped into the ocean sink without a trace, heard the faint calls of survivors bobbing in the freezing water. "Shall I ever forget the children's screams?" Dorothy wrote. Even when they were rescued the ordeal continued. They were taken aboard a freighter bound for America, 220 passengers on a vessel made to handle 30. Water was rationed; there were only three bathrooms. "I have lost everything," Dorothy wrote. "All I have is what I have on." But at least they were alive.[244]

This account of the *Athenia* disaster horrified readers of the *News-Herald*, and aroused in them the fear of a direct enemy attack on Vancouver. Immediate steps were taken to fortify the city. Even before war was declared, the federal government ordered the local militia to occupy new gun batteries at the tip of Point Grey, on Ferguson Point in Stanley Park and across the

Troops disembark from a landing barge during training at Kitsilano Beach in 1943. The fighting may have been far away, but the military were very visible in the city during the war.
Don Coltman photo, City of Vancouver Archives, AM1545-S3-: CVA 586-1220

First Narrows directly beneath the Lions Gate Bridge. These guns were expected to repel any attempt to invade the harbour. In the air, flying boats from the RCAF station at Jericho Beach patrolled the coast watching for the approach of enemy vessels. A young poet named Al Purdy was one of the soldiers sent to guard the Burrard Street Bridge from possible submarine attack, though in his case he was armed with a wooden weapon because his superiors did not trust him with a real one. ("I wasn't exactly a soldier tho / only a humble airman / who kept getting demoted / and demoted / and demoted / to the point where I finally saluted civilians."[245])

Volunteers for the Air Raid Precautions (ARP) ensured that residents obeyed the periodic blackouts and carried out fire-fighting drills. Deadman's Island became a naval training facility; Shaughnessy Hospital prepared to treat the war wounded; commandos used Kitsilano Beach for training; the army occupied downtown hotels; recruiting stations set up in Victory Square; gardeners grew vegetables in special "Victory Gardens" to feed the war effort. Signs of military preparedness were everywhere evident around the city, especially after Japan entered the war at the end of 1941. Pierre Berton, then city editor at the *News-Herald*, recalled the atmosphere: "Vancouver was blacked out that month, and the gloom was increased by the presence of fog. I crept through the Stygian streets, hearing ghostly footsteps behind me, beside me, in front of me, but unable to identify the passersby. Cars slid slowly past with slitted headlights. Shades or blackened curtains were pulled over office windows. Even the lights in the harbour were extinguished."[246] Obviously Vancouver endured minor disruptions compared to the London Blitz or the Nazi occupation of Paris. Nonetheless, the wartime sense of foreboding, even dread, was real.

The main victims of this anxiety were the city's Japanese residents. The Japanese community had not allowed official discrimination to keep it from building a thriving neighbourhood along Powell Street and around Oppenheimer Park. Although Asian Canadians were still not allowed to vote, a small victory had been won in 1931 when, after a lengthy campaign, Japanese Canadian veterans of World War I were granted the provincial franchise in recognition of their military service. This small concession was not followed, however, by any further extension of rights to the community. By 1939 there were just over twenty thousand people of Japanese ancestry living in the province, most of them in the Lower Mainland, and about 75 per cent of them were Canadian citizens. Following the Pearl Harbor attack, Canada declared war on Japan on December 8, 1941. Immediately, latent animosity in the city toward the Japanese grew into open hostility. Using the pretext that local "fifth columnists" were conspiring to assist a

Japanese invasion of the coast, and despite a complete lack of evidence that this was so, authorities introduced a series of measures to regulate the local population. Fishing boats were seized, curfews imposed, Japanese language newspapers and schools closed, cars, cameras and radios confiscated, and all people of Japanese descent were required to register with the police. In mid-February, Vancouver City Council requested by unanimous vote that the federal government remove all people of Japanese origin from the coast, a directive that Ottawa issued one week later, on February 24. The BC Security Commission, created to oversee the removal, established a holding camp at Hastings Park where all Japanese residents were required to report, bringing with them only the possessions they could carry. Internees, including the elderly and mothers with babies, were housed in buildings that until recently had held livestock, and still smelled like it. Between mid-March and the end of September, several thousand people passed through the facility as they were relocated to camps in the interior or across the

Women in traditional costume take part in a parade through Japantown in the 1930s. With the internment of most of its residents, the neighbourhood became a ghost town during the war.
City of Vancouver Archives, AM1663-: CVA 300-136

Rockies. It was not until 1949 that members of the Japanese community were allowed to return to live on the coast; in the meantime their confiscated possessions were sold to pay for the costs of the relocation. With the removal of its residents, Japantown disappeared overnight; many of its homes and businesses abandoned, others sold off at a discount by the government. "After the war," recalled Japanese Canadian resident George Nitta, "Powell Street was nothing but a ghost town."[247]

The standard bearer on city council for the anti-Asian campaign was alderman Halford Wilson. During the Depression, Wilson, who was first elected to council in 1934, had taken up the issue of white women being employed by Chinese businesses. Technically, the provincial Women and Girls Protection Act (1923) made this illegal, but the legislation left enforcement to the discretion of local officials. Employment in Chinatown restaurants was considered by many to threaten the moral purity of white women. The police, with Wilson's encouragement, ordered several restaurateurs to lay off their white waitresses. What followed was one of the oddest labour actions in the city's history, as more than two dozen women paraded to city hall to protest, blaming "a bunch of fussy old bridge-playing gossips who are self-appointed directors of morals" for costing them their jobs.[248] But no one paid any attention to the women, and the ban on white waitresses in Chinatown held.

Wilson also opposed the spread of Chinese-owned businesses to parts of the city beyond Chinatown. He was especially vigilant about grocers who opened stores in other areas, using whatever bylaws and regulations he could to confine Chinese residents to their downtown neighbourhood. In 1941, Tong Louie, the grocery wholesaler and future owner of London Drugs, moved with his new wife Geraldine to a home in Dunbar. The couple were the first ethnic Chinese to challenge the west side's racial exclusivity, and their arrival was met by petitions and protests from their neighbours demanding council stop the "Oriental" invasion. According to the *Sun*, property values in Dunbar had fallen by 20 per cent because of the "intrusion" of the Louies.[249] Halford Wilson supported the protestors, who were ultimately unsuccessful.[250] The following year it was Wilson who sponsored the civic motion to intern the Japanese and Wilson again who tried, unsuccessfully, to pass a bylaw banning "Orientals" from owning property outside of Chinatown.[251] Following the war, his strident anti-Asian views were no impediment to his consistently winning re-election to council. (Curiously the intransigent bigot seems to have gone through a conversion and, by the 1950s, he had put aside his racism and emerged as a leader in the city's nascent human rights community.[252])

Once Benito Mussolini joined the war as an ally of Germany, in June 1940, Canadian authorities also targeted the Italian community. After the turn of the century, several thousand Italian immigrants had arrived in the city, congregating mainly in Strathcona, where some of Vancouver's oldest Italian businesses (Bosa Foods, Venice Bakery and others) got their start. At the outbreak of the war the federal government banned various Italian organizations and interned several hundred Italian Canadians in prisoner-of-war camps in Alberta and eastern Canada, including forty-four men from BC, most of them from Vancouver. The internees were suspected of being Fascist sympathizers, though no charges were ever laid. Other Italians were moved away from the coast. In Vancouver the Italian community was overwhelmingly anti-Fascist. As soon as war began, Angelo Branca, a prominent lawyer and future provincial Supreme Court judge, convened a meeting of the Canadian-Italian War Vigilance Association and issued a declaration pledging loyalty to Canada. In spite of these efforts, about 1,300 local Italians who were considered enemy aliens were required to report monthly to the RCMP for the duration of the conflict.

The West Coast Shipbuilders yard on the south shore of False Creek. The vessels were freighters bound for the North Atlantic run.

Vancouver shipbuilders manufactured more wartime vessels than those in any other location in Canada.
Lew Parry Film Productions photo, City of Vancouver Archives, AM336-S3-2-: CVA 677-1108

ALONG WITH FEAR AND SUSPICION, the war brought renewed prosperity to the city. Armament manufacturing created thousands of jobs. Shipyards once again began producing large steel merchant-class and naval vessels. In southeast False Creek, James Coughlan & Sons, once the largest shipyard in the city, had burned in 1923 but it was resurrected as a brand new yard, West Coast Shipbuilders, with a steel fabrication plant, Hamilton Bridge, adjacent to it. West Coast was one of seven shipyards in BC producing freighters for the Allied merchant marine. These large vessels plied the North Atlantic, carrying supplies to a beleaguered Europe. Several sawmills also operated in False Creek, among them the Sitka Spruce Lumber Company, specializing in turning spruce logged in Haida Gwaii into aircraft for the war effort. On Granville Island, a sandbank that dredging had transformed into an early industrial park, more than two dozen plants manufactured a dizzying array of products for the war effort: rope, wire, cement, chain, rivets, nails, lumber—the list goes on. So much activity was turning False Creek into a stinking sewer, reeking of raw sewage and industrial waste. But with a war on, any plans to clean it up had to wait.

In North Vancouver, Burrard Dry Dock, formerly Wallace Shipyards, was running twenty-four hours a day, seven days a week, so busy that it had to open a second yard on the Vancouver waterfront. In the autumn of 1942, as more and more men were called away to join the armed forces, BDD became the first shipbuilder in the country to hire significant numbers of women to work in the yards. At the height of the construction boom the company employed fourteen thousand workers, up from just two hundred in 1939 and more than any other shipyard in Canada—so many that extra ferries had to be put into service to get them back and forth across Burrard Inlet every day. BDD and the other BC yards manufactured 255 cargo ships during the war. At peak production the Vancouver-area yards produced two new freighters every week, with crews working around the clock. Along with ships came airplanes. Boeing Canada opened a factory on Sea Island, where it manufactured amphibious aircraft for the RCAF and part of the fuselage for the American B-52 bomber. At the height of production, the plant employed seven thousand workers, many of them women. Vancouver even acquired a new suburb next door to the airport: Burkeville was an instant company town of 328 houses built by Boeing for its workforce and named for company president Stanley Burke.

The divisive political protests of the previous decade were quickly forgotten during the war years as a conservative, business-as-usual consensus settled over city hall. In the last civic election of the Depression, voters chose a CCF mayor, Lyle Telford, but seven out of the eight aldermen were backed by the NPA, and in subsequent wartime elections NPA candidates swept the mayoralty (Jack Cornett, a shoe merchant) and every one of the seats on council.

AT AROUND NOON ON MARCH 6, 1945, Vancouverites felt the air vibrate with a loud rumbling that seemed to emanate from the harbour, followed by three more loud concussions. As people looked at one another wondering what had just happened, the first sirens began to blare. Emergency vehicles rushed to the waterfront. The *Green Hill Park*, one of the large merchant freighters recently launched from local shipyards, had been taking on cargo at Pier B at the north end of Burrard Street when there was an explosion in one of the holds amidships. It was later determined that a dropped match had set off flares, which ignited the inflammable cargo; an inquiry found various officials in dereliction of duty. The blast shattered windows in buildings throughout the downtown. Shards of glass showered down on sidewalks and debris hurtled several blocks through the air. Eight men died instantly; another nineteen were injured. It was Vancouver's worst waterfront disaster, and it could have been far worse had the fire spread to the docks. Instead tugs towed the blazing ship away from the pier toward the First Narrows, where it was beached near Siwash Rock. For three days the fireboat *J.H. Carlisle* poured water into the hull until finally the fire burned out.

Two months after the *Green Hill Park* explosion, the war came to an end. On May 7 word arrived that Germany had surrendered. "Victory Comes to Vancouver," read the front page of the *Province*, above a photograph of Hastings Street showered by a snowstorm of paper thrown in jubilation from the windows of the office buildings.[253] The next day Canadians officially celebrated VE Day. The war in the Pacific dragged on for another three months until finally, on August 14, Japan in turn surrendered. Once again crowds filled the streets. The celebration was particularly intense in Chinatown. The novelist Wayson Choy recalls in his memoir the clamour of the drums and cymbals on Pender Street and the bang of firecrackers hanging from every balcony. "Past Columbia Street, people wearing party hats blew paper horns and spun wooden rattles, happily banging on all the store and restaurant windows . . . In various Chinese dialects and English accents, in European languages I couldn't then identify, I heard roaring—and above all the mixed and joyful tongues, the final English words: 'The war's over! The war's over!'"[254]

The Aristocratic Restaurant at the corner of
Granville and Broadway was the last of
a much larger chain of cafés that flourished
in the city from the 1930s to the 1950s.
Pictured in 1951, this location closed in 1997.
Artray photograph, Vancouver Public Library 81669

CHAPTER SIX

The Modernist City

EVA HOFFMAN was just entering her teens when she arrived with her parents from Poland to live in Vancouver at the end of the 1950s. Everything about the city—which she called a "bit of nowhere"—offended her.[255] With the certainty of adolescence, she dismissed its occupants as shallow and conformist, their homes as bland and superficial. She could not adjust to the dating rituals of her schoolmates; they left her feeling awkward and foolish. Far from being grateful for the chance at a life in North America, she was disdainful of her new surroundings. Everything seemed larger and blander than it was in her native Krakow. The city seemed to be an uncultured wasteland. While her parents struggled to get established in this new place, Eva could hardly wait to get out. Immediately after finishing high school she left to attend university in the United States and went on to a career as a teacher, critic and writer in New York and London.

In her memoir *Lost in Translation*, Hoffman is hard on the city, but in some ways she was no harder than native-born Vancouverites were. In the postwar period the city was disappointed in itself. Like a teenager on a first date, it was obsessed with its appearance. It fussed over how it looked and it did not like what it saw. The downtown seemed dowdy. The old wooden buildings in the city core were fading and dilapidated. Much of the housing stock was aged and ramshackle. In the words of one local politician, False

Creek—the industrial heart—was "a filthy ditch." Much of the time a noxious smog obscured the view. Harland Bartholomew and Associates, the consultants who had prepared the influential 1929 plan, submitted a series of postwar updates lamenting the city's rundown appearance as "an affront to the beauty of its natural setting." "The man-made city appears sordid and ugly," the consultants complained, with "a barren, awkward, frontier-like appearance."[256] As Vancouver entered its seventh decade, it seemed in desperate need of a makeover.

Many believed that the answer to all this decay and disrepair was modernism. As a style of architecture, modernism flourished among a talented local group of young designers, who set out to reimagine the city's possibilities. Prior to the war, downtown banks and office buildings were built of limestone and granite, often sourced from upcoast island quarries. The Marine Building, the Dominion Building, the World Tower, the second Hotel Vancouver—all these buildings dating from the 1920s and earlier represented a previous stage of city building. With modernism came the application of new materials and new ideas about the relationship between structure and setting. Glass and steel towers appeared, epitomized by the BC Electric Building erected on the height at Burrard and Nelson in 1957 as the company's new headquarters. Designed by Thompson Berwick Pratt, one of the leading-edge architectural firms in the city, this twenty-one-storey tower, ablaze with light all night, was stunning in its break with tradition. Modernism also flourished in domestic architecture in what became known as the West Coast Style, featuring the generous use of wood and glass, open floor plans, exposed beams and flat roofs. In 1949 one of these homes, known as the Sky Bungalow, was constructed in the parking lot of the downtown Hudson's Bay Company store. Stocked with furnishings from the HBC, it opened its doors to the public as a show home, revealing what the suburban good life could look like. After a year it moved to a permanent location in North Vancouver (where it still stands).

But modernism meant more than corporate headquarters and homes for the well-to-do. It also was reflected in the high-rise apartment buildings that began transforming the West End during the 1950s. And perhaps most important, it informed the ambitious schemes to renew the downtown hatched by the city's new planning department. Implicit was the belief that a city properly planned by technocrats could be a city without social problems. This was reflected in administrative changes that council made in the mid-1950s, first of all creating a professional planning department and then creating a Board of Administration to take much of the bureaucratic duties off the shoulders of elected councillors. The board came to enjoy unprecedented power. As one student of the period writes, "council and the public only knew as much as BOA told them."[25]

All of these related developments were nourished by the prosperity and growth that followed the war. Unlike the Depression that followed World War I, the post–World War II period was marked by an economic boom. Vancouver grew from a population of 275,353 in 1941 to 426,256 in 1971, a 54 per cent increase. The surrounding suburbs grew even faster. Burnaby, for example, quadrupled in population in the same period; North Vancouver (city and district) and Richmond sextupled in size. In recognition of this explosive suburban expansion, the province created the Lower Mainland Regional Planning Board (LMRPB) to manage growth and to plan for essential services on a region-wide basis. Created in 1949, the LMRPB was superseded by the Greater Vancouver Regional District (now Metro Vancouver) in 1967. Water, sewage, transportation, parks—these were some of the services that came to be planned for on a regional level.

During the 1950s the provincial economy was enjoying the stimulus of a worldwide demand for BC resources. Wood products, coal, oil and natural gas, copper and other minerals flowed down the rail lines and through the harbour. The export of grain, which had fallen off during the war, surged as

When the BC Electric Building (later the BC Hydro Building) went up in 1957, it changed the face of Vancouver. The old city was made of granite and limestone; the new one was a city of glass and steel. Illuminated all night, perched on the rise overlooking downtown, the dramatic building was a stunning landmark.
Daniel O'Neill photograph, Vancouver Public Library 84935

the oceans reopened to commercial shipping. In 1955 the harbour inaugurated a revolution in transportation when the 101-metre *Clifford J. Rogers* sailed for Alaska from a dock in North Vancouver. The *Rogers* was carrying six hundred cube-shaped steel containers filled with cargo, ready to be transshipped directly onto railcars in Skagway bound for Whitehorse. This was the first use anywhere of containerized shipping, soon to transform ocean-going transport worldwide. By 1969 Vancouver had surpassed Montreal as Canada's largest port in terms of tonnage handled.

More broadly, the election of a Social Credit government in 1952 set off a building boom throughout the province. Despite its free enterprise rhetoric, Premier W.A.C. Bennett's government invested unprecedented amounts of taxpayer dollars in large public enterprises: new highways and bridges, hydroelectric dams, a railway and a fleet of coastal ferries. With a buoyant economy and a faith in the ability of technology and planning to solve social problems, the stage was set for dramatic change in the postwar city.

THE END OF THE WAR brought the return of a familiar face to civic politics. Gerry McGeer was back, filled with his usual bombast and bravado. He had been away in Ottawa for a decade, serving as a Liberal Member of Parliament for the riding of Vancouver-Burrard. As an MP he was an erratic if ultimately loyal defender of Prime Minister Mackenzie King, and as a result he was rewarded with a seat in the Senate when the war was over. Not satisfied with a sinecure, however, the restless McGeer decided to take another run at the mayoralty. With the backing of the NPA he managed to win a fairly easy victory in the 1946 election, despite fighting much of the campaign from a hospital bed recovering from a ruptured appendix. McGeer relied on a familiar anti-crime platform, using the same "clean up the streets" rhetoric that had worked for him ten years earlier. "Get going you thugs," he warned the city's criminal element, "because I'm coming again, and there's no room in town for you."[258] Once elected, McGeer engineered the firing of police chief Alex McNeill and his replacement by veteran detective Walter Mulligan. Public hearings into the force revealed the by-now familiar pattern of bribes and kickbacks from the city's gamblers and brothel keepers, and once again McGeer could claim to have swept the city clean of vice. But before he could accomplish much else, he died midway through the first year of his term. At age fifty-nine his years of alcohol abuse had finally caught up with him. "He had the Irishman's love of a fight," eulogized the *Province*, "and he was in fights practically all his days."[259]

One of the issues McGeer did not survive to address was Vancouver's significant housing shortage. During the war, workers had been attracted to the city by the booming industries, boosting the population by 44,000 people. Construction of homes could not keep up and accommodation was at a premium. This acute shortage was exacerbated at the end of the war by the return of demobilized soldiers, many of them with families. As a result, by the middle of 1945, the vacancy rate in the city approached zero.[260]

One suggestion that emerged from the housing debate was to convert the "old" Hotel Vancouver into a temporary hostel for veterans. Once the most palatial stopping place in the city, the massive stone hotel at the corner of Georgia and Granville was slated for demolition, replaced by the newer version down the street. Many housing advocates wondered why it could not be used to lodge the homeless. When negotiations between the different levels of government and the CPR, which owned the building, dragged on, a group of veterans took matters into their own hands. On the afternoon of January 26, 1946, they marched into the deserted lobby and seized possession of the hotel, hanging a banner from the windows overlooking Granville Street: "Action at Last. Veterans! Rooms for You—Come and Get Them." Within four days, 1,400 squatters—ex-servicemen, their wives and families—had done just that. Local restaurants sent in free food and a festive atmosphere pervaded the halls. Intimidated by the popular support that rallied behind the squatters, the different stakeholders came to a quick agreement, and at the beginning of February the hotel was converted to an interim hostel for veterans. By the time it closed in 1948, the federal government had built several hundred homes in a new subdivision, Renfrew Heights, at the eastern edge of the city. Many of the vets moved directly from the hostel to their new homes in the suburbs. Once it was emptied the hotel came down, replaced for the next twenty-odd years by a parking lot.

Renfrew Heights was part of a larger initiative of the federal government through its housing agency, Central (later Canada) Mortgage and Housing Corporation (CMHC), created in 1946. CMHC was concerned initially with putting roofs over the heads of returned soldiers and their families. In Vancouver, Renfrew Heights was followed by a second project farther to the south. Fraserview, completed in 1950, was a development of 1,100 houses made available at reasonable rents. Streets were landscaped and efforts were taken to make the instant neighbourhood, in the words of former mayor Jack Cornett, "a workingman's Shaughnessy Heights."[261]

Subsequently, as the need for veterans' housing eased, CMHC began partnering with the provinces and local governments to construct public housing for low- and middle-income people. One of the first of these projects was the Little Mountain Housing Project just east of Queen Elizabeth Park.

Under the terms of the National Housing Act, costs were divided 75:25 between Ottawa and the province, with the latter allowed to pass on a portion of its share to the city. The Vancouver Housing Authority was established to administer the project and construction began during the summer of 1953. Social housing brought a storm of protest from the city's landlords and business groups. It was the era of the Cold War and opponents warned against "socialist" housing. Nonetheless the project went ahead, and in the spring of 1954, the first families moved in. Little Mountain showed there was a new, activist role for government to play in the provision of affordable housing and it was the model for several other projects that followed.[262]

Slightly to the west and south of Little Mountain, another part of the city was opening to residential development. In 1950 the CPR began selling off its lots south of Forty-first Avenue and east of Granville. A large chunk of this area had been an army barracks during the war until BC Electric purchased it for use as an expansive transit centre, where the company based its fleet of new trolley buses. Across Forty-first Avenue to the south, Woodward's built a shopping mall, Oakridge, which opened in 1960. The mall anchored a community of newly built bungalows in a part of the city that until then had remained largely uncleared bushland. Many of these new middle-class homes were owned by members of the city's Jewish population. During the interwar period Jewish families began migrating from Strathcona south of False Creek, a shift symbolized by the opening of a Jewish Community Centre in Fairview in 1928. Following World War II, this southward movement continued, and many Jews settled in the Oakridge area, where a new community centre opened at Forty-first Avenue and Oak Street in 1962. More recently this section of South Vancouver welcomed an influx of Asian residents.

SINCE THE CITY'S EARLIEST DAYS people had been creating their own "affordable" housing by squatting in cabins and floathomes along the foreshore of Burrard Inlet and False Creek. A report in the *World* newspaper in 1889 counted 233 "floating cabins"; five years later the *News-Advertiser* enumerated 364.[263] The houses either slumped on barges in the water, connecting to the shore via plank walkways, or tottered on pilings driven into the mud below the high-tide line. They ranged from single-room cabins to more substantial multi-room dwellings. According to the *World* reporter, their occupants consisted of "men and women of almost all shades of colour—negroes, Sandwich Islanders, Chinese, Japanese, Indians and half-breeds" along with "white people from England, Ireland, Scotland, the

United States, Spain, Switzerland, Germany, Italy, Norway and Sweden." One group of cabins was owned by the Hastings Mill and used by a small colony of Japanese workers employed by the mill. A boatbuilder named Andy Linton owned a float at the foot of Carrall Street on which he kept fourteen small cabins, which he rented out for a dollar a week. "These rooms are occupied by all classes of man," reported the *World*, "from the college graduate to the longshoremen, and who on the whole live very peacefully together." Most of the "cabineers" picked up whatever jobs they could find at one or another of the waterfront enterprises. "Some talk has been indulged in about removing these 'unsightly places' from the water fronts," concluded the reporter, "but if it were put into force great hardship would be the result, and many of their inhabitants would have to leave the city."[264]

Following World War II there were several hundred of these residences on either side of the Second Narrows Bridge, in Burnaby as well as Vancouver, in Coal Harbour and on both sides of False Creek. The anthropologist Rolf Knight recalled the boathouses strung along the shore below Wall Street in the former Hastings Townsite near the eastern edge of the city. "Since none of the inhabitants held title or paid taxes on the house sites," Knight explained, "they received no municipal services of any kind."[265] Residents collected water in rain barrels; heat came from wood-burning stoves, the fuel scavenged from around the harbour. This community of squatters persisted until the mid-1950s, when the National Harbours Board (now Port Metro Vancouver) claimed the foreshore for port development, evicting the residents and razing their shacks.

In False Creek another small village of floathomes clustered on the south shore, beneath the Burrard Street Bridge on the old Squamish site of Sen-ákw. During the Depression this community was known derisively as Bennettville, after Prime Minister R.B. Bennett, who was mocked for doing so little to ease the dire economic situation. In November 1949 the body of a woman, Blanche Fisher, was found floating in False Creek. She had been strangled and raped. A month later police arrested Frederick Ducharme for vagrancy. Ducharme had a long record of indecent exposure convictions in cities across western Canada. He lived in one of the False Creek shacks, and when police searched it they found items belonging to the dead woman. The case went to trial early in 1950. Ducharme's odd behaviour in court suggested he was mentally unstable, but he was convicted of murder nonetheless and hanged. The case reinforced local prejudices against the squatters and fears that their small, floating community was full of rapists and other felons. At about the same time, public health officials raised the alarm about possible typhoid cases in the shacks. But most important,

A squatter at his home on the south shore of
False Creek. During the Depression, when
this photo was taken, the small community
of squatters was known as Bennettville, after
the prime minister who was blamed for the
economic distress suffered by so many people.
City of Vancouver Archives, AM54-S4-: Wat P128

the squatters were caught up in a more general concern about the state of False Creek, which people agreed had become a blight on the city.

At the end of 1950 Fred Hume, an electrical contractor from Sapperton, won an upset victory in the civic election and settled into what would turn out to be four successive terms as mayor. Hume was a well-known sporting figure—he played for the famed Salmonbellies lacrosse team and later owned soccer, lacrosse and hockey franchises—and had already served a decade as mayor of New Westminster. During the 1950 campaign one of the prominent planks in his platform was a proposal to fill in False Creek. Foul with industrial waste, the inlet was home to as many as eighty businesses—sawmills, shipyards, metal manufacturers, tow boat companies, a cooperage and many others—accounting for ten thousand jobs.[266] The Vancouver Salt Company warehouse, built in 1931 on what had been the waterfront, processed salt for the fishing industry to use as a preservative. (The building is now used as a pub/restaurant.) Companies such as Opsal Steel, Westminster Iron Works, Vivian Gas Engine Works, Hayes Trucks and Vancouver Iron and Engineering manufactured equipment for the logging and fishing industries. False Creek could fairly be called the workshop that powered the provincial economy.

Complaints about pollution went back at least as far as the Bartholomew Report, which called False Creek "an eyesore and a menace to health."[267] A pall of soot-laden smoke infiltrated the surrounding working-class neighbourhoods and raw sewage drained directly into the basin. In his autobiographical novel *All That Matters*, set in interwar Chinatown, Wayson Choy described "the yellow-tinged air" and the taste of "the acrid smoke and fires spewing from the three- and five-storey-high brick chimneys of mills and refineries." For the young Choy, the factories of False Creek were "grim castles anchored deep in toxic black mud."[268] Every week more than three hundred scows and barges made their way in and out of False Creek. Mayor Hume did not challenge the area's role as an industrial centre. He argued simply that by filling in the creek the city would ease motor vehicle congestion, save on the cost of bridges and provide even more land for industry to grow.[269] But after the engineering department looked into the issue, the option of reclaiming the basin was discarded as being too expensive. The engineers' report did recommend some improvements, including clearing out the squatters, but for the time being not a great deal was done to clean up an area the *Province* called "a garbage dump, a sewer outlet, for the city of Vancouver."[270] Instead, to deal with the traffic issue, a new Granville Street Bridge was built across the basin, the first eight-lane bridge in Canada.

Air pollution was becoming a critical issue for the city, and not just in False Creek. "One of the most vital problems facing Vancouver today . . . is the pall of smoke which constantly hangs over the city," the *Province* warned its readers in 1955.[271] Soot produced by the sawmills and bee-hive burners was recognized to be a danger to health, not to mention a cause of the grime covering buildings and other outdoor surfaces, and a contributor to the dense fogs that smothered the city. The fogs posed a serious threat for drivers and pedestrians. Frank White was a truck driver who hauled freight to and from the Gastown warehouses in the 1930s and 1940s. He recalled the fog being so thick that drivers would have to hire youngsters to walk ahead of them with a flashlight showing the way. "Your horn wasn't any use because nobody would know where it was coming from," he explained. "I ran into a streetcar once and there was absolutely nothing that I saw until I hit it."[272] The *Province* was alarmed about the health risk: "If we don't fight this danger we shall wake up one morning and find that we have an active killer on our hands."[273] By the 1960s, nox-ious exhaust from motor vehicles was added to the list of pollutants. The *Province* lauded the work of the Air Pollution Control Society, perhaps

False Creek was the industrial heart of the city, home to sawmills, shipyards, metal-workers and a myriad of other industrial enterprises. It was not until the late 1960s that plans to replace industry with residential and recreational developments gained acceptance. W.J. Moore photo, City of Vancouver Archives, AM54-S4-: Wat N62.2

Vancouver's first environmental group, a voluntary organization created by the Kiwanis Club in 1952 to lobby for pollution controls. The city did take some steps—a new anti-smog bylaw in 1955, for example—but the provincial Social Credit government ignored the problem and very little was done.[274]

DURING THE 1950S the old downtown, at least the part of it between Hastings and the waterfront, solidified its reputation as the city's skid row, or skid road. Originally referring to the corduroy roads used to skid trees out of the forest, the term "skid row" had come to refer to a part of town frequented by loggers in from the bush and looking for a cheap room and a nearby bar. When they were ready to leave the camps permanently, many of these men retired to rooming houses, residential hotels and humble cabins in the east end. This was the way things had been in Vancouver from the beginning. Following the war, however, planners, local politicians and developers identified Skid Row as a neighbourhood of urban blight, crime and immorality, and a source of concern for uptown folk who seldom went there. Typical of this attitude was a series of articles in the *Province* in November 1952, depicting the downtown's East End as the source of 90 per cent of the city's crime, home to hopeless alcoholics and impoverished pensioners, and the heart of the drug traffic. The area was "a street of lost souls," according to reporter Bill Ryan. And worst of all, it was a "tax sink," meaning it produced far less in tax revenue than it ate up in civic expenditures.[275]

The economic deterioration of the East End was not a figment of the media's imagination, at least not completely. For a number of reasons the neighbourhood had fallen on hard times. Partly it was the result of civic policies, which had zoned as industrial the residential area to the east of Chinatown, known as Strathcona. This made it difficult for residents to obtain financing to upgrade their properties and contributed over time to their deterioration. At the same time waterfront industries that had congregated near the rail lines and shipping piers were relocating to cheaper land farther from downtown. The ferry from North Vancouver, which had been delivering passengers to its terminal at the foot of Columbia Street for several decades, ceased operation in 1958, followed by the Union Steamship Company, which for decades had serviced the BC coast from its docks at the foot of Carrall Street. The CPR coastal steamship service was also reducing its service, and the BC Electric Company moved its headquarters from the station on Carrall to the new building on Burrard Street. For decades, thousands of people had been circulating through the East End every day to shop, run errands, go to the theatre or a restaurant, catch the interurban or sail aboard a coastal steamer, but in the 1950s much of this activity shifted elsewhere, and the neighbourhood began to lose its economic vitality. By 1966 the *Sun* was reporting that the downtown East Hastings corridor was "a disaster area." "Cheap hotels, dingy beer parlours, shooting galleries, the claptrap that spells decay, threatened what was once the town's main drag."[276] The renowned architect Arthur Erickson told a reporter: "Migawd, it's such a shanty town. No city in North America is as basically shacky as this one."[277]

Civic politicians and planners responded to the perceived decay of the old downtown by proposing to destroy it, at least part of it. In 1950 a sociologist at UBC, Leonard Marsh, published a report based on interviews carried out by students at the university's school of social work. Marsh was one of the most influential social thinkers in Canada. Based at McGill University during the Depression, he was a founding member of the League for Social Reconstruction, the group of leftist intellectuals who provided the Co-operative Commonwealth Federation (CCF, the forerunner of today's New Democratic Party) with most of its policies. During the war he authored a report on social security that was in many ways a blueprint for the postwar welfare state. Marsh had moved to UBC after the war and his report on the inner city, titled *Rebuilding a Neighbourhood*, embodied what at the time were considered progressive views about urban renewal. He recommended the replacement of many of the aging single-family homes in Strathcona, east of the downtown core, with a planned neighbourhood featuring clusters of high-density rental housing projects.

Marsh's report was taken up by the city's planning department, which had recently been created to replace the advisory Town Planning Commission. Gerald Sutton Brown, a forty-one-year-old Englishman, was hired as the first director of planning. Sutton Brown was a self-confident professional who came to enjoy inordinate power in the city government. Bob Williams, a 1960s alderman, called him "a classic colonial type," by which he meant arrogant, insensitive and closed to any ideas that clashed with his own.[278] Sutton Brown's department endorsed the Marsh plan, even though the majority of residents had said they did not want to leave their homes, and the Strathcona redevelopment project began in 1959.[279]

Conceived in three phases and using a 50 per cent contribution from the federal government, the project began with the construction of a nine-storey apartment building on top of McLean Park. Even before the start of construction, residents—many of whom were Chinese-Canadians with businesses and/or jobs in Chinatown—had organized in opposition to the

1

2

1 Instead of fixing up dilapidated housing on the east side, the city preferred to knock it down and build anew, displacing the people who lived there. The Hogan's Alley area, shown here, was completely razed in the early 1970s to make way for the new Georgia Viaduct.
City of Vancouver Archives, COV-S168---: CVA 203-29

2 In the 1950s and 1960s, planner Gerald Sutton Brown was the most powerful bureaucrat in the city.
City of Vancouver Archives, COV-S578---: PRS 578-114E7f7.3

project, forming the Chinatown Property Owners Association. With blithe confidence in the values of modern planning, the *Province* advised the protestors to climb aboard the redevelopment bandwagon. "Slum clearance is Chinatown's opportunity," admonished the paper.[280] Strathcona residents might be forgiven for not seeing the upside to the bulldozing of their homes, but their complaints were dismissed. "The redevelopment must go ahead," proclaimed Mayor Tom Alsbury, a long-time supporter of the CCF.[281] "It was assumed," wrote the distinguished urban geographer Walter Hardwick, "that no one in his right mind would oppose urban renewal."[282] Accordingly, several more blocks of Strathcona were cleared of houses and two more high-rise developments went up. Thousands of houses were removed. It was not until the later 1960s and the "Great Freeway Debate" that a coalition of residents, heritage advocates and social activists managed to mobilize public opinion against the further destruction of the East End.

ON THE OTHER SIDE OF THE DOWNTOWN PENINSULA, in the West End, a similar process of "renewal" was taking place, though with less disruption for the people living there. The conversion of some of the large homes into apartment houses and the construction of low-rise apartment buildings had been going on in the neighbourhood since before World War I. In 1908, for example, the three-storey Manhattan Apartments opened at the corner of Robson and Thurlow. The building, built for sawmill owner W.L. Tait and still standing, was the first of dozens of similar blocks erected around the West End before the pre-war recession slowed the pace of construction. Apartment building resumed in the 1920s, but it was not until the 1950s that the high-rises that came to characterize the neighbourhood began appearing. In 1956 the city did away with a six-storey height restriction on buildings, unleashing a construction boom that transformed the neighbourhood into an island of soaring concrete towers. In part this change was motivated by a desire to encourage population growth close to the downtown commercial area, which was losing business to the burgeoning suburbs.

By the mid-1960s, more than 40 per cent of the apartments in the city were located in this one small area, where the population doubled in the decades following the war.[283] The construction of tall towers continued until 1973, when a new civic government, concerned about the increased density in the West End, placed limits that restricted the height of new buildings and brought the boom to an end. Between 1956 and 1976, developers constructed 181 high-rise residential towers; that is, buildings of between ten and thirty-two storeys.[284]

On its northern edge, facing Stanley Park, Coal Harbour was the West End's industrial precinct, and it was going through a series of changes of its own. From the 1860s the north end of Denman Street had been the site of a small settlement of Hawaiian families known as Kanaka Ranch, "Kanaka" being a term for Indigenous Hawaiian. Technically the site was part of the Three Greenhorns pre-emption and the Indigenous people were considered squatters, but when the matter came to court in 1899 it was settled in favour of Kanaka resident Mary Eihu who, along with her late husband, had first occupied the site. The land, at Georgia and Denman, remained with the Eihu family until it was sold to Crane's Shipyards in 1922.[285]

Crane's was one of several marine industries that occupied the southern shoreline of Coal Harbour from the World War I period. Others of particular note were W.R. Menchions, the last wooden boatbuilder in the harbour when it closed in 1990, and the Hoffar Motor Boat Company, which began manufacturing seaplanes in 1917 and later was taken over by Boeing. (On September 4, 1918, one of Hoffar's seaplanes was involved in the city's first air crash. The two-passenger biplane lost power during a test flight and crashed into a house at the corner of Bute and Alberni. The pilot came through it with minor cuts and bruises; there were no other injuries.[286]) Between the wars Coal Harbour was a bustling enclave of mills, boatyards and machine works. There was also a well-established community of floathouses. But by the 1950s most of the industries had closed or moved, and the floathome residents had been forced out. Its location at the entrance to Stanley Park made the area attractive for non-industrial use. The harbinger of this change was the Bayshore Inn, which opened on the shorefront in 1961. The luxurious hotel presaged the transformation of Coal Harbour from a working waterfront to a recreational playground as more of the shoreline was occupied by restaurants, residential towers and parkland.

Much was changing in the city as it went through its postwar remake, but one thing that remained the same was the inability of the police force to avoid scandal. As the *Sun* pointed out, the average tenure for a police chief in Vancouver was only four years.[287] When Walter Mulligan became chief in 1947—at forty-two years old he was the youngest chief in the force's history—he was supposed to be another new broom that swept it all clean. But the old patterns asserted themselves. In 1952, for example, the force was embroiled in highly public accusations of racist brutality. Early in the morning of July 19, a fifty-two-year-old stevedore named Clarence Clemons got into a scuffle with police at the New Station Café on Main Street. The New Station had a reputation as a lively afterhours joint close to Hogan's Alley. "It was world-renowned," affirmed Dorothy Nealy, a neighbourhood resident. "People would come from all parts of the city, used to come off the ships, the merchant seamen, and they'd stop you, 'where's this New Station?' You ordered something to eat, and you had your bottles with you, and you drank, and you met people and laughed and talked and danced up and down the aisles."[288]

On this occasion Clemons, who was Black, ended up in a jail cell charged with assault. Complaining of pain and partially paralyzed, he was taken to hospital where doctors could not find anything wrong with him. After his wife bailed him out of jail, Clemons continued to experience serious discomfort. A few days later he lapsed into a coma from which he never recovered. He died the day before Christmas.

Coincidentally, on the day of Clemons's arrest, the *Sun* ran an article profiling the city's Black community. According to reporter Bruce Ramsey there were about 700 "negroes" living in the city. While prejudice against them was not as bad as in the United States, wrote Ramsey, many local employers "continue to draw the colour line when hiring." An exception was the railway, where many of the men in the community found employment as porters and stewards. "The local negro population has given the police very little trouble," wrote Ramsey, an ironic observation given the outcry that erupted over Clemons's treatment.[289]

The *Pacific Tribune*, a Communist newspaper, was the first to take up the case, claiming that Clemons was victimized by police because of the colour of his skin. Human rights activists got involved, demanding that the city police commission investigate. In October, while Clemons lay in a coma, the commission decided there was not enough evidence to pursue the case. When he died, however, an inquest was convened. It opened on January 6, 1953, attracting an overflowing courtroom and front page headlines. The all-white jury heard from more than fifty witnesses, some of whom said they saw police bludgeoning Clemons, others claiming that he was a troublesome drunk who resisted arrest. In the end it was the medical evidence, or lack of it, that led the jury to exonerate the police. Doctors testified that Clemons had a pre-existing degenerative condition of the spine which was aggravated by the scuffle but not caused by it. The Black community remained unsatisfied, but public attention moved on.[290]

More troubling for Chief Mulligan were the rumours of corruption and influence-peddling that swirled around his force. According to the tabloid press, Vancouver was a "Gangland Eden" where officers, including the chief, regularly received bribes from gamblers, bootleggers and brothel keepers. In 1955 the provincial government appointed a commissioner, city lawyer Reginald Tupper, to look into the allegations. For seven months

Tupper, grandson of former prime minister Sir Charles Tupper, heard testimony revealing how deeply the rot had spread. Chief Mulligan's mistress was among the witnesses, along with various colourful underworld figures and crooked cops. One member of the force committed suicide; another tried to kill himself and failed. Every night listeners hung by their radios to hear journalist Jack Webster give a blow-by-blow account of the day's proceedings on station CJOR. Mulligan himself was accused of being on the take. Unable to stand the pressure, he resigned his job and decamped for California, where he found work at a flower nursery. Tupper's report confirmed that the chief had been accepting bribes, but no charges were ever laid.[291]

IN 1954, VANCOUVER hosted the biggest sporting event in its history, the British Empire and Commonwealth Games. The games were awarded to the city on the understanding that it would build a slew of new athletic facilities, including a rowing course, a swimming pool and a cycle track. Yet with less than a year to go before opening day, the whole thing looked to be falling apart. The sticking point was a new stadium. First of all, organizers couldn't agree on a site. Then, when it was agreed to locate the new track atop a former nine-hole golf course in a corner of the PNE Grounds, it looked as if they didn't have enough money to build it. All the construction bids came in well over budget. With Winnipeg offering to step in and host the games if Vancouver could not deliver, and the deadline for getting construction underway menacing, organizers managed to tweak the design to find some cost savings and Vancouver was spared a very embarrassing default.

When the games began on July 30, 1954, all the hiccups were forgotten. It was the first nationally televised sporting event in Canadian history. CBC Television, only two years old at the time, paid $50,000 for exclusive world rights to broadcast the competition. (By comparison, CTV and Rogers Communications paid $90 million solely for Canadian broadcast rights to the 2010 Winter Olympics.) Many families purchased their first black-and-white television sets just to be able to watch the games, which were available to local viewers on station CBUT, launched a mere six months earlier. And the main event they wanted to see was the mile race featuring the Australian world record holder, John Landy, and the British medical student Roger Bannister. Both men had recently run a mile in less than four minutes and their matchup had the sports world riveted. The race itself, which occurred on the final day of the games, did not disappoint. Landy sped off to an early lead and managed to hold for most of the race, until Bannister overtook him with a dramatic push on the final turn. For the first time two runners broke the four-minute barrier in the same race. It has been known ever since as the Miracle Mile.

Hardly had the 35,000 stadium spectators settled back into their seats after the excitement of the photo finish than another drama played out on the infield. The marathon was the final event of the games and it ended with a horrifying display of endurance and courage. Jim Peters, the British champion, had a fifteen-minute lead and seemed to be on his way to a gold medal when he entered Empire Stadium at the end of the 26-mile road race for a final lap to the finish line. But heat and exhaustion had left him a physical wreck. Staggering from side to side, stumbling onto his hands and knees, fading in and out of consciousness, Peters made his agonizing way toward the finish line. He was clearly in distress, but no one wanted to intervene for fear of disqualifying him when he was so close to victory. At last he collapsed into the arms of a British team official, apparently having crossed the line, and he was whisked away to hospital in critical condition. Unfortunately, it turned out that the actual finish was on the other side of the stadium and Peters had not reached it. He was indeed disqualified, and although he recovered fully, it was his last competitive race.

The marathon, the Miracle Mile and several other dramatic moments of competition made the 1954 British Empire and Commonwealth Games one of the most memorable events in the history of the city. Seventy million North Americans watched the mile race on television and many millions more listened on radio around the world. The famous photograph, snapped by *Sun* photographer Charlie Warner, showing Landy looking back over one shoulder as Bannister streaks by him on the other, appeared on the front page of every major newspaper. When *Sports Illustrated* magazine launched its first issue later in August, the games were the subject of its lead article. For those eight days of competition at least, boasted one local journalist, Vancouver was the centre of the universe.[292]

THE 1950S saw the demise of the electric street railway system that had carried commuters through Vancouver streets for more than six decades. Like so much of the city, the transit system emerged from the war in need of renewal. Wartime had been a heady period for the BCER. Fuel and rubber shortages forced many motorists to leave their cars at home, and ridership on public transit soared. Not to mention all the extra workers in the city commuting to jobs in the shipyards and munitions plants. But postwar revealed the weaknesses in the system. Many of the cars were old and rickety. Rail travel seemed slow and inefficient compared to the convenience of the private automobile.

One of the most famous photographs in the history of sport shows the thrilling climax to the Miracle Mile at the 1954 British Empire and Commonwealth Games in Vancouver. John Landy looks left, Roger Bannister passes him on the right. Both runners broke the four-minute barrier for the mile—the first time it had been done by two competitors in the same race.

Charles Warner photo, City of Vancouver Archives, AM281-S8-: CVA 180-3607

During the Depression, street railway companies across North America had joined to come up with a new vehicle to take on the challenge of modernity. The President's Conference Committee streetcar, the PCC, was a lighter, smoother, faster, roomier trolley that, it was hoped, would reinvigorate city rail travel. The BC Electric put its first PCC car into service in Vancouver at the beginning of 1939, and the sleek vehicle seemed to be the wave of the future. But once the war was over, management decided to take a new direction altogether. Instead of renewing the fleet, and the track, the BCER launched a ten-year program to convert the transit system from trolley cars to buses: "from rails to rubber" was the slogan of the day. Victoria and North Vancouver went first; both municipalities had converted their systems by 1948. In Vancouver the old trolleys survived until April 1955, when the last cars were taken out of service, replaced by buses both motorized and electric, many of them following the same routes as the trams. This period also saw the end of the interurban system. Passenger service on the Fraser Valley line out to Chilliwack disappeared in 1950, followed by shutdowns on all the other Lower Mainland routes, until finally in February 1958 the last of the interurbans, the line from Marpole to Steveston, closed. Ironically, when the SkyTrain opened in 1986, offering speedy rail service between downtown Vancouver and New Westminster, it followed much the same route first used by the interurban more than a century earlier.

Transportation was also at the heart of one of the worst construction accidents in the city's history. In 1956 work began on a new bridge across Burrard Inlet at the Second Narrows, replacing the original thirty-year-old crossing. On the afternoon of June 17, 1958, two partially completed spans collapsed into the water with a huge roar. As word spread across the city, people hurried to vantage points to get a look at the scene. A total of twenty-four people died: eighteen workers and engineers in the initial collapse, five of injuries and a diver who was killed searching the inlet for bodies. An inquiry blamed the catastrophe on a mistake made by one of the engineers who had died. Eventually work resumed, and the bridge opened in August 1960, but the collapse remains Vancouver's worst industrial accident. (To commemorate the terrible event, the bridge was renamed the Ironworkers Memorial Second Narrows Bridge in 1994.)

IN THE POSTWAR PERIOD, a critical mass of writers and artists was congregating in the city, centred at the university, the art school and the CBC. Young Eva Hoffman may have thought that the city was culturally barren, but for a mid-career writer like George Woodcock it was just what he was looking for. When Woodcock arrived from England with his wife Inge in 1953, after a failed attempt at homesteading on Vancouver Island, he found support for his literary projects from a group of friends that included the poets Roy Daniells and Earle Birney, founders of the Department of Creative Writing at UBC, painters Molly and Bruno Bobak and Jack Shadbolt and his wife Doris, and novelist and radio producer Robert Harlow. "Our cabin [on Burnaby Mountain], with its air of remoteness from civilization and yet its panoramic view of the city, appealed to these people," Woodcock recalled in his memoirs, "and we would entertain them at open air dinners which Inge ingeniously cooked on her tiny wood stove and a couple of hotplates . . . I found in Vancouver the mixture of stimulation and detachment that I need, and I have been fortunate enough to find it in a physical setting of whose beauty I have never tired. Settling in Vancouver was, in the creative sense, finding home."[293]

Abraham Rogatnick and Alvin Balkind were another pair of newcomers who catalyzed the local arts community. Not long after their arrival from the United States in 1955, Rogatnick, an architect, and Balkind, a curator and writer, established their New Design Gallery above a jewellery store in West Vancouver. "Vancouver was always referred to as 'the end of the world,' and things that were happening in New York or other places in the world that were exciting in the arts were just not available here," Rogatnick recalled years later. "And then suddenly they all started to happen in Vancouver, and that was such a wonderful, emotional explosion of the arts."[294] The New Design Gallery was at the centre of that explosion. When it moved downtown to Pender Street in 1958, Rogatnick, Balkind and others opened the Arts Club next door, introducing the city to many of the major figures in contemporary art. Marshall McLuhan gave his first Vancouver lecture at the Arts Club, and Lawrence Ferlinghetti performed his poetry there. The gallery continued to expose the city to modernist ideas until it closed in 1966.

In this period, Vancouver's first professional theatre troupe, the Everyman Theatre Company, also emerged, founded in 1946 by Sydney Risk. He was a Vancouver native and an experienced actor who had trained at the Old Vic Theatre School in London and performed with leading English touring companies, then returned to Canada and taught at the Banff School of Fine Arts and the University of Alberta. His troupe consisted of thirteen young actors who, when not touring western Canada, staged performances locally in a variety of venues. Always in financial difficulties, the company managed to scrape by until January 1953, when it pushed the limits of the avant-garde a little too far, at least for Vancouver.

The American novelist Erskine Caldwell's novel *Tobacco Road* had been adapted for the stage in New York, where it had done very well, setting the mark for longest-running play on Broadway to date. Thinking to emulate this commercial success, Risk decided to stage a local production, despite the fact that the play, a raw portrait of life among poor white Southern sharecroppers, had been banned as indecent in some American venues. At first the Everyman production was a hit. Responding to a complaint, however, detectives from the morality squad attended a performance and decided the contents were too obscene for local audiences. Knowing that the authorities intended to interfere, Risk went ahead with another performance anyway. In the middle of the action police walked on stage and arrested five actors amid an uproar in the theatre. The notoriety assured that the rest of the run was a sellout, but a judge ruled that the production was "indecent, immoral and obscene" and handed out fines of up to $50 to the director, several actors and the theatre operator. There was an appeal, then a counter appeal, and by the time the whole affair was settled the Everyman company had folded.[295]

As this incident suggests, the standards of what constituted vice were in flux in Vancouver during the 1950s. In some ways public morality was loosening up. During the 1950 election campaign voters had been asked to approve an "open Sunday" plebiscite, calling for a broad relaxation of the "blue laws" requiring businesses and entertainment venues to close on Sunday. The plebiscite was defeated, but it came much closer to acceptance than the pundits expected, and it presaged a gradual erosion of the Sunday closure bylaws. In 1958, for example, the Mounties baseball team was allowed to play its first fully legal Sunday games and in 1963 Sunday movies, stage performances and concerts were likewise permitted.

Around the same time, restrictions on public drinking were giving way to a more liberal attitude. The end of prohibition in 1921 had not brought a return to the "open bar"—far from it. Alcohol was sold only through government-owned stores, which went out of their way to discourage consumption. Liquor outlets were few and far between, and ringed round with so many constraints that buying alcohol from a government store was almost as furtive an activity as buying it from a bootlegger. Private clubs provided venues where members could consume liquor that they brought for themselves. Public drinking remained illegal; there were no taverns or bars until the first hotel beer parlours opened in 1925. The parlours were drab, dimly lit establishments, hidden from the street, where once again a temperance mindset prevailed. No food or entertainment was allowed, nor were women. Nothing was permitted that encouraged patrons to actually enjoy their beer. These cheerless watering holes remained the main venue for public drinking until the 1950s, when a new Social Credit government—ironically led by a teetotal premier—allowed the first lounges where men and women could sit together over mixed drinks and food. In Vancouver the first of these cocktail lounges opened in the Sylvia Hotel on English Bay, in the summer of 1954. Licences remained hard to obtain, however, especially for clubs in the less reputable East End, and illegal bottle clubs, where patrons supplied their own booze, remained a staple of the city's nightlife until the late 1960s.[296]

Drinking was grudgingly tolerated, but not indecency, especially when it came to erotic performance. In 1946 the State Theatre on East Hastings Street (formerly the Pantages, it was actually the same theatre that would become home to the Everyman troupe) became the city's first burlesque house, presenting dance shows featuring scantily clad showgirls along with comedians, singers and a wide variety of other entertainers. For the next several years the State was in and out of court as the morality squad tried to shut it down. City council kept renewing its licence on promises that the owner would clean up the acts, but finally the State Burlesque Theatre was shuttered for good in 1952.[297] Striptease and "girlie shows" continued to be available at the city's night clubs, whether the classy uptown joints like the Cave Supper Club, Isy's and the Palomar, or the rougher fleshpots of the East End, notably the Smilin' Buddha, the Kublai Khan and the city's only Black-owned club, the Harlem Nocturne. In practice, indecency was a geographical concept. The west side clubs, which catered to a white, middle-class clientele, featured glamorous touring acts and got away with a fair amount of nudity. The more racially diverse clubs in Chinatown and the East End endured constant harassment from police.[298] In other words, nightclubs and cabarets reflected the same socio-economic divide that characterized the city as a whole.

Along with nudity and booze, the juvenile delinquent was very much in the thoughts, and fears, of civic leaders in the 1950s, not just in Vancouver but everywhere in North America. Since the war teenagers had come into their own as a distinct cohort, with their own clothes, their own hairstyles, their own culture. Rock 'n' roll was their music, and in Vancouver at least, Red Robinson was their champion. At age seventeen, Robinson was the youngest disc jockey in Canada when he went on air in 1954 as host of his own radio show, *Theme for Teens*. He became so popular that when he appeared in person around town thousands of teens turned out to mob him. In 1956, when Bill Haley and the Comets appeared at Kerrisdale Arena in the city's first rock concert, it was Robinson who emceed the event. The following year it was Robinson again who introduced Elvis Presley from the stage at Empire Stadium. And in 1966, when the Beatles came to town, there he was again trying frantically to control a frenzied mob of teenyboppers. Of course the adult world thought rock 'n' roll was "the ultimate in musical depravity,"[299] in the words of *Sun* music critic Stanley Bligh; a dangerous threat to morals and public safety. But the kids couldn't get enough, and Robinson, who went on to enjoy a long career in local broadcasting and advertising, was their impresario.

The darker side of teen culture was the juvenile delinquent, or hoodlum, a figure of much concern during the 1950s, especially when delinquency manifested itself in gang activity. Small street gangs had been known in the city for years, but they became increasingly active following the war. Gangs identified with particular neighbourhoods—the Dunbar Gang, the Alma Dukes, the Victoria Road Gang—and fought territorial street battles with each other, sometimes armed with blackjacks and switchblades. Police warned against an increase in vandalism, drinking and petty theft, and formed special squads to crack down on the gangs. City council convened a "hoodlumism" committee and the school board fretted about fights on school grounds and disruptions in class. Concerns came to a head on Halloween night, 1963, when a riot involving about three hundred teens in Dunbar resulted in extensive property damage and the arrest of thirty participants. Gang activity seemed to decline later in the decade, though the teenager remained a problematic figure for the authorities.[300]

Some of the Halloween troublemakers may have ended up serving time in the Juvenile Detention Home, on Wall Street in the old Hastings Townsite. Young offenders involved in joyriding, shoplifting, burglary and any number of minor crimes were held at "Juvie" pending a hearing next door at the family court. Children as young as eight years old could be held in custody indefinitely. Young girls ended up in a separate institution, the Provincial Industrial School for Girls on Cassiar Street, near the boundary with Burnaby. Some had committed crimes; others were simply classified as "wayward" or "incorrigible." The school offered its inmates classes in cooking and cleaning, presumably preparing them for domestic service when they were released. Following an inmate riot late in 1953, an inquiry revealed scandalous conditions at the institution. Young girls mixed freely with drug abusers and sex workers; inmates were routinely brutalized; the building itself was a fire trap. Finally, in 1959, the industrial school moved to a new location in Burnaby where it reopened as the Willingdon School for Girls.

IN THE MIDDLE OF 1964, Vancouver erupted in a newspaper war. For several years the *Sun* and the *Province* had enjoyed a state of uneasy pseudo-competition. The more conservative *Province* was a chain paper, owned by the Southam company based in Ontario. Considered the voice of the establishment, it arrived on the doorstep in the early morning to be read over toast and coffee. The more populist *Sun* brought the evening news. It had been owned by the Cromie family since 1917 and was proudly local, advertising itself as the homegrown alternative to the "outsiders" from eastern Canada.

During the 1950s the *Sun*, housed in the venerable World Tower on Beatty Street and managed by the brothers Don and Sam Cromie, had surged ahead of its rival. The Cromies employed some of the leading journalists in the country, including popular columnists like Elmore Philpott, Jack Wasserman and Jack Scott, and the editorial cartoonist Len Norris, whose annual compilation of gently satiric cartoons became a staple present under many Vancouver Christmas trees. The *Sun* was well ahead in the race for readers but the competition was expensive and was wearing out both sides. "We were at each other's throats all day long," said Arthur Moscarella, the publisher of the *Province*. "It was just one vicious circle."[301] The possibility of cooperation had been discussed for several years but neither paper wanted to cede its independence. In February 1957 Sam Cromie, the younger brother, died in a boating accident on the Sunshine Coast. Whether or not this tragedy played any role in the undertaking that followed, that spring Don announced a deal with Southam by which the rivals agreed to an unprecedented business arrangement designed to make both of them money while maintaining their autonomy. The agreement created a new, jointly owned holding company, Pacific Press. It would acquire both the papers, which would occupy the same premises and share the same production facilities but otherwise operate separately. Profits, and losses if there were any, would be split equally. Because the *Sun* was the more successful paper, Southam agreed to pay Cromie a one-time compensation package of $3.85 million. (In a side deal Southam acquired the city's third paper, the *News-Herald*, which it promptly shut down.) Not surprisingly the deal aroused the suspicion of the Restrictive Trade Practices Commission in Ottawa. Hearings were held but in the end the amalgamation was approved.

The deal turned out to work very well for the *Sun*, which continued to dominate its long-time rival. Within a year daily readership had climbed above 200,000 and was soon double the *Province*'s circulation.

Nonetheless Don Cromie could not resist the blandishments of the eastern media, and in 1963 he sold his paper to the FP chain, based in Winnipeg. For the first time in decades Vancouver had no locally owned newspaper. Which is when the war broke out.

When Val Warren, a middle-aged advertising executive whose only experience as a journalist was ownership of a weekly giveaway for shoppers, decided to start up his own newspaper, it seemed like an act of madness. But Warren had heard about a new technology, photo offset printing, that dramatically reduced the cost of production, and he managed to raise enough money from investors and promises from advertisers to make his dream a reality. Warren was counting on a warm welcome from a newspaper readership that wanted something different from the *Sun-Province* monopoly while feeling bereaved at the disappearance of a homegrown news source. He hired a group of experienced journalists, including the talk show host Jack Webster and the sportswriter Jim Taylor, installed eighty-three-year-old General Victor Odlum, a veteran of the local newspaper scene, as chairman of the board, and on September 5, 1964, launched the *Vancouver Times*.

"Failure is impossible," Warren promised, but almost immediately the new paper faced a cash crunch. Readership was healthy enough in the beginning, but advertisers did not support the paper and the content did nothing to distinguish it from the two major dailies. As key members of staff quit and others plotted against the owners, the paper drifted toward insolvency. A desperate Warren tried to invigorate the newsroom by hiring the controversial hotliner Pat Burns—"The Mouth That Roars," as one columnist called him—who had more or less invented the phone-in radio format. Popular as he was, he was also rude and outspoken—in fact too rude and outspoken for his employer, CJOR, which eventually fired him in the spring of 1965. A protest rally attracted ten thousand fans of Burns, who had turned himself into a martyr for free speech. His notoriety briefly boosted the *Times*'s readership, but it could not stop the debts from mounting. In May, Warren first announced the paper would become a weekly, then quit as publisher. New management fought to keep "Vancouver's only home-owned newspaper" afloat, but finally, on August 6, the last issue appeared.[302]

The city's spirited, if brief, newspaper war was over.

THE POSTWAR PERIOD had brought substantial change to the appearance of the city. In the West End, high-rises began to replace the older rooming houses and low-rise apartments. The transformation of the urban economy was foreshadowed by the removal of the mills and boatyards from Coal Harbour and their replacement with a luxury hotel. The old stone and brick city was slowly giving way to the new city of steel and glass. In Strathcona the enthusiasm for urban renewal, also known as "slum clearance," which was sweeping the continent, was reflected in the destruction of hundreds of homes to make way for modern housing complexes. New residential neighbourhoods spread southward toward the Fraser River, occupying what had been vacant bushland. It was during this period that the residential city expanded to the full limit of its borders.

Most of this development took place with little or no consultation with the people in whose name it was being done. It was the age of the technocrat. City council ceded much of its power to the planning bureaucracy, which worked closely with the development community to execute projects that were assumed to be in the best interests of everyone.

By the mid-1960s, however, a backlash was developing against the arrogance of the planners and the politicians. People rebelled against government from the top down and began demanding a voice in what was going on in their own neighbourhoods. The new "counterculture" challenged authority on many fronts, including the corridors of city hall. A sea change was coming in the way that public business was conducted in the city.

In the mid-1980s, when this aerial photograph was taken, False Creek was in the middle of a transformation. Once the city's industrial heart, filled with sawmills and industrial plants, it was being reimagined as a residential and recreational playground.
Image I-11263 courtesy of the Royal BC Museum

CHAPTER SEVEN

The City of Grass

ON MARCH 20, 1967, the Vancouver Aquarium debuted a new star attraction. Skana the killer whale, purchased from a Seattle orca hunter, appeared for the first time in her new pool in Stanley Park. Over the summer, tens of thousands of curious whale watchers turned out to get a look. Aquarium director Murray Newman had been in the market for a killer whale since his abortive attempt to capture one live in 1964. That animal, dubbed Moby Doll, who had been taken by accident off Saturna Island and displayed in a makeshift pen at Jericho Beach for three months until its death, had contributed to a dawning public awareness that orcas were not the fierce marine monsters people had long presumed them to be. Instead, scientists began to suspect they were friendly, sentient, even intelligent. Unhappily for the animals, this also meant that they became valuable to marine parks. Over the next decade fishermen and professional hunters captured dozens of coastal orcas and shipped them to facilities around the world.[303]

At the aquarium, six-year-old Skana was a huge draw, sparking a dramatic increase in attendance over the previous year. But the aquarium was not just an amusement park. It was also a research facility where part of the rationale for keeping a whale in captivity was to study its behaviour. For this purpose Newman hired Paul Spong, a young neuroscientist from

New Zealand. Spong turned out to be a controversial addition to staff. His dishevelled personal appearance marked him as a member of the burgeoning hippie counterculture and placed him at odds with the straitlaced management at the aquarium. More important, as his research progressed, Spong became uncomfortable with the whole notion of whales in captivity. When he went public with his views, an angry Murray Newman fired him, making the aquarium, and Skana, the centre of an ugly public confrontation.[304] Subsequently Spong founded his own upcoast research station, OrcaLab, where he helped to pioneer the study of whales in the wild.

On the issue of captivity, Spong was ahead of his time. It would be twenty-seven years before the Vancouver Aquarium agreed to stop collecting orcas from the wild (1996) and another five years before its last resident killer whale was moved to another facility. But in his skepticism toward authority, and his fondness for psychedelic substances, he was also very much of his time. Vancouver in the late 1960s was, in the words of one memoir of the period, a "City of Love and Revolution."[305] The occupation of the UBC faculty club led by the Yippie provocateur Jerry Rubin, the "Human Be-ins" in Stanley Park, giant anti-war demonstrations, Cool-Aid and acid rock—these were all hallmarks of the era. When Paul Spong went swimming with the whales, it might have seemed weird to his fellow scientists, but it was very much in tune with the ethos of countercultural Vancouver.

IT IS HARD TO PINPOINT EXACTLY when the Age of Aquarius came to Vancouver, but arguably it was during the first three months of 1966. That's when two musical visitors blew into town, bringing with them the early warnings of the cultural tsunami soon to overwhelm the city. On the morning of January 14, early arrivals at the Point Grey campus of the University of British Columbia found the news spreading that "the Airplane has landed." When puzzled students showed up at Brock Hall that noontime to find out what was going on, they were greeted by the San Francisco band Jefferson Airplane on stage. It was the first concert north of the border by the psychedelic rockers—they had not yet released their first album—and their ethereal, drug-inspired music was unlike anything the locals had heard before. Ten weeks later, on March 26, a sold-out crowd at the Agrodome on the PNE Grounds welcomed Bob Dylan to town. Dylan was ending a six-month North American tour, his first with the Band as his backup group, but coming on top of the Airplane's visit it was the beginning of a cultural insurrection in Vancouver.

The era didn't last long, just a few years, but while it did the city was awash in paisley and bell-bottoms, the sound of electric rock and the aroma of marijuana. A decade earlier parents had been alarmed at the behaviour of duck-tailed juvenile delinquents. Now, suddenly, the older generation was agitated by the hippies with their long hair, wild music and aversion to gainful employment. The epicentre of the new lifestyle was Kitsilano—"Hippy Hollow," "Canada's Haight-Ashbury," "Love Street"—a neighbourhood of rooming houses, drop-in centres, cheap cafés and coffee houses, head shops and boutiques. Drug use became rampant, at least in the imagination of city elders. In 1967 the police, supported by Mayor Tom Campbell, launched a war on drugs—in this case LSD and marijuana —which Campbell described as "a cancerous growth that is invading society."[306] School officials sent home warnings to parents about the use of hallucinogens and threatened to expel any student caught supplying LSD. Police officers received instruction on how to recognize the distinctive odour of marijuana.

Drug use was part of a wider rebellion against the perceived complacency and conservatism of the older generation. The generation gap had widened into a chasm. Young people rejected the competitiveness of the workaday "straight" world, instead embracing a spirit of laid-back communalism. All manner of self-help organizations appeared, including health and legal aid clinics, food co-ops, communal houses, a free university, artist-run centres and credit unions. All this activity was recorded in the pages of the underground's own newspaper, the *Georgia Straight*, founded by a collective of writers in 1967. Mayor Campbell reflected the view of an affronted mainstream when he complained in an interview with the CBC that hippies "want to contribute absolutely nothing to the welfare of the community, yet they look to us for all the services . . . They are parasites on the community."[307] Campbell kept up a running battle with the *Straight*, trying several times without success to shut it down for obscenity. The battle was also joined by downtown business owners who claimed that long-haired loiterers were frightening away their paying customers. The Hudson's Bay Company went so far as to post a "window cleaner" outside its store to wash the sidewalks free of hippies with a pressure hose.

Politically the counterculture was animated by opposition to the American war in Vietnam. There were marches, teach-ins and local support for American draft resisters who crossed the border to live in Canada. (The legacy of protest persisted for many years in the area. On Saturday April 24, 1982, the largest peace march ever held in the city, an estimated thirty thousand people stretching five kilometres, made its way from Kitsilano Beach over the Burrard Bridge to Sunset Beach, to demand an end to the nuclear arms race.) In 1970, anti-war sentiment inspired a nascent environmental movement when the Don't Make a Wave Committee organized to protest American testing of nuclear warheads at Amchitka Island in Alaska. Combining peace activism with ecological concerns, the group chartered a fishing trawler called the *Phyllis Cormack*, renamed it the *Greenpeace* and departed the city on September 15, 1971. The plan was to sail into the test zone to be present at ground zero when the next explosion took place. In the event, bad weather frustrated the protestors, who returned to Vancouver before the blast occurred.

Nonetheless the voyage focused international attention on the issue of nuclear testing and gave rise to a new organization, Greenpeace. Within a few years this ragtag group of activists, notice of whose inaugural expedition was buried in the back pages of the *Sun*, had grown from a tiny office in Kitsilano to a worldwide movement with offices in several cities and a war chest that financed bigger ships and more ambitious expeditions. Led by Paul Spong and local journalist Bob Hunter, the Vancouver group shifted its attention to the international whale hunt. In 1975 it began a series of daring, and highly publicized, voyages that disrupted the activities of international whalers. It was thanks to these "Warriors of the Rainbow" that Vancouver first achieved its reputation as a centre of "green" activism. That said, the actual origins of environmentalism in Vancouver date back two decades earlier, to the Air Pollution Control Society of the 1950s and, more important, the Society for Promoting Environmental Conservation (SPEC) created by Gwen and Derrick Mallard in 1969. Less splashy than Greenpeace but every bit as effective, these local organizations planted the seeds of a new eco-consciousness that led to many changes in public policy.

Protest also overwhelmed the university campuses as students at UBC and the newly opened Simon Fraser University demanded a say in the operation of their institutions. At SFU activists thought that the university should open its doors to anyone who wanted to attend, since restrictive admissions seemed to favour the elites over the children of the working class. Further protests centred on the Department of Political Science, Sociology and Anthropology, where faculty and students agitated to make the university more democratic and socially relevant. When the administration fired several faculty members, some students went on strike, shutting down classes. Despite censure from the national teachers' organization, the administration managed to weather the storm and things eventually returned to normal.

In the city the generational conflict over the hippie lifestyle came to a head in 1971, when opposition to drug enforcement led to the infamous Gastown "riot." Despite police efforts, young people routinely flouted the

1 This young protestor was one of seventy-nine taken into custody by police during the Gastown Smoke-In. In part the protest was a response to a federal Royal Commission's suggestion that law enforcement relax the strict enforcement of drug laws. Mayor Campbell disagreed.

Vancouver Police Museum & Archives P00882

2 It was due to the influence of Paul Spong (left) and Bob Hunter that the Vancouver-based Greenpeace shifted its focus in the mid-1970s from nuclear testing to the international whale hunt.

Erol H. Baykal photo, City of Vancouver Archives, AM1671-: CVA 395-07757

2

1

laws against the recreational use of drugs, particularly marijuana. Gastown was a favourite gathering spot for street people, and in the summer of 1971 police stepped up their anti-drug efforts in a search-and-arrest tactic known as Operation Dustpan. In protest, activists organized the Gastown Smoke-In and Street Jamboree. On the evening of August 7 several hundred people gathered at Maple Tree Square, listening to music, smoking "weed" and chanting in favour of drug legalization. Expecting trouble, truncheon-wielding police officers moved in and the predictable mayhem ensued. In the end about a dozen people were treated for injuries, and close to eighty ended up in custody. Despite Mayor Campbell's assurance that "the police did a commendable job," a provincial inquiry condemned the official use of force as an overreaction, calling the event a "police riot."

THE LATE 1960S marked a clash of generations in Vancouver, and a turning point in civic politics. A series of development projects, backed by council and its planning department, provoked unprecedented opposition from the public. Discontent boiled over into open defiance. An alliance of community groups, academics, student activists and heritage proponents refused to accept the destruction of large parts of the downtown in the name of urban renewal. Giving voice to this opposition, new political organizations sprang up to challenge the experts and the long-time hegemony of the NPA on city council. As Walter Hardwick, one of the key participants in the debates, pointed out, this was a period of fundamental shifts in the relationship between local voters and their government.[308]

The first of the redevelopment projects was the plan to bulldoze Strathcona. Several blocks of the neighbourhood had already been razed, and massive housing developments replaced many of the single-family homes, but by the time the third phase of the project was ready to begin, opposition from the community had grown. In mid-December 1968, residents formed the Strathcona Property Owners and Tenants Association (SPOTA) to demand their voices be heard. Led by Bessie Lee, Harry Con and Walter and Mary Chan and their daughter Shirley, these activists mobilized homeowners against the city's plan. They also formed alliances with people outside the Chinese community who could help them, people such as storefront lawyer and later mayor Mike Harcourt, social planner and later alderman Darlene Marzari and another social worker, and future Member of Parliament, Margaret Mitchell. A new Liberal government in Ottawa, led by Prime Minister Pierre Trudeau, was sympathetic to the opposition. By mid-1969 officials had made it clear that there would be no more federal money for the scheme unless the complaints of local residents were addressed. As an example of an alternative approach to redevelopment, Ottawa did make money available to upgrade the existing housing stock and to improve public works in the neighbourhood.[309] "We have to remind the city," said Bessie Lee, one of the presidents of SPOTA, "that when they decide to change things in a community they must always consider the total planning of that community and the concerns of the people who live in it."[310]

By this time, events in Strathcona had been overtaken by another controversy. In the summer of 1967 the city announced, without any public consultation whatsoever, that an elevated freeway would be built through the heart of Chinatown. The plan involved continuing the Trans-Canada Highway from Boundary Road across the east side of the city, through Chinatown and west along the Burrard Inlet waterfront, to connect to a proposed third crossing to the North Shore. The plan accorded with the urban freeway building that was going on in many other North American cities. "The simple needs of automobiles are more easily understood and satisfied than the complex needs of cities," wrote Jane Jacobs in her hugely influential 1961 polemic *The Death and Life of Great American Cities*, "and a growing number of planners and designers have come to believe that if they can only solve the problems of traffic, they will thereby have solved the major problem of cities."[311]

Vancouver's freeway plan was supported by Mayor Campbell, who had won election the previous December, and his top bureaucrat, Gerald Sutton Brown, both of whom badly underestimated the opposition. (Sutton Brown, who had been appointed director of planning in 1952, became city manager in 1963.) The outcry was immediate, not only from the Chinese community but also from business groups, tourist associations and heritage advocates, all of whom objected to the wholesale destruction of a historic neighbourhood. At a raucous public hearing in November, council endured heated criticism from an overflow crowd. At one point, harassed by hecklers, Campbell and some of his councillors walked out of the meeting, though they later returned. Afterward the mayor called it "a near riot."[312] So many voices wanted to be heard on the issue that a second public meeting was held a couple of weeks later. At this gathering, Peter Oberlander provided the most drama. The UBC planning professor and chair of the Town Planning Commission first read a brief from the commission supporting the city's plans, then resigned on the spot because of his own personal opposition to the freeway.

Though the city promised to take the criticism under advisement, later in the year council announced the freeway was going ahead on the planned

Members of the Chinese Benevolent Association meet in 1960 to discuss the city's plan to remove homes in Strathcona. The CBA, which opposed the plan, was one of the most influential community groups in Chinatown.
Province Newspaper photograph, Vancouver Public Library 41632A

route down Carrall Street. Campbell dismissed the opposition as "a tempest in a Chinese teapot" but civic officials had failed to comprehend the changing role of Chinatown in the civic imagination. The public, or at least large parts of it, no longer considered Chinatown an ethnic ghetto that required "cleaning up" by urban renewal. Instead the neighbourhood had evolved into a major attraction that gave the city much of its "colour and romance," in the words of one *Province* reporter, not to mention producing much of its tourist revenue.[313] After decades of neglect and vilification, Chinatown was now celebrated as one of the city's prime assets, not to be destroyed by the schemes of developers and planners. Early in 1968, in the face of the continued outcry, council reversed its decision, for the time being.

The freeway plans were intimately linked to discussions about a third crossing to North Vancouver. The planning department had been mulling over options for another crossing since the 1950s. Improved access to the North Shore was considered fundamental to whatever plan emerged from the freeway debate. One proposal was to twin the Lions Gate Bridge, necessitating an expanded causeway through Stanley Park. Another imagined a combination bridge and tunnel east of Brockton Point. Others proposed construction of a double-decker highway through the heart of the park or, conversely, a tunnel beneath the peninsula. Even when the proposal to gut Chinatown was killed, planners came up with another scheme to route the freeway around downtown by building along the north side of False Creek, before swinging north to Burrard Inlet via a tunnel beneath the West End. When this plan, which had been developed covertly, became public in 1971, opponents once again rallied, this time to demand a public vote. Mayor Campbell described opponents of the scheme as "Maoists, Communists, pinkos, left-wingers and hamburgers" (hamburgers, he explained, being people without university degrees), but in fact dissent was widespread, and was expressed vociferously at another marathon public meeting held in March 1972. Both the provincial and federal governments had heard enough. Ottawa withdrew its funding for the project and later in the year a new NDP provincial government introduced the SeaBus passenger ferry to the North Shore as an alternative to another bridge. Enthusiasm for a third crossing, along with a downtown freeway to feed into it, faded away.[314]

One part of the freeway scheme that did get built was a new Georgia Viaduct carrying traffic from the East End over the railway tracks into downtown. The original viaduct dated to World War I and was in need of repair. A 1965 plebiscite approved replacement of the structure and a pair of new viaducts opened on January 9, 1972. By then their construction was linked to the discredited freeway proposal and the motorcade of dignitaries celebrating the opening needed the help of police to force its way through a crowd of protestors blocking the roadway. A defiant Mayor Campbell decried the protest. "We're a growing, developing city and if we were to listen to the knockers we'd never get anything done," he told the press. "As long as I am in office we'll pay no attention to these vocal minorities."[315]

The construction of the viaducts resulted in the destruction of an historic community associated with the city's small Black population, Hogan's Alley. The alley itself was a laneway of wooden shacks only a couple of blocks long running east from Main Street between Prior and Union avenues. In the city at large it had acquired an unsavoury reputation as a place where people came at night to get a taste of the tenderloin. Residents of the area, on the other hand, saw it more as an immigrant neighbourhood where Black people in particular settled because of its proximity to the railway station, where many of the men worked as porters. Unlike Chinatown, the destruction of Hogan's Alley did not arouse much blowback from the public; it passed almost unnoticed.

The rebuilding of this period was not confined to the east side of the city. Along the Granville corridor downtown, a number of ambitious projects went up, including the Pacific Centre at Granville and Georgia. After the war and the destruction of the second Hotel Vancouver in 1949, the site had languished as a parking lot for twenty years. In the 1970s Granville was designated a transit mall. All vehicle traffic aside from buses was prohibited and shopping went underground into the Pacific Centre, anchored by the Eaton's department store on the parking lot site. To the west, the courthouse, designed by Frances Rattenbury in 1906, was considered inadequate by the 1960s. When the city rejected a provincial plan to demolish it and centralize the courts and law offices in a new fifty-storey high-rise, Arthur Erikson instead refashioned the old court building as a municipal art gallery, then designed a new provincial law court complex, Robson Square, to the south, including a multi-level public plaza.

No matter how one felt about the mallification of Granville, it rolled out relatively free of controversy. Not so another more contentious project at the entrance to Stanley Park, known as Harbour Park. In 1971, after almost a decade of debate and negotiation with developers, city council approved the construction of a large Four Seasons hotel and several apartment towers at the corner of Georgia and Denman. Many people were appalled that the gateway to the park would be occupied by a large commercial development, and a legal challenge was mounted to stop the project. City council backed down to the degree that it promised a plebiscite on the future of the site. Unwilling to wait for the courts, or the outcome of a plebiscite, a group of young people occupied the corner. They christened it All Seasons Park and began a prolonged sit-in, or in their terms a liberation of the site. (Meanwhile, the plebiscite result showed that 51.2 per cent of voters wanted the city to buy the property, less than the required 60 per cent.) As many as three hundred people occupied the site at any one time, living in tents and other makeshift structures. Although Mayor Campbell called it a "breakdown of society," the protest attracted widespread community support, at least at the beginning. As time passed conditions in the park deteriorated and by the time police moved in, all that remained were a few homeless transients. However, in the end the protest was successful. Early in 1972 the federal government, whose approval was required, withdrew its support, and in August, Four Seasons abandoned its plans. After subsequent negotiations, debate and another plebiscite, the site was preserved as parkland.[316]

With Harbour Park, as with all the main development controversies, the historic tension between alternative visions of the city bubbled to the surface. Should Vancouverites allow their "paradise" to be paved over in the name of economic development, what the celebrated journalist Bruce Hutchison once called "the North American disease of proliferation and giantism"?[317] Or should the human dimensions of the city—its parks, views and water-front—be preserved for the enjoyment of all its residents? It was essentially the same debate that the city had been having since its earliest days.

TOM CAMPBELL, the mayor during much of this rancorous period, had been a lawyer and property developer before getting into politics. A stead-fast proponent of large redevelopment projects, Campbell served six years (1966–1972) as mayor, mostly with the backing of the NPA. These were "electric years in Vancouver politics" in the words of Paul Tennant, who was both a student of and a participant in the tumultuous events.[318] In part the electricity was generated by Campbell's personal style. He was equally unrestrained when it came to clearing the hippies off the streets or demol-ishing much of the downtown to make way for gleaming new high-rises. An iconic image from the era shows a grinning "Tom Terrific," waving a hard hat, swinging through the air on a wrecking ball. His disdain for the youth subculture, for left-wingers, really for anyone who opposed his grandiose plans for the city, were invariably expressed in colourful lan-guage. But the ethos was changing around him. A younger generation was challenging the values of the "establishment" and demanding a voice in

This iconic photograph of Mayor Tom Campbell captures his enthusiasm for redeveloping the city without much concern for public opinion. Campbell's time as mayor, 1966–1972, marked a sea change in municipal politics.

decisions. The public was no longer willing to simply go along with what the experts advised. Essentially there was a changing of the guard as the old elitist, backroom politics where the planner and the property developer were king, was overthrown by a new politics of participation and consultation. Campbell was, in the words of one of his successors, Mike Harcourt, "the last gasp of the old vision."[319] Opposition to the freeway, the bulldozing of Strathcona and a series of other land development controversies led to the decline of the NPA and the emergence of a new political formation, the Electors Action Movement (TEAM). TEAM was led by a group of reform-minded professionals (academics, lawyers, business people) who were mobilized by opposition to the freeway in particular and support for more open government in general. TEAMsters believed that people directly affected by a development project should no longer be shut out of the planning process.[320] Along with TEAM there appeared a second, more radical group, the Committee of Progressive Electors (COPE). Unlike the middle-class TEAM, COPE was a socialist party with support from the labour movement. Its main voice on council was labour lawyer Harry Rankin, one of the longest-serving aldermen in the city's history.

At the same time, the freeway debate gave rise to activist community groups, which banded together to fight the proposal, and others like it, at the grassroots level. Most prominent were the Strathcona Property Owners and Tenants Association (SPOTA) and, later, the Downtown Eastside Residents Association (DERA). SPOTA gave voice to neighbourhood residents determined to save their homes and businesses from the destructive urges of city hall. DERA was formed a few years later, in 1973, with a former logger and ironworker named Bruce Eriksen as its first president. Along with community activists Jean Swanson and Libby Davies, Eriksen and DERA advocated for the rights of people living in the rooming houses and cheap hotels that characterized the inner city. Eriksen served several terms on city council backed by COPE, as did Davies, who became the NDP Member of Parliament for the area. Thanks to the efforts of DERA, the old Skid Row (also known as central Hastings) was reimagined as the Downtown Eastside, a community rather than an eyesore, whose residents demanded the same level of services as people in any other part of the city. One of the organization's significant victories was to persuade the city to repurpose the old Carnegie Library at the corner of Hastings and Main. By the late 1970s the building was unused and falling apart, ready for demolition. But DERA found the money for repairs, and at the beginning of 1980 the Carnegie reopened as a community centre. DERA went from being an advocate for residents to becoming a developer of downtown co-op housing in its own right, and a thorn in the side of city hall. The struggle to renew its civic grant became an annual political drama as unsympathetic councillors tried to shut the organization down.

The emergence of reformist voices on council and in the community suggest that the freeway debate changed the city's politics more than it changed its geography. That said, the extent of the change should not be exaggerated. For one thing, members of TEAM were not revolutionaries. They were moderate, middle-class reformers, many of them Liberal Party members, who gained most of their electoral support from the more affluent west side of the city. As Paul Tennant, a founding member of the group, points out, TEAM constituted a "new elite" of professionals instead of businessmen, an elite that was "even less representative of the population in socio-economic terms than was the elite of the preceding period."[321]

The rise of TEAM was also helped along by the implosion of the NPA. By the time the 1972 election rolled around, the incumbent Mayor Campbell had decided he had had enough and did not stand for a fourth term. In his place the NPA supported lawyer Bill Street, who as the campaign progressed was discredited for his ties to the development industry. Eventually Street resigned as the NPA's candidate, then quit the campaign altogether, leaving the NPA without a horse in the race. Meanwhile the popular *Sun* columnist Alan Fotheringham revealed shady backroom dealings between Campbell and a local car dealer who also happened to be the NPA president. It was all too much for the voters, who abandoned the NPA in droves, electing Art Phillips and his TEAM slate in a landslide.[322] But the result, while dramatic, was short-lived. Two years later, the TEAM presence on council was reduced to five aldermen and the NPA was back up to four. And by the end of the decade, TEAM was reduced to a rump.

A sign of this reversion to the historic norm was the career of Jack Volrich. In the late 1960s Marathon Realty, the CPR's real estate arm, developed plans for a huge shopping centre and housing complex on low, swampy land that it owned below Arbutus Ridge in north Kerrisdale. The neighbourhood homeowners' association fought the plan and Volrich, a local lawyer, emerged as a leading voice for the community. Marathon eventually had to scale back its plans for Arbutus Village, and Volrich entered politics, joining city council as part of the TEAM sweep in 1972. Four years later he won election as mayor with TEAM backing, but his more conservative instincts reasserted themselves and he left TEAM to serve his second term more or less in alliance with the NPA. At the same time councillors Mike Harcourt and Darlene Marzari abandoned TEAM in the opposite direction, sitting as independents but known to be left-wing progressives. Still, for the brief period before it fragmented, TEAM managed to make important changes in the way politics was done in the city (not least the firing of the autocratic city manager Gerald Sutton Brown).

One of the planks in TEAM's platform was the reintroduction of a ward system for civic elections. Wards had been abolished in the 1930s because they were seen to encourage neighbourhood parochialism and corruption, but in the 1970s they were recast as a reform measure, favoured as being more democratic than the at-large system. TEAM itself promoted a mixed system with some aldermen elected by ward and some at large. A plebiscite was held in October 1973, and although members of the punderati were expecting voters to endorse a return to at least a partial ward system the result was almost 60 per cent opposed to any change at all. The resurgence of the NPA at around this time was at least partially due to its opposition to wards.[323] But the issue would not go away. During the 1978 civic election voters were asked once again in a plebiscite to choose between a full ward system, backed by reformist elements on council, and the status quo, backed once again by the NPA. This time the result was ambiguous, with a slight majority favouring wards though a majority of the newly elected council was opposed.[324] Instead of acting on the referendum result, council appointed a commission to investigate the issue and make recommendations. After hearing from the public, the commission reported in favour of wards, but its proposal for implementing them was so complicated that council chose not to proceed with it, ending the discussion of wards for the time being. (The ward system was very much an issue that would not go away. The restoration of wards was put to the electorate on two other occasions, in 1988 and 2004. Both times the majority voted the proposal down.)

Another TEAM initiative, this one more successful, was the transformation of False Creek from an industrial eyesore to a mixed-use residential/ commercial area. A key factor that allowed this change was resolution of the land tenure issue. Under the terms of a 1928 agreement the CPR managed the tenures of the land along the creek shoreline, leasing most of it to mills and other industrial operations, though the foreshore itself was owned by the province. This agreement was scheduled to lapse in 1970, before which time the interested parties entered into agreements that simplified the ownership. In 1967 the province and the CPR agreed to a land swap that resulted in the north shore of the creek ending up with the railway, while the south shore came to the province. The province then transferred its land to the city in return for cash and property on Burnaby Mountain that the province required for the expansion of Simon Fraser University.

A repurposed Granville Island was the centrepiece of the transformation of False Creek South, part of Vancouver's continuous public waterfront that now stretches around the shores of False Creek and on to the Stanley Park Seawall. Daniel – stockadobe.com.

The end result of this complicated wheeling and dealing was that the city came into possession of False Creek's south shore and could begin planning for development there.[325] Mayor Campbell and the NPA labelled as obstructionists and crackpots those who wanted to rid the creek of its industrial eyesores. "Parks can be built anywhere and shouldn't be placed beside a valuable industrial waterway," said alderman Earle Adams.[326] But a new vision for the area emerged under the leadership of Walter Hardwick, the TEAM councillor and urban geographer. Instead of the same old polluting industries, what emerged was a neighbourhood characterized by mixed incomes, low-rise family housing and a substantial amount of open space. Construction of this new community began in 1975. At about the same time the Fairview Slopes south of False Creek underwent extensive redevelopment as many of the older houses which had characterized the neighbourhood were replaced by modern condominium buildings. In both cases planners preferred to adopt a low-rise approach to densification as opposed to the high-rise strategy familiar from the West End building boom a decade earlier.

Along with the transformation of False Creek's south shore came the rebirth of one of its prime industrial areas, Granville Island. Thanks to the involvement of local MP and Liberal cabinet minister Ron Basford, jurisdiction over the island was transferred in 1973 from the Harbours

Board to the Central Mortgage and Housing Corporation, the federal agency responsible for housing. Under Basford's watchful eye, CMHC administered the transformation of the island. One by one resident industries gave up their leases, clearing the way for new tenants to move in, tenants who would conform to a new vision for the island as an "urban park" with a variety of commercial, cultural and recreational uses, highlighted by a large public market. Many of the old industrial buildings were recycled to conform to the new vision. For example, a haulage company's warehouse became a restaurant, and two old factories combined to provide a new home for the Emily Carr College (now University) of Art and Design. In 1979 the "new" island sprang to life. As with the Bayshore Hotel in Coal Harbour before it, the rebirth of Granville Island, and False Creek South generally, signalled that the city was transitioning to a post-industrial economy reliant on commerce, the arts and service industries. As in Coal Harbour, the Granville Island project rescued a great chunk of the city's waterfront for public use.

The TEAM regime also gave new precedence to heritage values, particularly in Gastown and Chinatown. Gastown, the city's "first neighbourhood," had been allowed to fall into disrepair. Many of the warehouses that once defined the area had moved away from the city centre and Gastown was considered a neglected extension of the problematic Skid Row area. In 1966 the *Sun* published a front-page article announcing a dramatic new development plan for the downtown waterfront. Engineered by Marathon Realty, the land development arm of Canadian Pacific, Project 200 proposed a forest of new office towers, apartment blocks and a hotel, all tied into the new freeway proposal. It would have destroyed Gastown as the first phase of urban renewal had destroyed parts of Strathcona, and just like Strathcona it was initially supported by all levels of government.

But when "people power" halted the freeway, Gastown and Chinatown were rediscovered for their heritage possibilities. Thanks to the efforts of a group of developers fronted by entrepreneur Larry Killam and the involvement of the Community Arts Council and the Gastown Merchants Association, many of the old buildings in Gastown were repurposed and eventually protected by legislation. A variety of restaurants, galleries and shops opened, and the city contributed funds to beautify Water Street and others adjacent. To some this attempt to impart a "ye olde" atmosphere, epitomized by the outsized steam clock at the corner of Water and Cambie Streets, made Gastown more a tourist attraction than an authentic *quartier*, but at least the neighbourhood was preserved from the wrecker's ball. In 1971 it became an official heritage district.

A similar process went on in neighbouring Chinatown. Since the war, political rights had been extended to Asian Canadians. They had won the vote and with it the right to enter professions that had previously been closed to them. The Chinese Immigration Act was repealed in 1947 and two years later the Japanese Canadians who had been expelled from the coast were allowed to return. One by one the discriminatory regulations fell, though not without resistance on the part of the government and persistence on the part of the Asian-Canadian community. A key moment was the election to Parliament of local lawyer Douglas Jung in 1957, the first Chinese Canadian to hold elected federal office. With these changes came an increase in the city's Chinese population. During the 1950s it had doubled to more than fifteen thousand, then it doubled again during the next ten years. Not all of these people lived in or near Chinatown, but the neighbourhood remained the focus of the community.

Mainstream Vancouver began to see Chinatown as an asset, not the sleazy den of vice it had so often been imagined as being. "Difference" was suddenly a virtue, not a stigma. Outsiders came to shop for produce at the market stalls or to get a meal in one of the Chinese restaurants. This was in keeping with the federal government's enunciation of its policy of multiculturalism in October 1971. Canada, according to the Trudeau government, was no longer officially a bicultural (French-English) country but rather a multicultural mosaic of complementary ethnic groups. And the Chinese community comprised one of the most prominent tiles in the mosaic. Following the successful fight to stop the freeway, planners came forward with ideas to "Chinesify" the streetscapes and buildings of Chinatown. In 1971 the province declared the neighbourhood a historic site, and three years later the city charter was changed to allow the civic designation of particular heritage buildings or areas. But local residents, having saved their neighbourhood from the wrecking ball, had no desire to turn it into a museum or a tourist trap, despite the best efforts of outsiders. The fight to stop the freeway had united the community against the intrusive plans of bureaucrats wanting to mark out Chinatown as an ethnic enclave. That said, funding from different levels of government did make possible the creation of two facilities that became central to the identity of the community: the Chinese Cultural Centre (1981) and the Dr. Sun Yat-Sen Classical Chinese Garden (1986).

DURING THE 1960S, one of the raunchiest nightspots in the city was the Penthouse Cabaret on Seymour Street. The strip club had been owned by Joe Philliponi and his brothers since before the war. In the best tradition of the brown bag and bottle club, patrons served themselves drinks discreetly from bottles concealed beneath the tables. Many showbusiness celebrities visited and performed at the club over the years. For instance, in 1959 the actor Errol Flynn dropped by the night before he died at a West End apartment in the arms of his teenage girlfriend. In those days police routinely raided the club looking for illegal booze. Joe Philliponi cut a memorable figure; one reporter described him as "shaped like an egg: small, round and smooth. A garnished egg, because Joe's wardrobe—orange shirt, brown checked jacket, green plaid pants and patterned tie—looks as if it was pulled at random out of a spin dryer."[327] The Penthouse was also a clearing house for sex trade workers. According to a police-commissioned study, as many as one hundred women used the club every evening to make contact with customers. Taxis lined up three deep outside to ferry the working women and their dates to nearby hotels.

For the most part police tolerated this arrangement—at the Penthouse and at other clubs—as a nuisance-free alternative to streetwalking, but in the autumn of 1975 the force mounted an investigation involving photo surveillance, hidden tape recordings and undercover officers. Just before Christmas they arrived at the front door with warrants for the arrest of three of the brothers and three other employees, alleging the Penthouse was little better than a common bawdy house. Media reports of the trial, which began in September 1976, kept Vancouver titillated for months. In the end a judge found five of the defendants guilty of living off the avails of prostitution. Following an appeal the convictions were overturned and the club reopened.

The unintended consequence of this otherwise minor episode in the history of Vancouver's nightlife was that sex workers who had been working quite safely at several cabarets around town were flushed out onto the streets to carry on business in the shadows. These new "strolls" were outside the neighbourhoods, usually on the east side, where prostitution traditionally had been tolerated. As women started to jostle for space on the sidewalks of the west side, police realized they had created a problem where none had existed before. In 1972 the federal government had passed a new law that left the definition of solicitation unclear. Matters became more confused in the spring of 1978, when the Supreme Court of Canada brought down its ruling in the case of a Vancouver sex worker, Debra Hutt, who had been arrested servicing an undercover police detective in his car outside the Dufferin Hotel. In overturning Hutt's conviction, the court ruled that solicitation had to be "pressing and persistent" in order to be illegal. If a sex worker was not being a nuisance, then there was no case. By this time Mayor

Jack Volrich and the police department were waging a war on vice, arresting hundreds of workers and charging them with soliciting. The Hutt decision put paid to this effort. Not knowing when behaviour was "pressing and persistent" enough, police more or less gave up charging offenders. Local politicians, led by the crusading Mayor Volrich, declared the situation a "crisis." "They're moving from the dingier, more shadowy areas on the fringes of downtown into the neon glare of some of the city's prominent squares and intersections," wrote a reporter for the *Globe and Mail*, referring to outdoor sex workers.[328]

One of these high-profile areas was the hotel district around Georgia and Hornby, described by another reporter as "a high-priced hooker heaven."[329] There police had some success moving the women along. A more intractable situation developed on Davie Street in the West End. With the closure of the Penthouse, the number of sex workers, both male and female, along this strip began to climb. At the same time the West End had gone through a period of gentrification as new high-rises had replaced many of the older rooming houses and low-rise apartment blocks. As the tone and income level of the neighbourhood changed, residents grew less tolerant of the sex workers and the disruption that accompanied them: the noise, the used condoms littering the sidewalks, the young women and boys negotiating for sex in doorways. People complained of feeling unsafe. Popular *Sun* columnist Denny Boyd visited the area and expressed the exasperation of many: "As a citizen of this city I am tired of having Georgia Street taken away from me, fed up to the gills with having Davie Street turned into an avenue of squandered young lives. There is a sleaziness growing in this town where I live."[330] Residents actively lobbied police and the city government to get rid of the sex workers, but council, while sympathetic, could not find a way to deal with the issue.

In the spring of 1982, council passed a bylaw banning the sale of sexual services on the street, hoping to move the sex workers indoors. "Be discreet, don't use the streets," was Mayor Mike Harcourt's advice (he had succeeded Jack Volrich in 1980).[331] But the bylaw turned out to be beyond the city's legal powers and had to be rescinded. Civic officials were furious that the federal government was refusing to step in, while neighbourhood activists warned of violence if their concerns were not addressed. The police chief admitted that "there's been no problem more frustrating to me than prostitution."[332] The threat of mayhem finally induced the provincial government to get involved. The attorney general asked the BC Supreme Court to crack down on the West End sex trade, and on July 5, 1982, Chief Justice Allan McEachern issued an injunction banning sex workers from the streets west of Granville. Calm returned to the neighbourhood, though events would prove this was far from being a resolution of the issue.

By this time the West End, or at least the Davie Street area, had become well known as the centre of gay and lesbian culture in the city. Until the changes to the criminal code introduced by Pierre Trudeau's government in 1969, homosexuality had been a crime in Canada and gays and lesbians were regularly discriminated against. Vancouver nightspots that welcomed a gay clientele—and there were a few of them—experienced harassment from law enforcement and licensing inspectors.[333] Notable among gay-tolerant bars from the 1960s through the 1980s was the beer parlour at the Castle Hotel on Granville Street, and Faces, the city's first gay-owned club at the corner of Seymour and Robson. Even with the 1969 changes, homosexuals faced ingrained prejudice and a range of discriminatory laws. In August 1971 a small band of gay men and lesbians gathered on the steps of the Vancouver Art Gallery in what is thought to be the city's first pride protest demonstration, demanding an end to discrimination targeting homosexuals. Gradually social attitudes changed, helped along by the determination of the gay liberation movement, which insisted on equal

The Pride Parade has been happening annually in the city's West End since 1978. Daniel O'Neill photograph, Vancouver Public Library 85698

rights for gays and lesbians. It was during this period, the 1970s, that the West End, with its abundance of rental accommodation in the new high-rises and its range of restaurants, bars and clubs along Davie Street, attracted a disproportionate number of gay residents and became identified as the city's "Gay Village."

At the centre of gay life in the city was Little Sister's bookstore, founded in 1983 by Bruce Smyth and Jim Deva just off Davie. Firebombed three times, and constantly harassed by the authorities, the store seemed to focus what prejudice there was in the city against homosexuality. Finally, in 1986, the store sued the border authorities who had been refusing entry to its merchandise on the grounds that it was obscene. The store claimed discrimination under the Charter of Rights and Freedoms. Ultimately the Supreme Court of Canada upheld the authority of Canada Customs but ruled that it was misused in the case of Little Sister's. This court victory seemed to symbolize a new acceptance of homosexuality by the "straight" mainstream.

DURING THE 1970S Vancouver's arts scene reflected the volatility and experimentation of its youth culture and politics. Fresh ideas were imported from south of the border but much of the ferment was home-grown. A key development was the emergence of artist-run centres as alternative venues for the production and presentation of art. More than the commercial gallery or the art museum, these centres were the engines of experimentation, chiefly devoted to multimedia production and performance art. Intermedia, founded in 1967, was the first of the interdisciplinary hothouses, along with the Sound Gallery, Image Bank and others. In 1973 a group of artists purchased the Knights of Pythias Hall in Mount Pleasant, renamed it the Western Front Lodge, and created a dynamic artist-run production centre and performance/ exhibit space. At the same time the Vancouver Art Gallery, under director Tony Emery, made itself available to local artists as never before, opening its doors to a wide range of experimental happenings. In the view of the art critic Joan Lowndes, the gallery during this period was "a downtown drop-in centre and pavilion of delights."[334]

During the election of 1974, the new art infiltrated the world of civic politics with the appearance on the ballot of Mr. Peanut. Conceived by John Mitchell and embodied by Vincent Trasov, both artists associated with the Western Front, Mr. Peanut appeared as a mayoralty candidate at election events in the costume of the Planter's Peanuts emblem, including top hat, monocle and cane. Running on the art platform, the dapper Mr. Peanut did not speak—Mitchell was the campaign spokesperson—though he was supported by a group of musicians and a chorus line called the Peanettes. The spectacle of a mute, tap-dancing nut running for public office struck a chord with voters, at least with the 2,685 who voted for him. Conventional politicians did not all appreciate the satire; NPA candidate George Puil, who lost his attempt to unseat TEAM's Art Phillips as mayor, complained that Mr. Peanut was making a mockery of the election. After the vote, the Western Front suffered for its irreverence when the city turned down its grant application.

(Unconventional candidates were nothing new, of course. In the 1970 mayoral election Tom Campbell faced no fewer than eleven opponents, one of whom was Betty Andrew, known familiarly as Zaria, a candidate for the anarchist Yippies. Zaria, who obtained 848 votes, was photographed for the campaign cradling her infant son in her lap while holding a rifle (unloaded) in one hand. Her platform promised to repeal the law of gravity and abolish the police and the courts. And then there was the town fool, Joachim Foikis, who won a Canada Council grant in 1968 to be the city jester. Asked if he would run for mayor, Foikis answered that "no fool would accept the job."[335]

The literary scene also was experiencing new creative energy. The Beat writers of the 1950s had made some impression on the city. The first Beatnik coffee house, the Black Spot, opened in Dunbar in 1958—the poet bill bissett lived upstairs and read there regularly—and the centre of progressive music, The Cellar jazz club (1956–1964), also featured poetry readings and even the occasional play. But a more important influence was a group of American poets who began to appear in the city in 1961, invited by the UBC literature professors Warren and Ellen Tallman. Two years later the Tallmans organized the Vancouver Poetry Conference, where some of the same poets—Allen Ginsberg, Charles Olson, Denise Levertov and Robert Creeley among them—led workshops, gave readings and generally electrified the local writing community. Their most immediate impact was on a group of local poets known as the TISH group (Jamie Reid, Daphne Marlatt, Frank Davey, Fred Wah, George Bowering, Gladys Hindmarch and others), after the name of the literary magazine that they founded. By the early seventies, small literary book and periodical presses were appearing, including Pulp Press (now Arsenal Pulp), Talonbooks, Vancouver Community Press (later New Star Books) and bill bissett's blewointment, among others. Local feminists supported a variety of their own initiatives, including the Women's Bookstore, the magazine *Makara,* the newsletter *Kinesis,* the journal *Room of One's Own* and the printer and book publisher

Press Gang. More mainstream initiatives included the 1959 creation of *Canadian Literature*, a critical journal based at UBC and edited for many years by George Woodcock, and the Literary Storefront, founded in 1977 by a young poet named Mona Fertig, and housed in a former dress shop in Gastown. The Storefront provided a meeting place for writers to engage with each other and the reading public. It staged hundreds of literary events—readings, book launches, workshops and special events—before it dissolved in 1985.

Contemporaneous with the explosion of experimental art was a new respect for Indigenous cultural creation. Following the war, UBC became an important patron of Indigenous artists. In 1947 the university acquired several paintings by Nuu-chah-nulth artist George Clutesi, and at the same time decided to establish a collection of totem poles on campus. Initially UBC purchased its poles, then it began hiring carvers to produce them on site. One person associated with the UBC project was Ellen Neel. She was a Kwakwaka'wakw artist from Alert Bay who came to Vancouver and began carving miniature totem poles, which she sold through her Totem Arts Studio in Stanley Park. UBC hired Neel to restore the poles it had acquired, but when she found that the work interfered with her own business, she suggested the university hire her uncle Mungo Martin. Martin worked at UBC for the next two years, then moved to Victoria, where he was chief carver at the provincial museum. Under his tutelage a new generation of Indigenous carvers emerged.

For many years Indigenous arts were relegated by the mainstream to the realm of folk art or curio, made principally for the tourist market. This attitude began to change during the 1960s, thanks in part to a landmark exhibition at the Vancouver Art Gallery in 1967. Curated by Doris Shadbolt, *Arts of the Raven* featured work by First Nations artists such as Bill Reid (who was a consultant to the project), Charles Edenshaw, Doug Cranmer, Robert Davidson and Tony and Henry Hunt. It made a point of presenting Indigenous work as art, not ethnological artifact, equal to anything non-Indigenous culture had to offer. "We were presenting an exhibition of art, 'high art,'" declared Shadbolt.[336] The premiere of *The Ecstasy of Rita Joe* took place at the Vancouver Playhouse that same year. Written by the Okanagan playwright George Ryga, the play, with a cast that included Chief Dan George, portrayed the struggles of a young Indigenous woman who had come to live in the city. It was one of the first dramas in Canada to present the challenges facing the growing number of "urban Indians"; two years later it was the first English-language play presented at the new National Arts Centre in Ottawa.

Taught to carve by her grandfather, the renowned Kwakwaka'wakw artist Charlie James, Ellen Neel opened her own studio in Stanley Park after World War II. She carved many small poles for tourists, and one of her full-sized poles stands today at Brockton Point.

Artray photograph, Vancouver Public Library 82070

IN 1966 THE PROVINCIAL GOVERNMENT in Victoria passed an unassuming piece of real estate legislation called the Strata Titles Act. The act produced a legal framework for a new division of property, the strata unit or condominium. For the first time a single piece of property could be subdivided into units, each of which might belong to a different owner. For example, an apartment building, once owned by a single landlord who rented units to tenants, could be converted to a strata property in which each unit was owned separately. Or a single property might contain several units each belonging to a different owner (with some of the property owned communally). What followed was an explosion of condominium conversion and construction during the 1970s, particularly in the residential neighbourhoods south of False Creek. Strata title was, writes the legal historian Douglas Harris, "a legal innovation without peer in its capacity to increase the density of private ownership in land."[337] With the arrival of condominiums, Vancouver was remade.

The first condo development was a twenty-four-unit building in Kerrisdale in 1970. Ten years later there were more than ten thousand condos in the city.[338] As more of these units became available, more people had access to home ownership. That was the upside of condofication, and for the property industry it meant windfall profits. But most of these strata developments replaced or converted older buildings that had provided rental accommodation. As the number of rental units disappeared, lower-income residents who could not afford to buy one of the new condos were priced out of the market. Fairview, for instance, was in the 1960s a neighbourhood of older houses, most of them divided into apartments offering reasonably priced accommodation for students, pensioners and other lower-income residents. With the condo craze in the following decade, almost all of these buildings came down, replaced by hundreds of modern strata units attractive to middle-class professionals and empty nesters looking to live close to downtown. This transition was helped along by the redevelopment of Granville Island and False Creek South that was occurring at the same time. Equally abrupt change occurred in Kitsilano, where 1,500 condo units were built between 1971 and 1976.[339] Rental apartments in older buildings were either converted to strata ownership or the buildings were replaced with new condo developments. Either way, many former residents could no longer afford to live there.

Reaction against the gentrification of these old neighbourhoods was strong. In Kitsilano the West Broadway Citizens Committee, an activist community group founded in 1972, led attempts to hold back the condo tide with demonstrations, picketing and lobbying of city hall. City government recognized the problems caused by the changing ownership structure encouraged by condofication, including evictions of tenants whose apartments were being converted. By and large, however, the process of gentrification was allowed to occur with minimal interference in the free market, though neighbourhood activism did succeed in preventing the construction of high-rises.

The people who settled in these units were part of a dramatic change. The flight to the suburbs, a hallmark of the postwar city, was losing steam. Young, upwardly mobile professionals were choosing to live in apartments or townhouses in the central city instead of moving to single-family detached homes in the suburbs, preferring to remain close to jobs and cultural attractions. Since the 1950s the rate of the city's population growth had declined, decade by decade, to the single digits. In fact, between 1971 and 1976, the population had actually fallen by more than sixteen thousand people. This trend reversed itself during the decade, however, as the population once again began to climb, in part because of middle-class households choosing to remain in or return to the inner city.

Furthermore, whereas in 1961 about 75 per cent of dwelling units in the city were single-family homes, by 1986, just twenty-five years later, that figure had fallen to barely over 50 per cent, and by 2020 it was less than one-third. In other words, in the past half-century a revolution in the way Vancouverites house themselves has taken place, and a large part of that revolution has been the emergence of the condominium.

One nasty and unforeseen consequence of the condo boom was that many of the developments were not built to proper construction standards, and within a few years they began to leak rainwater. Homeowners were faced with thousands of dollars in unexpected repairs. In 1998 the province was forced to establish a commission, led by former premier Dave Barrett, to look into the mess. Meanwhile, the blue tarp that encased buildings undergoing repairs became an iconic city landmark.

FOR ALL THE MIDDLE-CLASS GENTRIFYING that was going on, in 1983 the city experienced a rebirth of working-class protest not seen since the Great Depression. Operation Solidarity was a province-wide movement against the restraint program introduced by the Social Credit provincial government, led by Premier Bill Bennett. Its largest manifestations occurred in Vancouver, where hundreds of thousands of people—teachers, loggers, nurses, office workers, firefighters, bus drivers—took to the streets in waves of defiant opposition.

In the early 1980s the Canadian economy fell into a deep recession, along with most of the rest of the world. Unemployment soared, along with inflation, while prices for resource products fell. The economists called it "stagflation"; most people called it a disaster, the worst downturn since the Dirty Thirties. In BC, corporations shed workers by the tens of thousands. Mines and mills closed all over the province. By 1982 half of all loggers and close to 30 per cent of all millworkers had lost their jobs.[340] Nationally the unemployment rate reached 13 per cent; in BC it climbed even higher.

Premier Bill Bennett reacted to this crisis by introducing a policy of austerity. He began early in 1982 by imposing wage controls on public sector workers, which precipitated a strike by the BC Government Employees' Union later that summer. That clash ended with both sides claiming victory and labour more determined than ever to oppose the government. Following his re-election in the spring, Bennett unleashed a full-scale restraint program. On July 7, 1983, budget day, his government presented twenty-six new pieces of legislation that together amounted to an unprecedented assault on collective bargaining rights and social justice programs. Rent controls were abolished, as was the human rights commission. The government took control of local school districts so it could regulate their spending. Wage controls for public employees continued, but more than that, their employers were given the power to terminate without cause.

Predictably the labour movement reacted to "Black Thursday" with a howl. A week after the budget dropped, representatives from every labour organization in the province met to discuss strategy. From this meeting Operation Solidarity emerged, a well-funded coalition to fight the restraint program at the bargaining table and in the streets. It was joined by a separate but allied Solidarity Coalition of social justice activists. On July 23 the first Vancouver protest occurred, attracting an estimated twenty thousand people. This was followed by a summer of protest across the province, culminating in a giant rally at Empire Stadium on August 10. An estimated forty thousand people crammed into the aging football stadium. Liquor stores and libraries closed; bus service ceased until late in the afternoon; government offices stayed open with only skeleton staffs. It was "a triumph of organization," wrote *Sun* columnist Denny Boyd, but the premier was less impressed. He dismissed the protestors as "irrelevant," a minority of soreheads who were refusing to admit that they lost the last election.[341] Defying the threats of a general strike, Bennett forged ahead with plans to fire 1,600 government workers. In the legislature he forced all-night sittings and even invoked closure to ram through his agenda amid cries of "dictatorship" and "Fascist goon squad" from the NDP opposition.

On October 15, a reinvigorated protest movement took to the streets of Vancouver once again. This time sixty thousand people were on the march, winding along Georgia Street past the Hotel Vancouver, where earlier Premier Bennett had told delegates to the Social Credit annual convention, "We will never back down." The city had never experienced such a mixture of euphoria and apprehension. Whether the size of the protest surprised him or whether he was chastened at the continuing threat of a general strike, the premier went on television on October 20 to offer what *Sun* columnist Marjorie Nichols characterized as a "peace initiative" to his opponents. The 1,600 would not be laid off, at least not yet, and his government seemed willing to negotiate some changes to the austerity program.

Talks resumed while Operation Solidarity prepared its members to hit the bricks if progress was not made. At the same time the social activists in the Solidarity Coalition, encouraged by the enthusiasm of the Vancouver demonstrations, refused to take a general strike off the table. As events moved toward a confrontation, both the government and Operation Solidarity dug in their heels. On November 8, teachers across the province walked off the job, the first of a scheduled series of strikes planned to roll out over the next two weeks. But at the last moment, worried that the momentum was building for a head-on collision that no one wanted, both sides agreed to compromise. At a meeting in Kelowna on November 13, representatives of Operation Solidarity and the government came to an agreement that ended the standoff. Both sides claimed a qualified victory, while the Solidarity Coalition activists were left fuming over what they considered to be a betrayal by labour leaders. It was a controversial, unhappy end to a four-month period of unprecedented unrest in the city and the province.

But Vancouver's activists had little time to reflect on their disappointment. Hardly had the dust settled on the solidarity struggles than the Bennett government proceeded with plans for another initiative that threatened to exacerbate the social problems faced by residents of the Downtown Eastside even as it promised to open the city to the world.

Operation Solidarity protests overwhelmed
Vancouver streets during the summer and
fall of 1983. For a few weeks a general strike
seemed probable and talk of social revolution
was in the air as it had not been since the 1930s.
Item MSC160-893_3A courtesy of the Pacific Tribune
Collection, Special Collections and Rare Books,
Simon Fraser University Library

"City of Glass" is the name the artist/writer Douglas Coupland coined for the affluent city of high-rise towers and dazzling views Vancouver became. The north side of False Creek, a former industrial district, was redeveloped as a residential community in the aftermath of Expo 86.

Rod Ferris – stockadobe.com

CHAPTER EIGHT

• • •

Vancouverism
and its
Discontents

WITH THE "GREENING" of the former industrial lands on the south side of False Creek during the 1970s, the north side of the creek remained the most tantalizing undeveloped parcel in the central city. Most of the land was still owned by Canadian Pacific through its development arm, Marathon Realty. After its plans to erect several residential high-rises on the property stalled, Marathon sold the land to the province for the equivalent of more than $60 million. Early in 1980, Premier Bill Bennett announced his government's plans to build a domed football stadium on the site and to stage a world's fair to celebrate Vancouver's centennial in 1986. He saw both projects as a means of stimulating economic development for the city, which had been losing population to the surrounding suburbs, and securing political support for his government. By this time Mike Harcourt, an NDP supporter and initially an opponent of the fair, had become mayor, and the years leading up to the exposition, dubbed Expo 86, were marked by bitter antagonisms between Vancouver and the province.

The 60,000-seat stadium, named BC Place, was completed first, at a cost of $126 million. Located just to the north of the False Creek waterfront, its signature feature was an inflated domed roof, the largest of its kind in the world. When it opened in June 1983, BC Place was the first covered stadium in Canada. (The dome was replaced with a retractable roof in 2011.) It was also something of a monstrosity, crouching over its neighbourhood like a giant crab, cutting off some streets, overshadowing others, and generally getting in the way rather than blending in.

The Crown Corporation that built the stadium was also responsible for proceeding with Expo. The origins of the fair tracked back to the mid-1970s, when different provincial cabinet ministers had begun floating the idea of hosting a World Exposition in downtown Vancouver. In June 1978 Grace McCarthy, the irrepressible minister of almost everything, met with the president of the Bureau of International Expositions (BIE) in London to discuss the idea. It was hoped that the fair would act as a springboard for the redevelopment of False Creek North. Once the BIE gave its approval, Expo 86 was off and running. Vancouver had already hosted one successful international gathering, in 1976: the United Nations Conference on Human Settlements, known as Habitat. It welcomed delegates from 150 countries to discuss issues of urban development. But whereas Habitat was a serious conference, with academic (as well as celebrity) participants, formal presentations and weighty resolutions, Expo promised something more like a festival.

The main Expo grounds sprawled along the shore of False Creek between the Cambie and Granville Street Bridges. On land that had once been a stygian spread of sawmills, shipyards and other industrial worksites, a series of sixty-five pavilions were erected, occupied by foreign governments, Canadian provinces and various corporations, as well as theatres, amusement park rides and restaurants. A second site, Canada Place, was located across the peninsula on the harbour, on what had been the CPR's Pier B-C. Canada Place had its own convoluted backstory. Once again it was Grace McCarthy, then minister of tourism, who announced in 1976 that the province was contemplating a new convention centre for Vancouver, paid for by the three levels of government. As the years passed, the project fell in and out of favour, and the cost rose from an estimated $25 million, when it was first announced, to about $135 million by the spring of 1982. Which is when Premier Bennett revealed that the federal government would be building the Canada Place pavilion as part of Expo, after which the facility would become a trade and convention centre and cruise ship terminal for the city. During the fair, visitors were carried between the two sites by yet another megaproject, an elevated monorail transit system known as Sky-Train, which was finished just in time for opening day. Originally SkyTrain connected New Westminster to the Vancouver waterfront along a line that more or less followed the route first used by the interurban train almost a hundred years earlier.

1

VANCOUVER

city of the century

2

1 Expo 86 welcomed more than 22 million visitors to its grounds on the north side of False Creek. The fair had enormous and far-reaching impacts on the city, not all of them positive. The influx of capital into the local property market led to a rapid increase in housing prices.
City of Vancouver Archives,
AM1576-S6-12-F68-: 2011-010.1065

2 In 1986 Vancouver celebrated its one hundredth birthday. While Expo attracted most of the limelight, the centennial was more of a community-based celebration.
City of Vancouver Archives, AM1551-S1-: 2010-006.392

The construction of all these megaprojects—and more: the Coquihalla Highway was also built during the early 1980s—took place when the entire country was suffering through the worst recession in decades. The Bennett government had decided to fight the recession with a self-described policy of "restraint." But there was little restraint shown when it came to Expo and its associated multi-million-dollar projects. One way the province did attempt to save money was by hiring non-union contractors for the Expo site, provoking determined opposition from the province's building trades union leaders. The unions thought they had worked out an agreement with the Expo Corporation, chaired by entrepreneur Jim Pattison; if all jobs on the site went to union workers there would be no strikes during the duration of the project. But Premier Bennett would not agree. He announced that contracts could go to non-union bidders and threatened to cancel the fair if labour did not agree. Faced with new legislation passed especially to hamstring the unions, their leadership had to buckle and non-union contractors were allowed to bid on Expo construction.[342]

As Expo's opening day approached, another downside loomed large. Ever since it had been announced, activists in the nearby Downtown Eastside had been concerned about the fair's impact on the neighbourhood. The principal worry was that landlords of hotels and rooming houses would take advantage of the inrush of tourists and short-stay customers to evict residents and jack up rents. Most of the residents were single men on fixed incomes who could not afford to pay more rent and had nowhere else to live. Early in 1982 the Downtown Eastside Residents Association (DERA) joined with the Carnegie Centre and First United Church to form a coalition, the Save the Downtown Eastside Committee, to lobby for protection for the residents. The coalition supported a proposed civic bylaw to establish rent and eviction freezes. Mayor Harcourt and some councillors supported the bylaw, but others did not. Alderman Gordon Campbell, a future mayor and one-time developer with Marathon Realty, argued that the eviction crisis was a "non-issue" and "a scare campaign that frankly is strictly politically motivated."[343] He was supported by Michael Walker, director of the Fraser Institute, a right-wing think tank, who told a reporter that it would save everyone a lot of trouble if displaced tenants were just loaded on buses and sent to the Kootenays.[344] After much acrimonious debate, in February 1986 city council passed the bylaw. But the province still needed to give its approval before the freeze could be imposed, and once again the Socred government would not budge. Instead, the expected rent increases occurred, and somewhere between 500 and 850 people were evicted in the months leading up to the fair.[345]

In spite of all the controversy, Expo 86 opened its gates on time, on May 2, 1986. Prince Charles and Princess Diana were there for the ceremony, as was Prime Minister Brian Mulroney. They were among the first of more than 22 million visitors to pour onto the grounds during the fair. When it ended on October 13, boosters declared it to have been an unqualified success. They pointed to the legacies left behind for residents of the city to enjoy: the SkyTrain, the new convention centre, the Science Centre, the Roundhouse Community Centre, the Cambie Street Bridge—all built or rebuilt as part of the fair. They also pointed to the impact Expo had on Vancouver's international reputation. Millions of tourists visited the city during the summer ("the world came to British Columbia," boasted Premier Bennett[346]) and carried away with them mostly positive images of the beautiful setting, the safe streets, the hospitable people and the festive atmosphere. "You feel good just walking around," enthused E.J. Kahn in *The New Yorker*.[347] Supposedly the fair gave Vancouver a prominence on the world map that it had not enjoyed before. It was, wrote one local journalist, "a coming out party for a backwater."[348] More important, it stimulated an influx of foreign investment, much of it channelled into developments in False Creek. Skeptics were less enamoured of the fair. They pointed to the displacement of hundreds of residents, the deficit that ballooned to $331 million and the deployment of so much public spending when social programs were being cut back in the name of restraint. But the skeptics were largely drowned out by the chorus of approval that has rained down on the fair ever since.[349]

Ten days after Expo concluded, the Social Credit Party under its new leader, Bill Vander Zalm, won a stunning victory in a provincial election, claiming what the *Vancouver Sun* called "the biggest Social Credit majority in BC history."[350] Bill Bennett had resigned two months earlier, but his gamble to press ahead with the fair and other megaprojects in the midst of a recession appeared to have paid off for his party. The new government now had to decide what to do with the land on which the fair had taken place and which it owned. Instead of developing the 83-hectare site itself, or subdividing it for sale to multiple developers, Vander Zalm's government sold it as one block. The deal was hotly debated, with two groups of local investors bidding on the sale and the Socred cabinet divided, but in the end the government sold the land to Hong Kong's richest tycoon, Li Ka-shing, for a reported $320 million. Once the millions of dollars of cleanup costs, for which the province was responsible, were deducted, it is not clear exactly how much the land went for. What is clear is that the deal led to a radical transformation of False Creek North as Li Ka-Shing's company, Concord

Pacific, filled the Expo site with a small village of high-rise condo towers and townhouses that more or less established Vancouver as the opulent "city of glass" it has become. It also turned out to be a catalyst for a massive influx of foreign capital into the local property market and the transformation of Vancouver into what some people came to call a "global city."

At the same time as Expo was attracting millions of visitors, the city was celebrating its one-hundredth birthday with a party of a different kind. Expo was the splashy, international, hot ticket festival, and the centennial was much more of a community-based affair. Planning dated back to 1979 and a bid by Vancouver to host the 1988 Winter Olympics. When the Canadian Olympic Committee turned down this proposal in favour of one from Calgary (the ultimate host of the games), Mayor Volrich and local broadcaster/Conservative Party organizer Don Hamilton decided to repurpose the organizing committee in support of a centennial bash, quite independent of the province's Expo planning, which was just getting underway.[351] When Mike Harcourt became mayor in 1980 he opposed Expo, at least until he secured guarantees that the city would not have to pay for it, but he was much more supportive of a local centennial party. When 1986 rolled around, organizers were ready with a variety of community-based initiatives, including arts and athletic events and heritage-related programs, often involving the city's ethnocultural communities and neighbourhood groups. The highlight of the centennial was a huge incorporation day party in Stanley Park on April 6, which attracted 400,000 people. Fittingly, the dignitaries gathered at Xway'xway (Lumberman's Arch) where the First Nations had greeted Captain Vancouver on his arrival in the harbour in 1792. On this occasion organizers planned for a parachutist carrying a large bouquet of flowers to jump from a plane and land at the feet of Governor General Jeanne Sauvé. The first jumper overshot the mark and put down with his flowers in a clump of trees, but the possibility had been foreseen and a second parachutist landed right in front of Her Excellency.[352] It was generally agreed that the centennial party, though it lacked the long-term impact of Expo, was a gratifying success.

PART OF THE TRANSITION TO "GLOBAL CITY" STATUS was a rapid increase in the number of residents belonging to what have come to be called visible minorities—visible in the sense of being non-white. Indeed, by the 2016 federal census, the population of Vancouver had become 51.6 per cent visible minority. In other words, the visible minority was now the majority. This was a dramatic change from the immediate postwar period, when less than 5 per cent of the city's population was non-white.[353] The transformation of the ethnic makeup of the city took place gradually, and then in a hurry. Until the mid-1960s, the restrictions on non-white immigration to Canada remained in place and most newcomers arrived from "Western" countries. As a result, the 1971 census revealed that the background of 85 per cent of Vancouverites was European. But by the time that census appeared, the situation was already changing. Immigration policy was liberalized during the 1960s, with the introduction of a points system by which prospective immigrants were ranked according to a variety of criteria, none of them related to ethnicity or skin colour.

As a result, the number of arrivals from non-traditional countries began to climb. This was especially true of people from Asia. The percentage of the greater Vancouver population claiming Asian heritage went from 5.4 per cent in 1971 to over 10 per cent in 1986, by which time the trend had become even more pronounced.[354] As Britain prepared to hand its colony of Hong Kong back to China in 1997, many residents of that city, nervous about the future, made plans to emigrate, though this was just one factor fuelling a surge in immigration to Vancouver. One study shows that between 1986 and 1996, the number of residents "born in India, China and Vietnam doubled, born in Malaysia, the Philippines and Pakistan tripled, born in Iran, Hong Kong and Korea quadrupled and born in Taiwan rose by more than ten times."[355] This process, which has been called the internationalization of Vancouver, completely transformed the face of the city. By 2017 an estimated 43 per cent of the residents of Greater Vancouver were of Asian background, making Vancouver, as the *Sun* declared, the most "Asian" city in the world outside Asia.[356]

The Asian population was not only larger than ever before but also more widely distributed across the city. Rather than settling on the east side, newer, wealthier Asian immigrants purchased homes in more upscale neighbourhoods from which they had traditionally been excluded: places like Oakridge, Kerrisdale and South Main, or farther afield in Richmond and Surrey. The South Asian community, for example, created a new commercial and cultural district along Main around Fiftieth Avenue, christened the Punjabi Market area. Unlike earlier in the century, the backlash from older residents was muted and often framed in the language of aesthetics rather than race. First of all, newcomers were ridiculed for the "Vancouver Special," a popular type of housing that appeared in large numbers during the 1970s. The house was a boxy two-storey designed to take full advantage of zoning bylaws and inexpensive building materials. Features included a low-pitched roof, a second-floor balcony, usually aluminum, an offset front door and a brick or stucco finish on the ground floor. The design was adaptable to both single-family and multi-family use, and large numbers of the Specials popped up all over the city, to the dismay of aesthetic tastemakers who found them cheap and ugly, rather than efficient and affordable.

In the 1990s complaints about the Vancouver Specials faded, to be replaced by anger at the ubiquity of the so-called "monster home." Wealthier newcomers were accused of replacing traditionally styled houses with larger structures built to the maximum size permitted on their lots. Critics claimed that these opulent homes overshadowed their neighbours' homes and disrespected the character of their neighbourhoods. Making matters worse, many of the large houses belonged to absentee owners and sat unoccupied at least part of the year. The popular press was full of stories about "astronaut families" and "parachute children," families characterized by members living in different countries. A popular Facebook page called "Vancouver Vanishes" recorded the steady replacement of "character" homes on the west side with monsters and lamented the destruction of the city's history as reflected in its traditional architecture. As Vancouver achieved "global city" status, many of its inhabitants worried that the old city, the city they knew and felt comfortable in, was disappearing.

Some commentators also blamed the new wave of Asian immigrants, especially wealthy Hong Kong immigrants, for a sharp escalation of property values. In 1989 alone house prices rose by a shocking 30 per cent.[357] The city was gripped by debate about the impact of foreign buyers on the skyrocketing cost of housing. Real family income in Vancouver actually fell during the period 1990–2000, while the cost of a home increased dramatically, leading analysts to blame an injection of offshore capital.[358] This debate was complicated by accusations of racism, but it soon became indisputable that foreign capital, mainly from China, was at least partially responsible for the affordability crisis that had made Vancouver the most expensive city in Canada, and one of the most expensive cities in the world.

AS THE 1980S DREW TO A CLOSE, Vancouver was congratulating itself on the way it had negotiated the transition from provincial centre to global metropolis. The bundle of policies that characterized this transition became known as "Vancouverism." Several city planners received credit for initiating Vancouverism, including Ray Spaxman, director of planning from 1974 to 1989, and later Ann McAfee and Larry Beasley, who shared the director's job from 1994 to 2006. Beasley wrote a book in which he described the principles that drove the new urbanism.[359]

In a nutshell, they emphasized the importance of high-density downtown living; safe, attractive streetscapes; ethnic and socio-economic diversity; plentiful green spaces; revitalized waterfront areas; the maximization of scenic views; a balance of heritage preservation and urban renewal; and a sustainable environmental footprint. It was an accepted truth of Vancouverism that the city had been correct to reject the downtown freeway schemes of the 1960s and 1970s. Planning thereafter concentrated not on how to move motor vehicles but on how to plan communities of sufficient diversity and density that motor vehicles were unnecessary.

As they were applied chiefly to the western downtown, these principles made Vancouver, in the words of the urban designer Lance Berelowitz, "the poster child of urbanism in North America."[360] Another key element to Vancouverism was public input into planning decisions. The Great Freeway Debate of 1967–71 had marked an end to top-down decision making and introduced an era of consultation, which reached its epitome in 1992, when the city embarked on an ambitious planning process, initiated by Mayor Gordon Campbell, known as CityPlan. Thousands of residents took part in meetings, workshops and strategy sessions that solicited their views on the kind of city in which they wanted to live. This input was sifted and massaged to come up with development plans both city-wide and neighbourhood focused. It seemed the apotheosis of Vancouverism, which according to its champions successfully resolved the historic tension between the beauty of the city's location and the pressures of urbanization. Vancouver "is now a city worthy of its setting," wrote planner John Punter in his book *The Vancouver Achievement*. It has "increased its vitality and civility and largely retained its safety as it has achieved its urban renaissance."[361]

Not everyone agreed that Vancouver was doing all it should to achieve the status of a major metropolis. One heretic was Arthur Erickson, the city's very own "starchitect." In the fall of 1989, Erickson shocked a civic workshop by announcing that Vancouver should be setting its sights on a population of ten million; in other words, more than twenty times what it was at the time. (Intentional or not, Erickson's choice of ten million evoked the famous early promotional slogan, "By 1910, Vancouver then, will have 100,000 men.") City council was guilty of small-town thinking, argued Erickson: "You do not face the fact that you do not live in a suburb but a major urban centre," he lectured the local politicians who were present. "We have to grow up," he told them, dismissing claims that people were attracted to Vancouver because of its lower density and "liveable" ambience.[362] The following February, Erickson repeated his prediction at a public debate with civic officials, one of whom, chief planner Ray Spaxman, spoke to the necessity of preserving "one of the most verdant places I have ever been in" from rampant overdevelopment.[363] The debate was light-hearted but reflected the always present fault line in Vancouver's history between the globalists, who promoted a vision of unlimited growth, and the localists, who preferred to emphasize their version of liveability.

For all its successes, Vancouverism had notable failures, which its champions were the first to admit, and they were principally in the Downtown Eastside, which remained untouched by the flashy planning achievements of the upper city. The old downtown remained in "a state of deep crisis," wrote John Punter.[364] It was "the biggest black eye in this whole story," regretted Larry Beasley.[365] The downtown's East End had always attracted a population of the poor, the transient and the elderly to its cluster of old hotels and rooming houses. But during the 1980s the situation had grown worse. For one thing, the number of homeless people in the neighbourhood had begun to climb. The scarcity of affordable rental housing and inadequate income assistance programs combined to leave many more people without permanent shelter. Emergency shelters were filled to capacity, while the number of people waiting for subsidized housing expanded. Another factor was the province's decision to close Riverview Hospital, which in the 1950s housed more than 4,600 patients. For good reasons, large mental institutions like Riverview fell into disfavour and governments began to shut them down, promising to replace them with community-based care centres. Unhappily, this promise was not fulfilled in Vancouver. Instead, former patients were released without the support to properly care for themselves. Studies indicated that about one-third of the city's homeless population struggled with mental health issues, and many of these people gravitated to the Downtown Eastside, where they were particularly susceptible to the traffic in illicit drugs.

Vancouver had long been home to a flourishing drug trade. The poet and novelist Peter Trower recalled that in the late 1940s, when he worked as a logger and lived during the off-season in one or other of the downtown flophouses, the centre of the traffic was the corner of Hastings and Columbia. In his novel *Dead Man's Ticket*, Trower evokes the scene: "The usual crew of tenderloin regulars thronged the sidewalk around me—knots of carousing loggers lurching noisily from bar to bar; shabbily dressed East End housewives looking for bargains at the Army and Navy or the Save-on-Meat store; scrofulous winos with grimy paws cadging dimes in raspy voices; cut-rate hookers wearily heading for toast and black coffee at some greasy spoon café; a furtive heroin pusher bound for the Broadway Hotel —Vancouver's notorious "Corner"—to set up shop at a dim beer parlour table . . ."[366] In 1958 *Maclean's* magazine dubbed this intersection "Canada's most notorious underground rendezvous." The *Maclean's* reporter paid a visit to Harry Rankin, then a young lawyer but soon to be one of the city's longest-serving aldermen, who gazed down ruefully from his office window and declared "it's not a street anymore, it's a scene from Gorky's Lower Depths."[367]

At that time the most common, and destructive, drug was heroin. But then things went from bad to worse. In the 1980s heroin was joined by an upsurge in the availability of cocaine, followed by crack cocaine and methamphetamines. The illicit use of these drugs was not confined to the Downtown Eastside, but it was there that the social and health costs were most evident. During the late 1980s the potency of the drugs increased, resulting in a spike in the number of overdose deaths. Users were shooting up in the streets and drugs changed hands openly on every corner. Levels of crime and violence also escalated as junkies stole to support their habit and dealers fought for control of their turf. The Downtown Eastside became, in the words of coroner (later mayor) Larry Campbell, a "drug-fueled craziness."[368]

By the mid-1990s, the use of injection drugs and the sharing of needles by users led to soaring rates of infection from HIV (human immuno-deficiency virus) and hepatitis C. The earliest cases of HIV/AIDS in North America appeared in 1981, and within two years it had spread to the city's gay community. Vancouver's first fatality was a twenty-seven-year-old man living in the West End, whose body was discovered in his apartment in early March 1983, his lungs overwhelmed with AIDS-related pneumonia. The mysterious disease, about which the local gay community had only read and heard, had arrived. It was greeted with fear and discrimination but also by courage and mutual aid as the community stepped up to address the crisis. Within the year a group of gay men created AIDS Vancouver, the first AIDS service organization in Canada, and in 1986 several patients founded the Vancouver Persons with AIDS Coalition (now the Positive Living Society of BC) to share information and fight for treatment. St. Paul's Hospital, located close to the West End, was in the vanguard of patient care. One of the earliest patients was a young medical doctor, Peter Jepson-Young. When he was no longer well enough to continue his medical practice, Jepson-Young became a high-profile AIDS activist, chiefly through his television appearances as "Dr. Peter" chronicling his experiences with the disease. Following his death in 1992, a foundation named for him created the Dr. Peter Centre to provide care for people with AIDS. As research led to more effective treatment and knowledge led to safer sex practices, the transmission of the disease within the gay community stabilized, though the disease continued to take its tragic toll.

In the 1990s there was a second spike in the incidence of HIV/AIDS, this time among injection drug users who were using contaminated needles. In an attempt to stem the spread of infectious diseases, a former addict named John Turvey began walking the streets handing out new syringes. His work led to the creation of Canada's first needle exchange, but still the infection rates soared. The number of overdose deaths climbed—more than two hundred people were dying of overdoses in the city each year—and HIV/AIDS infection rates became the worst of any city in the developed world. In 1994, in an influential report, chief coroner Vince Cain called the "so-called War on Drugs . . . an expensive failure." The crisis was a public health issue, not a justice issue, said Cain, and bold new policies were required to deal with it.[369] One idea that emerged was harm reduction, an approach that put the safety and survival of the user ahead of the law. During the winter of 1997–98, after the local health authority had declared a public health emergency, a group of activists organized the Vancouver Area Network of Drug Users (VANDU) and spearheaded a campaign to set up needle exchanges, and ultimately a supervised injection site where patrons could take their drugs in a safe setting.

Another key player in this mix of housing and public health activists was the Portland Hotel Society. By the 1980s the Downtown Eastside Residents Association had emerged as a leading creator and manager of social housing in the neighbourhood. One of these facilities was the Portland Hotel at the corner of Carrall and East Hastings. It became home to a group of tenants suffering from an array of difficult health challenges, both mental and physical. The Portland was considered a haven of last resort since the couple who managed it, Liz Evans and Mark Townsend, refused to turn anyone away. Eventually Evans and Townsend left the umbrella of DERA and created their own Portland Hotel Society, which became an essential force in providing social housing and agitating for the safe injection site. (By 2013 the PHS operated more than two dozen residential facilities in the Downtown Eastside, for people with mental health and addiction issues, managing a multi-million-dollar budget and employing more than three hundred people.[370])

At city hall an unlikely ally appeared in the person of Philip Owen, a businessman who had been elected mayor with the backing of the conservative NPA in 1993. Despite coming from a background of wealth and privilege, Owen had an open mind on the drug issue and became convinced by activists from the community that addiction was a health issue, and that harm reduction was part of the way to deal with it. Owen asked Donald MacPherson, former director of the Carnegie Community Centre and the city's first drug policy coordinator, to come up with a plan. The result was a report, passed by city council in 2000, endorsing a "Four Pillars" approach to addiction: prevention, treatment, enforcement and harm reduction. Support for this approach, and especially for harm reduction, may have cost Owen his job. For whatever reason, and despite the fact that he was the incumbent, the NPA replaced him as its candidate in the 2002 election. But the COPE candidate in that election, former coroner Larry Campbell, running on a harm reduction platform, won the mayoralty, and in September 2003 the first legal supervised drug injection clinic in North America, Insite, opened on East Hastings Street.

At the same time as the Four Pillars approach was gaining traction, the three levels of government came together to tackle the broader situation in the Downtown Eastside. In 2000 they signed the Vancouver Agreement, an initiative to coordinate and promote community welfare in the neighbourhood. The agreement supported almost one hundred projects aimed at economic revitalization, public health, housing and security. The agreement expired in 2010, though many of its intiatives were absorbed into other government and community programs. The Downtown Eastside continued to grapple with deep and troubling challenges but, concluded planner Larry Beasley, "god forbid what might be the situation today if the Vancouver Agreement and all of its spinoffs had not happened."[371]

AT THE SAME TIME Mayor Owen was taking a beating from his traditional constituency over his support for the Four Pillars, he was also getting a lot of criticism over another issue: the mysterious disappearance of women from the Downtown Eastside.[372] Since the 1980s women had been going missing from the streets in alarming numbers. Because most of the missing were sex workers and many were Indigenous women and/or struggling with addiction, the police at first did not pay much attention. The tipping point was reached with the disappearance of a thirty-six-year-old Indigenous woman from Alert Bay named Janet Henry.

Henry was last seen toward the end of June, 1997, in the beverage room at the Holborn Hotel on East Hastings. She was not the first to vanish, nor would she be the last, but she was the first whose disappearance received any public attention. Her sister, Sandra Gagnon, who had been scouring the downtown in search of Janet, talked to a journalist and the subsequent story in the *Sun* set in motion a chain of events that ultimately forced police to acknowledge that a rising number of women had gone missing from the Downtown Eastside. Coupled with the increasing number of sex workers known to have been murdered since the mid-1970s—by the fall of 2001, this figure exceeded sixty—it was becoming clear that along with its health crises, the city was in the grip of a murder epidemic.

By early March 1999, the tally of women unaccounted for had reached twenty. Family members and advocates for the women argued they must be victims of foul play, but police insisted that they had no evidence that this was the case. Someone suggested offering a reward for information. But how could there be a reward when there was still no acknowledged crime? The public was growing impatient at the lack of progress in the case and the seeming lack of respect being shown the missing women and their families. Under heavy pressure from the community, Mayor Owen reversed his position and in April announced that the city and the province would put up a reward of $100,000. For the first time, someone in authority was acknowledging publicly that the women may have been crime victims.

Despite the reward and a flurry of media attention, women continued to disappear: six during 1999, another two toward the end of 2000, eight more during 2001. As the number grew, RCMP and city police combined their efforts in a joint task force and the media paid even closer attention to the disappearances. Finally, on February 7, 2002, police called a press conference to announce that they had begun searching a farm property in suburban Port Coquitlam. Two weeks later one of the owners of the farm, Robert "Willy" Pickton, was arrested and charged with two counts of murder. Both of the initial victims were identified as women from the Downtown Eastside. As the search continued, the charges against Pickton piled up until, when his trial finally began early in 2006, he stood accused of killing twenty-seven women and was suspected of killing many more. In the end he was convicted of six murders—the prosecution, in a controversial decision, chose not to proceed with charges in twenty other murders, and one case was rejected by the court—and was sentenced to life in prison. Afterward the VPD issued an apology to the families of the victims for its inept conduct of the investigation, and a provincial commission of inquiry, led by former attorney general Wally Oppal, was highly critical of the police when it reported at the end of 2012.

The case of the missing women left a horrible stain on the reputation of the city. Pickton may have been the murderer, but the community was complicit in his crimes. Decades of indifference to the welfare of sex workers had left them exposed to violent predators. A 1995 study of the Downtown Eastside found that 99 per cent of sex workers were assaulted on the job. They had been beaten, raped, pistol-whipped, dragged by cars, robbed and strangled. Yet by and large the law did nothing for them. Instead they were forced deeper into marginal neighbourhoods, away from public places, out of sight and out of mind, where they had no protection against the men who preyed on them. By the 1990s Vancouverism may have become a byword for successful urban development, but the term obscured the city's dark side: the malignant social conditions that enabled the worst serial killer in the history of the country.

ANOTHER GROUP OF RESIDENTS for whom Vancouverism had little meaning were the First Nations. With the exception of the Musqueam living on their reserve on the Fraser River, mainstream Vancouver had removed the Indigenous people who originally lived within the city's borders and pretty much erased them from its memory. The ancient village of Xway'xway in Stanley Park was partly paved over and renamed Lumberman's Arch. On Kitsilano Point, the village of Sen-ákw and the Kitsilano Reserve were purchased, emptied and sold off for a variety of purposes. One of the purchasers was the Department of National Defence, which in 1966 gifted its land, most of the northern part of the former reserve, to the city.[373] Today this land comprises Vanier Park, home to theatre festivals, the MacMillan Space Centre and Planetarium, the Museum of Vancouver and the civic archives. In 2000 the Squamish signed the Kitsilano Agreement by which the nation formally surrendered almost all of the former reserve (along with other alienated lands on the north shore and in Squamish) in return for a payment of $92.5 million.[374] The agreement left about 4.5 hectares at the south end of the Burrard Street Bridge in the possession of the Squamish. In 2019 the nation announced that it intended to build a residential development there.

The Musqueam had an equally contentious relationship with other levels of government over their territory. In 1958 the Shaughnessy Golf & Country Club, formerly located on land leased from the CPR east of Granville Street between Thirty-third and Thirty-seventh, leased land on the Musqueam Reserve for a new course. Years later the Musqueam learned that the federal government, which had arranged the lease on their behalf, had agreed to charge the golf club a rent well below the market rate. The deal had been struck without the knowledge or consent of the Musqueam, who sued Ottawa for not properly protecting their interests. The case went to the Supreme Court of Canada, which in 1984 awarded the Musqueam $10 million in compensation, ruling that the government had failed in its fiduciary duty to the First Nation.[375]

At the same time another land lease controversy was looming at the reserve near Southwest Marine Drive. In 1960 the Musqueam agreed to lease some of its land to non-band members, leading to the construction of a small subdivision of high-end homes known as Musqueam Park. Leases were obtained at a very reasonable rate for the first thirty years and then were supposed to be renegotiated every decade at a fair market rate. In 1995, when the leases came up for the first renewal, tenants faced a steep increase in rent as the Musqueam believed they should receive an amount consistent with the value of surrounding, non-Musqueam land. For some tenants this meant an annual payment as high as $23,000. The *National Post* called it a "shakedown" and accused the band of "ethnic cleansing by fiscal means,"[376] a sign of how heated the disagreement became. For their part the Musqueam believed they were within their rights to expect to receive what anybody else would receive for their land. Again, the dispute had to be settled by the Supreme Court, which ruled in 2000 that the land was only worth half of the value of surrounding land, granting the lease-holders a reduced increase to their annual rent.[377]

Two other land projects illustrate the new prominence of local First Nations in the Vancouver property market. Both date to 2014, when the three First Nations—Musqueam, Squamish and Tsleil-Waututh—formed the MST Partnership to pursue economic opportunities within their traditional territories. The federal government then transferred to MST and its partner the Canada Lands Company, a federal Crown Corporation, two large chunks of property that had belonged to Ottawa. One was the so-called Heather Lands, an 8.5-hectare block west of Little Mountain between Thirty-third and Thirty-seventh Avenues. A focal point of the property was the Fairmont Academy, a large Tudor-style building used originally as a school for boys (1914–18), then as a military hospital where patients were treated for shell shock. In 1920 the building began a long association with the RCMP, which over time occupied most of what is now the Heather Lands, until vacating the site for new headquarters in Surrey in 2012. The second property is known as the Jericho Lands, a 36-hectare site on West Fourth Avenue in Point Grey. Part of the site was a military garrison belonging to the Department of National Defence, while the other part belonged to the province. Both sold their land to the MST–Canada Lands partnership and planning began for residential development. Along with the Squamish plans for what remains of the Kitsilano Reserve, these projects constitute an unprecedented participation by local First Nations in the development of their ancestral homelands.

FOR YEARS, WOODWARD'S DEPARTMENT STORE was a go-to destination for downtown shoppers. The food floor, the revolving W on the roof, the special deals on $1.49 Day—all were part of Vancouver's nostalgic reminiscence when the store went into decline during the 1980s, and finally closed in 1993, leaving a huge hole in the fabric of the Downtown Eastside. For several years the building sat empty while developers, local business owners, the city, the province and housing activists debated what to do with it. Affordable housing was at the centre of the debate, especially since the federal government was no longer funding social housing. The developer who purchased the site wanted to build market-priced condominiums; neighbourhood activists and their allies in government wanted at least some of the development to be subsidized accommodation.

Discussions over the future of the Woodward's site dragged on, and in 2001 the provincial NDP government purchased the site from the developer. Finally activists took matters into their own hands. On September 14, 2002, in protest against homelessness and the lack of social housing in the Downtown Eastside, a handful of protestors scaled an extension ladder to a second-floor window and began an occupation of the building. The occupiers hung banners overlooking Hastings Street and invited others to join them, which they soon did. Supporters kept up an almost constant drumbeat of solidarity in the streets outside. A list of demands issued by the squatters included immediate development of the Woodward's building as social housing, immediate accommodation for all homeless squatters, reversal of provincial government cuts to social services and conversion by the city of empty buildings into accommodation for low-income people.

The Woodsquat, as it came to be called, lasted seven days.[378] It ended early on the morning of September 21, when police broke into the building and took fifty-eight people into custody. Once they were released, with orders not to revisit Woodward's, some of the activists returned to the site and occupied tents on the sidewalk outside. The building was empty but the protest continued. The following evening police again intervened, clearing the sidewalk, arresting more people and trashing all the personal belongings in garbage trucks. But the protest reconvened and continued outside Woodward's for the next three months. It ended in mid-December when fifty-four homeless protestors moved into the Dominion Hotel after the city agreed to pay their rent for four months.

The site of an old department store, Woodward's, was the focus of a drawn-out dispute about affordable downtown housing, leading to the Woodsquat in September 2002 when protestors occupied the building, demanding government action. In the end the city purchased the site and transformed it into a mix of subsidized and market housing, a variety of offices and shops and SFU's School for the Contemporary Arts.
Courtesy woodsquat.wordpress.com, photo by Reid

The occupation and squat were over, but the future of the building remained undecided. That fall the left-leaning civic political party, the Committee of Progressive Electors, had swept to power at city hall, electing Mayor Larry Campbell and eight of ten councillors. One of the councillors was the housing activist Jim Green, who had been involved with different proposals for the Woodward's site for two decades. In 2003 the city purchased the old building from the province and following a long consultation partnered with private capital to redevelop the site as a combination of market condos, subsidized housing, shops, offices and SFU's School for Contemporary Arts. The complex opened in 2010. It has been praised for injecting vitality into a deteriorating neighbourhood without displacing the people who were already living there, and criticized, rightly or wrongly, for intensifying the gentrification of the Downtown Eastside.

One of the showpieces of the new Woodward's was a huge photographic installation mounted over the entrance to the building's atrium. *Abbott & Cordova, 7 August 1971* is artist Stan Douglas's re-creation of the notorious Gastown Riot, which had occurred at the downtown intersection right outside the door.[379] Douglas was a leading practitioner of a new school of photography known as photo-conceptualism, which emerged in the 1970s and included fellow Vancouver artists Ian Wallace, Jeff Wall, Roy Arden, Ken Lum and Rodney Graham. Their work, often large-scale, back-lit photographic images, sometimes depicted meticulously staged fictional scenes and sometimes, as in the case of *Abbott & Cordova*, presented striking images of the city itself. The international success of these creators brought unprecedented attention to the city as a progressive art centre.

IN THE MID-1990S, a group of people involved in amateur sports and tourism began to organize a bid to host the 2010 winter Olympics for Vancouver and the nearby ski resort at Whistler. Eventually chaired by Arthur Griffiths, former owner of the Canucks hockey team, the group put together a proposal that beat out Calgary and Quebec City to win the support of the Canadian Olympic Committee. Subsequently a team headed by developer Jack Poole and sports bureaucrat John Furlong campaigned to persuade the International Olympic Committee to give the games to Vancouver. As the competition approached its final stages in early 2003, Larry Campbell, the newly elected mayor, decided he had to honour his election promise to put the matter to a local plebiscite. Bid organizers opposed the idea but the vote went ahead at the end of February. Campbell and his COPE councillors, including housing activist Jim Green, agreed they would support the Yes side as a quid pro quo for a provincial agreement to fund social housing in the Woodward's project.[380] The public vote endorsed the Olympics by a substantial amount. That July the IOC awarded Vancouver/Whistler the 2010 games, and later John Furlong was appointed head of VANOC, the organizing committee that carried the games to fruition. Opposition to the games bid was vocal, and led by Chris Shaw, a UBC professor of ophthalmology, who argued in general that the Olympics were more about real estate speculation than athletics and in particular that the games were an extravagant waste of public money.[381] But in the end the boosters drowned out the naysayers and the games captured the imagination of the community.

The competition itself got off to a tragic start when a young Georgian athlete died during a training run at Whistler. This accident was followed by an embarrassing mechanical glitch that marred the opening ceremony on February 12, and continuing fears about a lack of snow at local mountain venues. But once events got well underway, a spirit of celebration took over the city. For seventeen days the streets buzzed with activity. The opening ceremony was the most watched television event in Canadian

Local enthusiasm for the Olympics manifested early. This photograph shows the crowd that assembled for the arrival of the torch relay at BC Place Stadium to kick off the games with the ceremonial lighting of the Olympic flame. Within Canada the relay had started in Victoria and travelled in a huge circle north to the Arctic, east to Newfoundland and back west again across the country, a total of 45,000 kilometres over 106 days.

© Leszek Wrona | Dreamstime.com

history, and 22 million Canadians watched the gold medal hockey game, won by Canada over the US in overtime on the final day of competition. Canada won more gold medals than any other country and the games came in on budget, leaving an aftertaste of success that was strengthened by the various infrastructure projects, which have become an integral part of the Lower Mainland, including the Canada Line rapid transit train to the airport, several well-used sports facilities and the reconstruction of the Sea to Sky highway to Whistler.

The final cost to the taxpayer was, according to the provincial government's own estimate, $925 million, substantially more than the $600 million originally estimated, but still "one of the best provincial decisions ever," according to finance minister Colin Hansen.[382] Of course this tally did not include the $1 billion contributed by the federal government for security and other costs. Nor did the provincial government total include the cost of the salaries of hundreds of public employees seconded to work for the Olympics, or the $700 million spent to widen the Sea-to-Sky Highway so that visitors could more easily access the events at Whistler. In the end, the NDP opposition claimed, the true cost to all levels of government was several billion dollars.[383] To Vancouver, the biggest hangover from the games was the redevelopment of the athletes' village in the southeast corner of False Creek, but after initial financial difficulties even this troubled project turned out to be a successful addition to the city.

AS WITH EVERY PUBLIC SPECTACLE OF ITS KIND, organizers claimed that the 2010 Olympics had put Vancouver "on the map" and changed the city forever. But Vancouver had been on the map for a long time. At least since Expo 86 the city had been benefitting from, and struggling with, the consequences of being a destination city for global capital and global migration. Not only had the population become as ethnically diverse as any place in the world, but the local economy had been transformed beyond recognition. Since the 1980s parts of the city that once hummed with industrial activity had become residential communities or consumer playgrounds. The deindustrialization that began in Coal Harbour in the 1960s accelerated to include the working waterfront in Burrard Inlet, both sides of False Creek and the north arm of the Fraser River. Mills, factories and machine shops disappeared, replaced by condominium towers, restaurants, parks and bike paths. The latest neighbourhood to experience this transition has been the False Creek flats. Once occupied by railyards and industrial sites, the flats have been reimagined as a "green enterprise zone," home to art galleries, hi-tech industries, a relocated Emily Carr University and the future St. Paul's "health campus" (what used to be called a hospital).

At the same time the Vancouver economy was deindustrializing, it was also de-coupling from its reliance on the province's traditional resource industries: logging, mining and the fishery. Manufacturing provided far fewer jobs than it once had. According to a study prepared for the region in 2016, only 5 per cent of employment in Greater Vancouver was provided by manufacturing.[384] Instead, the service industries—including tourism, the motion picture industry (Hollywood North), computing and media technology—became significant employers. At the same time Vancouver's role as a gateway to the Asia-Pacific region was solidified as goods and capital continued to flow back and forth across the Pacific through the port and the airport.

The transition from an industrial to a post-industrial economy can seem like a success story, but it has not occurred without disruption. Most significant, Vancouver became an exceedingly expensive place to live. Inflows of capital forced the price of real estate ever upward, putting it beyond the reach of more and more working residents. What were once affordable neighbourhoods gentrified, displacing the lower-income residents who could once afford to live there. And the west side of the city, which has always been more expensive than the east side, was priced beyond the means of even well-off middle-class income earners. Pointing out that a similar inflation of property values took place in other "world cities" such as San Francisco, Toronto and London provided little solace for young adults who could not afford to live in the city, while houses and condos owned by absentee owners sat vacant. Governments intervened with a variety of measures to try to cool off the property market, with limited success. It became conventional wisdom to caricature the city as a seaside resort where only the global super-rich could afford to live.[385]

Vancouver prides itself on having the world's longest uninterrupted waterfront path, extending from the convention centre downtown to Spanish Banks. The most popular portion of it is the Stanley Park Seawall, shown here, begun in 1917 by master stonemason James Cunningham and finally completed in 1980.

Debbie Ann Powell – stockadobe.com

Next Vancouver

SINCE THE 1980S, Vancouver has gone through transformative changes. The makeover of False Creek from an industrial precinct to a residential community was completed. An influx of immigration completely changed the ethnic composition of the population. An injection of foreign capital into the real estate market, mainly from Asia, touched off a soaring inflation of housing costs that made it almost impossible for middle- and low-income people to take up residence in the city. At the same time, the successful densification and gentrification of the downtown core was accompanied by the creation of an urban lifestyle with its own sobriquet, Vancouverism. The Downtown Eastside had always been a disadvantaged neighbourhood. Hit by the traffic in hard drugs such as heroin and cocaine, an influx of residents with mental health issues and a public health emergency brought on by HIV/AIDS, it faced challenges unlike any seen before.

All of these transformations, good and bad, left the city in the curious position of being considered a roaring success and a dismal failure at the same time. For those privileged enough to afford the lifestyle, the city offered an array of stylish restaurants, expensive shopping and a dizzying variety of outdoor recreation. It regularly finished at or near the top of every "best place in the world to live" list. In 2010, when playing host to the winter Olympics, Vancouverites seemed especially proud of what they had accomplished.

The games were, according to the *Sun*, "a humongous success."[386] Along with the athletic events, the city's streets swarmed with bustling crowds of visitors and locals together, celebrating how much fun they were all having. The Olympics seemed like the epitome of Vancouverism, the optimistic, "neighbourly" approach to civic reinvention that characterized the 1980s and 1990s.

A decade later that utopian vision of Vancouver seemed to have evaporated, revealing a darker version of the city. In the shadow of the glass towers was a wasteland of human suffering. During the summer of 2019 the crowds in the streets were not celebrants, they were homeless people living in tents or desperate drug users overflowing the sidewalks. The Downtown Eastside, always challenged for housing and health care, seemed to be in perpetual crisis. The arrival of fentanyl, a synthetic pain killer ten times more powerful than heroin, led to another epidemic of overdose deaths. During the 1990s, about two hundred people died of drug overdoses in the city each year. That was serious enough to be considered a public health emergency, and it led to the creation of Insite, the safe injection site. For a few years the number of drug fatalities declined. But in the 2010s came fentanyl, followed by another opioid, carfentanil, and an overdose calamity even more serious than the previous one. In doctor's offices and pharmacies, fentanyl and carfentanil are effective painkillers. On the street they are cheap to manufacture and easy to mix with heroin and cocaine, though many times more dangerous. There were 1,541 overdose deaths in BC in 2018, including almost 400 in the Greater Vancouver area—more than one every day.[387]

At the same time, homelessness continued to plague the neighbourhood. Dozens of people camped out in Oppenheimer Park because they had nowhere else to live. The scene was reminiscent of the jobless "jungles" of the 1930s. The city's annual homeless census recorded 2,223 people with no home, with 614 of them actually living on the street, as opposed to an emergency shelter or some other temporary accommodation. Indigenous people made up about 40 per cent of the total. Homelessness was at an all-time high.[388] During the summer, CBC Radio host Stephen Quinn focused his program on the Downtown Eastside. He concluded that "in more than two decades covering the neighbourhood as a reporter, I've never seen it look worse. Or feel worse." Many people, including Mayor Kennedy Stewart, agreed with him.[389]

And the plight of the Downtown Eastside was just one issue facing the city. More broadly, affordability remained a challenge as the real estate market failed to make room for modest income earners. Prices cooled off slightly in 2018 but were still far out of the range of most people hoping to be home buyers. Homes are for living in, but in Vancouver homes were being used as profit opportunities for absentee investors. This infusion of outside capital partly drove the skyrocketing inflation of real estate prices through the mid-2010s. For several reasons this inflow of foreign capital decreased after 2016 and the effect was seen in a gradual decline, or at least a slower rise, of housing prices in the city. But affordability continued to be one of the most serious challenges facing the city. Simple demographics complicate the situation. The boundaries of Vancouver have not changed since the amalgamation of 1929. In the same period, the population of the city has risen from about 245,000 to more than 635,000. Most of this increase was absorbed by the development of vacant land, then by the repurposing of so-called brownfield sites, land that was formerly occupied for industrial or other purposes. By the beginning of the 21st century, however, both these sources of land were more or less exhausted. The city had almost nowhere else to build; there was no more vacant land. Yet the population continued to climb, at a pace of about 5,500 people a year. In other words, growing room is one of the basic challenges facing the city.

LIKE THE REST OF THE WORLD, Vancouver faces another challenge that will potentially dwarf all the others, and over which it has less control: climate change. The city's concerns about global warming go back more than two decades. In 1989 council created a task force on atmospheric change that produced a pathbreaking report called *Clouds of Change*. It was the initial alarm, stating categorically that "human activity is changing the atmosphere" at a time when these were still fighting words for many. "The bottom line is: atmospheric change means *we* have to change," the report concluded.[390] *Clouds of Change* called for a reduction in carbon emissions by the city, an increase in energy efficiency and steps to reduce automobile use, among many other recommendations. It has been called "the first serious attempt at tackling an environmental approach to city building in our town."[391] Since it appeared, successive civic administrations have committed themselves to a series of "green city" initiatives, including a promise to reduce carbon emissions by 50 per cent by 2030.

At the same time the signs of a warming climate are becoming ever more evident in everyday life. Two phenomena in particular that affect the city are rising sea levels and wildfires. The global sea level has risen by 10 to 20 centimetres over the past century, due to warmer water temperatures and melting bodies of ice. And the rate of warming seems to be increasing. In Vancouver, sea water is already flooding low-lying parts of the city during winter storm surges and extreme weather events, and this threat will only worsen. At the same time British Columbia has experienced several summers of devastating wildfires, especially in the interior forests. Smoke from these fires, and from similar fires south of the border, made its way to the coast, where it blanketed the city in a noxious smog. Flood and fire are just two early symptoms of the serious environmental challenges that will face the city as climate change proceeds. In acknowledgement that the threat is real, in January 2019, Vancouver City Council joined cities around the world in declaring a climate emergency.

Climate change is a threat created by human activity. The city also faces a potentially catastrophic threat over which it has no control at all, the Big One. Scientists expect a giant megathrust earthquake (above 9.0 on the magnitude scale) to occur near Vancouver within the next century, possibly sooner than later. The civic administration has taken steps to upgrade infrastructure and develop an emergency plan. Schools have been strengthened; so have bridges and other civic buildings. Yet the Big One can only be prepared for, not prevented. When it occurs, it will almost certainly cause enormous destruction and many deaths.

It turns out that the city's prime asset, its gorgeous location at the edge of the Salish Sea, now puts it in danger of disastrous fallout from two major environmental threats. As Vancouver approaches its 140th anniversary (2026), its location, so long considered its defining asset, may also be its Achilles heel.

THE MOST DISRUPTIVE EVENT IN THE CITY'S HISTORY began early in 2020. Originating in a wild animal market in Wuhan, China, and quickly spreading around the world, the coronavirus pandemic arrived in Vancouver on January 28 with a traveller who had been on a business trip to Wuhan. By the middle of February the respiratory disease caused by the virus had been christened COVID-19 and cases were spreading rapidly. It turned out that elderly people were especially vulnerable. As a result, care homes in the Lower Mainland emerged as significant centres of infection. By the end of March there were over a thousand cases in the province and twenty-four deaths.

Realizing how quickly the virus was spreading, health officials announced a public health emergency. Travellers rushed home from mid-term school holidays as one by one the airlines grounded their flights, attempting to keep the virus from spreading between countries. In the city public transit emptied as commuters stayed home from work. Downtown streets grew deserted. All gatherings of more than 250 people were cancelled and all places where people congregated were closed, including schools, parks, museums and libraries. Many businesses that dealt with the public were asked to shut down. Restaurants and bars closed. Churches stopped holding services. Scientists hurried to develop tests for detecting the disease, while everyone was urged to wash their hands regularly, to keep their distance from each other and to wear a mask in public.

As residents isolated in their homes, the pandemic began to acquire its own daily routines. Every afternoon the chief medical health officer, Dr. Bonnie Henry, gave a televised briefing bringing the province up to date on how rapidly the virus was spreading. These briefings, which turned the soft-spoken, dependable Dr. Henry into a cultural hero, became "must-see" television for the remainder of the year. In the evening people stood on their porches and balconies banging pots together as an expression of support and gratitude for health care workers who were risking their own lives in the hospitals and care homes.

By early April the city had laid off 1,500 employees and Mayor Kennedy Stewart was reporting that lost revenue and epidemic-related expenses were costing between $4 and $5 million a week. By the end of the month, however, the dramatic protective measures seemed to have paid off. Hospitals were managing the case load and the number of infections was falling. Throughout May businesses reopened their doors and on June 1 students were back in school. During the month the situation improved steadily, though large events were still discouraged. However, health authorities warned that a second wave of the infection was inevitable and sure enough in July case numbers started to rebuild. By mid-October the province was officially in the second wave, which eventually became more extensive than the first. The number of new cases reported daily rose from around 200 in October to 300 by early November and then to a high of 941 by the end of the month.

Meanwhile, the "other epidemic," the drug overdose crisis, reached a new level in the city. In May 2020, 170 people died of accidental drug overdoses, the highest monthly provincial total ever, and more than died that month due to COVID-19. Most of the deaths involved fentanyl, the supply of which had become even more deadly in the context of the pandemic because of interruptions to the illicit supply and the fact that more users were injecting alone. In the first six months of the year there were 728 overdose deaths in BC, most of them in the Vancouver area. In July paramedics responded to 2,706 overdose callouts, the highest monthly number in four years, and by the end of the year overdoses were claiming five lives every day.

As 2020 drew to a close, a pair of vaccines became available to fight the coronavirus. In BC the first doses were delivered on December 15. It was going to take several months to inoculate enough people to provide widespread protection against the disease but there was hope that the summer would bring the beginning of the end to the pandemic, at least in the Lower Mainland, even with the appearance of new strains.

As people contemplated a return to "normalcy" they considered whether any of the changes that the pandemic brought to city life might become permanent. Were places catering to large groups—theatres, museums, restaurants and nightclubs, for example—ever going to return to business as usual? Would people ever feel completely safe congregating as they had before? Perhaps the dramatic reduction in vehicle traffic in the downtown core will become permanent as many more people choose to carry on their jobs from home. During the health crisis the city closed some streets to cars and allowed only bicycle traffic. Stanley Park, for instance, banned automobile traffic and threw open its roads only to bicycles and pedestrians. Will many more commuters of the future get out of their cars and switch to pedal power? At the same time sidewalks were widened to provide more room for pedestrians and for restaurants to move their tables outdoors. At the heart of all these changes was space, an issue that has challenged the city almost from the beginning. It is expected that we will require more of it, whether it is larger outdoor spaces in which to gather or more space between tables at our favourite restaurant. What kind of new protocols may be needed to attract people back onto public transit, or back into sporting events or concerts? Will mask wearing become a permanent feature of urban life? Will the aversion to density initiate a turn away from the inner city and toward suburban living?

It became obvious that the pandemic deepened the inequalities that already existed in society as the poor and the disadvantaged tended to be more vulnerable. In Vancouver some people predicted that the crisis was an opportunity to break the cycle of high real estate prices and make the city more affordable for lower-income residents. The pandemic also exposed the importance of different kinds of low-wage workers who were revealed to be much more essential to the public welfare than previously realized: delivery drivers, health care workers, grocery story clerks, and so on. Would the new respect enjoyed by these workers carry over into the post-pandemic era, and would it be reflected in changes to what is considered a living wage in the city?

The answers to all of these questions remained in the future. What was known for certain was that 2020 had been a year unlike any in the city's history.

Acknowledgements

I GREW UP ON VANCOUVER'S WEST SIDE in a tall house with a view of the ocean. My parents purchased the house in 1948, the year after I was born, because my arrival—I was the fourth, and last, child—required more space for the family. The house had been built twenty years earlier in a comfortable corner of West Point Grey by Elmer Reid and his wife Dorcas. Elmer was a school principal who also wrote textbooks and published an educational magazine called *School Days* for the Vancouver School Board. My father, who was a doctor, bought the house from another doctor, one of his colleagues at the Vancouver General Hospital perhaps. We were a well-to-do family in a solidly middle- to upper-middle-class neighbourhood.

As a boy, I had a bedroom that looked out across English Bay at the dark shape of Stanley Park and the buildings of the downtown peninsula. Before I fell asleep each night I would sit at the window admiring the twinkling carpet of lights. Periodically an air raid siren would begin wailing from the army base at the foot of the hill and great searchlights would sweep the sky, Cold War precautions left over from the shooting war.

My earliest memories are of Vancouver in the 1950s. It was a low-rise city. The building boom that transformed the West End into an oasis of high-rise apartments had not yet begun and the first modern business tower, the BC Electric Building on Burrard Street, did not go up until 1957. It was a city of brick and stone, not glass and steel. My grandmother used to take me downtown to the movies on the streetcar; I recall the sound of its bell and the stomach-shifting sway as it rounded a corner. Dense fogs still muffled the city. My father told me that he sometimes had to navigate the foggy streets by opening the driver's-side door of his car so that he could look down and keep himself positioned above the streetcar tracks. The mournful sound of the foghorn at Point Atkinson was such a defining part of the urban soundscape that when it was silenced the Coast Guard was accused of cutting the vocal chords of Vancouver.

West-siders like myself were incredibly insular. Our city did not include the east side. We crossed Cambie Street just once a year, in August, to travel out to Hastings to visit the Pacific National Exhibition. Stanley Park still had a zoo, populated by penguins, otters, monkeys and melancholy bears in their deep pit. It is difficult for today's "foodies" to imagine how few restaurants there were in the city. My family's idea of dining out was to stop at the White Spot drive-in for a hamburger and a strawberry milkshake. Occasionally my father took me to Capilano Stadium—now Nat Bailey Stadium—to watch the Vancouver Mounties play baseball. The Mounties were a triple-A farm team of the Baltimore Orioles. I may have been in the stands in 1959 when Brooks Robinson, the future hall-of-fame third baseman, suffered a near career-ending injury chasing down a foul ball.

In our house a set of bookshelves lined one wall of the living room. They contained the usual middle-brow reading of the 1950s: Nevil Shute's apocalyptic nuclear novel *On the Beach*; the odd Thomas Costain and Pearl Buck title; some volumes of Reader's Digest Condensed Books. But the only book of my parents' that I ever took down from the shelf was a copy of Alan Morley's *Vancouver: From Milltown to Metropolis*. Written to commemorate the centennial of British Columbia in 1958, it was the first book about the city that I read, curious about the place I could see from my window. Morley's history certainly had its failings, but it was impressive in its own way, mainly because it was proof that Vancouver deserved a book, which would not have been self-evident to a teenager growing up there. When I read Morley I was not seized with the desire to write my own version of the city. That came much later. But who can tell? Perhaps his example sowed a seed that has been slowly germinating for all the many years since.

A much more important influence than Alan Morley was my publisher, Howard White, who invited me to embark on this book. Howie and I have done several projects together, not least the *Encyclopedia of British Columbia*, which required me to learn an enormous amount about Vancouver, its past and present. Once that project was done, it was also Howard who suggested that perhaps there was a book in the life of Louis Taylor, Vancouver's longest-serving mayor. Taylor died in 1946, before I was born, but delving into his biography for my 2002 book *L.D.: Mayor Louis Taylor and the Rise of Vancouver* (Arsenal Pulp Press) required that I become familiar with the early history of the city for the first time. Two years later my friend George Fetherling persuaded me to write a history of the city's sex trade for his small publishing house Subway Books. *Red Light Neon* is a book that I can honestly say was "banned in Kerrisdale": a bookstore in that tony neighbourhood refused to sell it because of its salacious subject matter. More importantly, *Red Light* and *L.D.* before it, turned out to be rehearsals for what has become the main event and I owe Howard and George many thanks for setting me on the path.

In the twenty or so years that I have been delving into the history of Vancouver I have acquired many debts to the helpful and knowledgeable archivists and librarians at the City of Vancouver Archives and the Special Collections at the Vancouver Public Library. Other friends and colleagues have contributed their suggestions and opinions during many conversations over the past couple of years as well. They include Stephen Osborne, Thad McIlroy, Frank Mackey, Jim Taylor, Mark Stanton and Michael Hayward. Thanks to them, and to my brother Michael Francis who shared his extensive knowledge of the city. Michael, Stephen and Thad also generously read and commented on all or part of the finished manuscript. Jean Barman was kind enough to read—and share her input on—the manuscript as well. Much gratitude to my friends at Harbour Publishing, especially my editor Mary Schendlinger and the book's designer, Roberto Dosil. Obviously responsibility for any mistakes of fact or interpretation rests with me. Thanks also to the Vancouver Heritage Foundation and the Grunt Gallery for inviting me to give talks on different aspects of Vancouver's past, the research for which contributed in important ways to this book.

Finally, the book is dedicated to my wife Quita, who has lived in Vancouver longer than I have (by about two months), whose family roots in the city go back farther than my own, and who has always been willing to join me in my rambles through the urban streets in search of the city's past. I owe her everything.

Notes

1   Sean Kheraj, *Inventing Stanley Park* (Vancouver: UBC Press, 2013), pp. 63ff.

2   *Vancouver World*, April 24, 1899.

3   Cited in Kheraj, *Inventing Stanley Park*, p. 69.

4   *Vancouver World*, May 15, 1899.

5   Walter Hardwick, *Vancouver* (Toronto: Collier-Macmillan Canada, 1974), p. 7.

6   Nicolas Kenny, "Forgotten Pasts and Contested Futures in Vancouver,"
    British Journal of Canadian Studies, vol. 29, no. 2 (2016), p. 177.

7   Lance Berelowitz, *Dream City* (Vancouver: Douglas & McIntyre, 2005), p. 4.

8   Berelowitz, p. 266.

9   Foreword to Kate Bird, *Vancouver in the Seventies* (Vancouver: Greystone Books, 2016), p. 6.

10 J.S. Matthews, comp., *Conversations with Khahtsahlano, 1932–1954*
    (Vancouver: City of Vancouver Archives, 1955), p. 6.

11 Matthews, p. 3.

12 Daphne Sleigh, *The Man Who Saved Vancouver* (Vancouver: Heritage House, 2008), p. x.

13 Matthews, *Conversations*, p. 31.

14 *Vancouver Province*, January 14, 1933.

15 *Vancouver World*, July 4, 1906.

16 *Vancouver Province*, July 4, 1906.

17 F.W. Howay, "Early Settlement on Burrard Inlet," BC *Historical Quarterly*, April 1937, p. 108.

18 Major J.S. Matthews, *Early Vancouver: Narratives of Pioneers of Vancouver* (Vancouver:
    City of Vancouver Archives, 2011), vol. 2, p. 22.

19 W. Kaye Lamb, ed., *The Letters and Journals of Simon Fraser, 1806–1808* (Toronto: Dundurn
    Press, 2007), p. 126.

20 Graeme Wynn and Timothy Oke, eds., *Vancouver and Its Region* (Vancouver: UBC
    Press, 1992), p. 39.

21 Howay, "Early Settlement," p. 102.

22 *Vancouver Province*, March 13, 1915.

23 Quoted in Jean Barman, *Stanley Park's Secret: The Forgotten Families of Whoi Whoi,
    Kanaka Ranch and Brockton Point* (Madeira Park, BC: Harbour Publishing, 2005), p. 32.

24 W. Kaye Lamb, "EDWARD STAMP," in *Dictionary of Canadian Biography*, vol. 10,
    University of Toronto/Université Laval, 2003–, accessed October 21, 2019,
    www.biographi.ca/en/bio/stamp_edward_10E.html.

25 Raymond Hull and Olga Ruskin, *Gastown's Gassy Jack* (Vancouver: Gordon Soules
    Economic Research, 1971), p. 43.

26 Matthews, *Early Vancouver*, vol. 1, p. 135.

27 Archives Society of Vancouver, *Vancouver Historical Journal* no. 3 (January 1960), p. 12.

28 Matthews, *Early Vancouver*, vol. 1, p. 137.

29 Norbert MacDonald, "The Canadian Pacific Railway and Vancouver's Development
    to 1900," BC *Studies* no. 35 (Autumn 1977), pp. 9–11.

30 Douglas C. Harris, "Property and Sovereignty: An Indian Reserve and a Canadian City,"
    UBC *Law Review*, vol. 50, no. 2 (July 2017), p. 346.

31 Harris, p. 348.

32 See Frank Leonard, "'So Much Bumph': CPR Terminus Travails at Vancouver, 1884–89," *BC Studies* no. 166 (Summer 2010), pp. 7–38.

33 Quoted in MacDonald, "The Canadian Pacific Railway," p. 32.

34 Quoted in Pierre Berton, *The Last Spike* (Toronto: McClelland and Stewart, 1971), p. 305.

35 *Daily Colonist*, March 20, 1886.

36 Consolidated Acts of Incorporation of the City of Vancouver (Vancouver: Critic Printing Co., 1898).

37 Matthews, *Early Vancouver*, vol. 1, p. 205.

38 Archives Society of Vancouver, *Vancouver Historical Journal* no. 3 (January 1960), p. 21.

39 A book-length account of the fire is given in Lise Anne Smith, *Vancouver Is Ashes* (Vancouver: Ronsdale Press, 2014).

40 *Vancouver Advertiser*, June 29, 1886.

41 Matthews, *Early Vancouver*, vol. 2, p. 212.

42 Smith, *Vancouver Is Ashes*, p. 72.

43 Archives Society of Vancouver, *Vancouver Historical Journal* no. 3 (January 1960), p. 35.

44 *New York Times*, June 16, 1886.

45 Matthews, *Early Vancouver*, vol. 4, p. 240.

46 *Vancouver Advertiser*, June 29, 1886.

47 *Vancouver Sun*, April 2, 1953.

48 Ethel Wilson, *The Innocent Traveller* (Toronto: The Macmillan Company of Canada, 1949), p. 119.

49 Matthews, *Early Vancouver*, vol. 4, p. 160.

50 Matthews, *Early Vancouver*, vol. 7, p. 93.

51 *Vancouver News-Advertiser*, April 28, 1891.

52 Archives Society of Vancouver, *Vancouver Historical Journal* no. 3, p. 18.

53 *Vancouver News-Advertiser*, January 5, 1887.

54 Norbert MacDonald, "The Canadian Pacific Railway," p. 23.

55 *Vancouver News-Advertiser*, May 1, 1887.

56 Matthews, *Early Vancouver*, vol. 1, pp. 85–86.

57 Matthews, *Early Vancouver*, vol. 4, p. 171.

58 *Vancouver News-Advertiser*, January 1, 1888.

59 Sean Kheraj, *Inventing Stanley Park*, p. 45.

60 Kheraj, p. 60.

61 Barman, *Stanley Park's Secret*, p. 89.

62 Barman, pp. 91ff.

63 *Vancouver News-Advertiser*, December 29, 1887.

64 Robert McDonald, "Victoria, Vancouver, and the Economic Development of British Columbia, 1886–1914," in *British Columbia: Historical Readings*, W. Peter Ward and R.A.J. McDonald, eds. (Vancouver: Douglas & McIntyre, 1981), p. 376.

65 Robert A.J. McDonald, "Victoria, Vancouver and the Economic Development of British Columbia," p. 381.

66 Patricia Roy, "The British Columbia Electric Railway Company, 1897–1928: A British Company in British Columbia," PhD thesis, UBC, 1970, p. 175.

67 Alan Morley, *Vancouver: From Milltown to Metropolis* (Vancouver: Mitchell Press, 1961), p. 114.

68 Wilson, *The Innocent Traveller*, p. 120.

69 *Vancouver Province*, June 29, 1907.

70 Frank Yeigh, *Through the Heart of Canada* (Toronto: S.B. Gundy, 1913), pp. 303–4.

71 Matthews, *Early Vancouver*, vol. 1, p. 18.

72 Daniel Francis, *L.D.: Mayor Louis Taylor and the Rise of Vancouver* (Vancouver: Arsenal Pulp Press, 2004), p. 49; *Vancouver Province*, September 21, 1907.

73 Matthews, *Early Vancouver*, vol. 1, p. 19.

74 C.F.J. Galloway, *The Call of the West* (London: T.F. Unwin, 1916), p. 262.

75   Matthews, *Early Vancouver*, vol. 7, p. 128.

76   Wilson, *The Innocent Traveller*, p. 150.

77   Mrs. M.G. Mackenzie, "Behind the Scenes of the WCTU of Vancouver, BC," self-published, 1901.

78   Matthews, *Early Vancouver*, vol. 5, p. 11.

79   *Vancouver World*, September 26, 1891.

80   *Toronto Mail*, December 2, 1891; see also James Matthews, "The Fight for Kitsilano Beach: The Celebrated Greer Case," self-published pamphlet, City of Vancouver Archives, AM1519-: PAM 1931–59.

81   See G.E. Mills and D.W. Holdsworth, "The B.C. Mills Prefabricated System: The Emergence of Ready-made Buildings in Western Canada," *Canadian Historic Sites: Occasional Papers in Archaeology and History* no. 14, Ottawa, 1975.

82   Emily Carr, "Vancouver," *The Emily Carr Omnibus* (Vancouver: Douglas & McIntyre, 1993), p. 425.

83   Maria Tippett, *Emily Carr: A Biography* (Toronto: Oxford University Press, 1979), p. 73.

84   Douglas Sladen, *On the Cars and Off* (London: Ward, Lock and Bowden, 1895), p. 43.

85   Matthews, *Early Vancouver*, vol. 5, p. 143.

86   See Mills and Holdsworth, "The B.C. Mills Prefabricated System," pp. 149–51.

87   Matthews, *Early Vancouver*, vol. 4, p. 81.

88   Graeme Wynn, "The Rise of Vancouver," in Wynn and Oke, eds., *Vancouver and Its Region* (Vancouver: UBC Press, 1992), p. 90.

89   Galloway, *The Call of the West*, pp. 272–73.

90   Francis, *L.D.*, p. 56.

91   For more on Taylor, see Daniel Francis, *L.D.*

92   Robert A. Campbell, *Demon Rum or Easy Money: Government Control of Liquor in British Columbia from Prohibition to Privatization* (Ottawa: Carleton University Press, 1991), p. 18.

93   M. Allerdale Grainger, *Woodsmen of the West* (Toronto: McClelland and Stewart, 1964; orig. published 1908), p. 15.

94   Robert K. Burkinshaw, *False Creek: History, Images and Research Sources* (Vancouver: City of Vancouver Archives, Occasional Paper #2, 1984), p. 31.

95   Matthews, *Early Vancouver*, vol. 6, p. 80.

96   Matthews, *Early Vancouver*, vol. 5, p. 211.

97   Roy, "The British Columbia Electric Railway Company," p. 205. For more on the jitney phenomenon, see Donald F. Davis, "Competition's Moment: The Jitney-Bus and Corporate Capitalism in the Canadian City, 1914–29," *Urban History Review* vol. 18, no. 2 (October 1989), pp. 102–22.

98   Robert A.J. McDonald, "'Holy Retreat' or 'Practical Breathing Spot'? Class Perceptions of Vancouver's Stanley Park, 1910–1913," *Canadian Historical Review* vol. 65, no. 2 (June 1984), pp. 127–53.

99   E. Pauline Johnson, "The Lost Lagoon," *Flint and Feather: The Complete Poems of E. Pauline Johnson (Tekahionwake)* (Toronto: Musson Book Co., 1937; orig. published 1912).

100   See McDonald, "'Holy Retreat' or 'Practical Breathing Spot'?"; Kheraj, *Inventing Stanley Park*, pp.107–14; Wynn, "The Rise of Vancouver," pp. 118–21.

101   Quoted in Wynn, "The Rise of Vancouver," p. 118.

102   Quoted in Francis, *L.D.*, p. 103.

103   *Vancouver Province*, October 12, 1914.

104   Archives Society of Vancouver, *Vancouver Historical Journal* vol. 1 (January 1958), p. 60.

105   *Daily News-Advertiser*, February 25, 1887.

106   *Daily Colonist*, March 1, 1887.

107   *Daily Colonist*, March 1, 1887.

108   Kay J. Anderson, *Vancouver's Chinatown: Racial Discourse in Canada, 1875–1980* (Montreal: McGill-Queen's University Press, 1991), pp. 65–68.

109 Anderson, p. 74.

110 Norbert MacDonald, "The Canadian Pacific Railway," p. 28.

111 Canada, "Royal Commission on Chinese and Japanese Immigration," *Sessional Papers* 1902, #54, p. 278.

112 *Vancouver World*, September 1, 1906.

113 Patricia Roy, *A White Man's Province: British Columbia Politicians and Chinese and Japanese Immigrants, 1858–1914* (Vancouver: UBC Press, 1989), p. 186.

114 Quoted in Peter W. Ward, *White Canada Forever: Popular Attitudes and Public Policy Toward Orientals in British Columbia* (Montreal: McGill-Queen's University Press, 1978), p. 66.

115 *Vancouver World*, July 22, 1907.

116 *Vancouver World*, September 10, 1907.

117 See Patricia Roy, *A White Man's Province*, pp. 213ff.

118 J. Lewis Robinson, "Vancouver: Changing Geographical Aspects of a Multicultural City." *BC Studies* no. 79 (Autumn 1988), p. 61.

119 This account relies on Hugh Johnston, *The Voyage of the* Komagata Maru (Vancouver: UBC Press, revised edition 2014) and Ali Kazimi, *Undesirables: White Canada and the* Komagata Maru (Vancouver: Douglas & McIntyre, 2012).

120 Patricia Roy, *Vancouver: An Illustrated History* (Toronto: James Lorimer & Co., 1980), p. 170.

121 *Vancouver World*, September 10, 1892.

122 Matthews, *Conversations with Khahtsahlano*, p. 23A.

123 Sean Kheraj, *Inventing Stanley Park*, pp. 28–29.

124 Barman, *Stanley Park's Secrets*, p. 102.

125 Barman, p. 223.

126 Quoted in Douglas C. Harris, "Property and Sovereignty," p. 336.

127 Jean Barman, "Erasing Indigenous Indigeneity in Vancouver," *BC Studies* 155 (Autumn 2007), p. 17.

128 *Vancouver Province*, March 8, 1913.

129 *Vancouver Sun*, March 11, 1913.

130 Wilson, *The Innocent Traveller*, p. 157.

131 Matthews, *Early Vancouver*, vol. 1, p. 212.

132 *Vancouver Province*, November 3, 1906.

133 *Vancouver Province*, November 19, 1906.

134 *The Truth*, November 28, 1912.

135 *Daily Colonist*, April 15, 1903.

136 *Vancouver World*, April 15, 1903.

137 *Daily Colonist*, April 19, 1903.

138 *Daily Colonist*, May 8, 1903.

139 See J. Hugh Tuck, "The United Brotherhood of Railway Employees in Western Canada, 1898–1905," *Labour/Le Travail* 11 (Spring 1983), pp. 63–88.

140 Robert A.J. McDonald, "Working Class Vancouver, 1886–1914: Urbanism and Class in British Columbia," *BC Studies* nos. 69–70 (Spring/Summer 1986), p. 49.

141 J.A. Hobson, *Canada To-Day* (London: T. Fisher Unwin, 1906), p. 32.

142 W.C. Archibald, *Home-making and its Philosophy* (Boston: self-published, 1910), p. 499.

143 McDonald, "Working Class Vancouver."

144 McDonald, p. 36.

145 McDonald, p. 47.

146 See Mark Leier, "Solidarity on Occasion: The Vancouver Free Speech Fights of 1909 and 1912," *Labour/Le Travail* 23 (Spring 1989), pp. 39–66.

147 See James Conley, "'Open Shop' Means Closed to Union Men: Carpenters and the 1911 Vancouver Building Trades General Strike," *BC Studies* nos. 91–92 (Autumn/Winter 1991–92), pp. 127–51.

148 *Vancouver Province*, January 5, 1912.

149 *Vancouver Province*, January 12, 1912.

150 Alfred Henry Lewis, *South Vancouver Past and Present* (Vancouver: Western Publishing Bureau, 1920), p. 12.

151 *Vancouver World*, October 7, 1911.

152 *Vancouver Province*, November 28, 1911.

153 *Vancouver Province*, February 27, 1939 to March 16, 1939.

154 Herbert Rae, *Maple Leaves in Flanders Fields* (Toronto: William Briggs, 1916), p. 2.

155 Rae, p. 6.

156 Rae, p. 13.

157 *Vancouver Province*, July 30, 1914.

158 Robert A.J. McDonald, *Making Vancouver: Class, Status and Social Boundaries, 1863–1913* (Vancouver: UBC Press, 1996), p. 147.

159 Irene Howard, *The Struggle for Social Justice in British Columbia: Helena Gutteridge, the Unknown Reformer* (Vancouver: UBC Press, 1992), p. 104.

160 *Vancouver World*, January 11, 1915.

161 *Vancouver Province*, March 4, 1915, and March 8, 1915.

162 *Vancouver World*, March 27, 1915.

163 Howard Shubert, *Architecture on Ice: A History of the Hockey Arena* (Montreal: McGill-Queen's University Press, 2016), pp. 77–78.

164 *Vancouver Province*, April 7, 1915.

165 Chris Madsen, "Wages, Work, and Wartime Demands in British Columbia Ship-Building, 1916–19," *BC Studies* no. 182 (Summer 2014), p. 75.

166 James Conley, "Frontier Labourers, Crafts in Crisis and the Western Labour Revolt: The Case of Vancouver, 1900–1919," *Labour/Le Travail* 23 (Spring 1989), pp. 29–30.

167 *Vancouver World*, August 2, 1918.

168 *Vancouver World*, August 3, 1918.

169 See Daniel Francis, *Seeing Reds* (Vancouver: Arsenal Pulp Press, 2010), pp. 61–62.

170 *Vancouver Province*, August 29, 1911.

171 For a full biography of Gutteridge, see Irene Howard, *The Struggle for Social Justice in British Columbia: Helena Gutteridge, the Unknown Reformer* (Vancouver: UBC Press, 1992).

172 *Vancouver World*, August 26, 1915.

173 Matthews, *Early Vancouver*, vol. 6, p. 178.

174 On the epidemic, see Margaret W. Andrews, "Epidemic and Public Health: Influenza in Vancouver, 1918–1919," *BC Studies* no. 34 (Summer 1977), pp. 21–44; and Betty O'Keefe and Ian Macdonald, *Dr. Fred and the Spanish Lady: Fighting the Killer Flu* (Vancouver: Heritage House, 2004).

175 Andrews, p. 27.

176 John Everitt and Warren Gill, "The Early Development of Terminal Grain Elevators on Canada's Pacific Coast," *Western Geography* nos. 15–16 (2005/2006), pp. 30, 37.

177 Bruce Macdonald, *Vancouver: A Visual History* (Vancouver: Talonbooks, 1992), p. 40.

178 *Vancouver Province*, January 3, 1922.

179 Eleanor A. Bartlett, "Real Wages and the Standard of Living in Vancouver, 1901–1929," *BC Studies* no. 51 (Autumn 1981), p. 10.

180 Patricia Roy, "Vancouver: 'The Mecca of the Unemployed,' 1907–1929," in *Town and City*, A.F.J. Artibise, ed. (Regina: Canadian Plains Research Centre, University of Regina, 1981), p. 405.

181 Roy, p. 406.

182 J. Lewis Robinson, "Vancouver: Changing Geographical Aspects of a Multicultural City," *BC Studies* no. 79 (Autumn 1988), pp. 63–64.

183 Daphne Marlatt and Carole Itter, eds. *Opening Doors: Vancouver's East End* (Victoria: Ministry of Provincial Secretary and Government Services, Sound Heritage Series, 1979), p. 20.

184 Anderson, *Vancouver's Chinatown*, p. 118.

185 For the Smith case, see Edward Starkins, *Who Killed Janet Smith?* (Toronto: Macmillan of Canada, 1984).

186 See Catherine Carstairs, *Jailed for Possession: Illegal Drug Use, Regulation, and Power in Canada, 1920–1961* (Toronto: University of Toronto Press, 2006).

187 *Vancouver Sun*, March 22, 1920.

188 See for example *Vancouver World*, January 16, 1922; February 6, 1922; February 2, 1922.

189 *Vancouver Sun*, March 24, 1920.

190 Emily Murphy, *The Black Candle* (Toronto: Thomas Allen, 1922), p. 29.

191 Murphy, p. 188.

192 *Vancouver Sun*, March 2, 1923.

193 Maria Tippett, *Emily Carr: A Biography* (Toronto: Oxford University Press, 1979), p. 68.

194 Sheryl Salloum, "John Vanderpant and the Cultural Life of Vancouver, 1920–1939," *BC Studies* no. 97 (Spring 1993), pp. 38–50.

195 Simon Baker, *Khot-La-Cha: The Autobiography of Chief Simon Baker* (Vancouver: Douglas & McIntyre, 1994), p. 2.

196 The term originates with John C. Weaver, "The Property Industry and Land Use Controls: The Vancouver Experience, 1910–1945," in Peter Ward and R.A.J. McDonald, eds., *British Columbia: Historical Readings* (Vancouver: Douglas & McIntyre, 1981), p. 430.

197 *Vancouver Sun*, June 13, 1950.

198 Weaver, "The Property Industry and Land Use Controls ," p. 436.

199 James Duncan, "Shaughnessy Heights: the Protection of Privilege," in Shlomo Hasson and David Ley, eds., *Neighbourhood Organizations and the Welfare State* (Toronto: University of Toronto Press, 1994), p.62.

200 Duncan, p.63.

201 Henry Ewert, *The Story of the BC Electric Railway Company*, p.114.

202 Matthews, *Early Vancouver*, vol. 3, pp. 297–98.

203 *Vancouver Province*, March 27, 1915.

204 Jean Barman, "Neighbourhood and Community in Interwar Vancouver: Residential Differentiation and Civic Voting Behaviour" in R.A.J. McDonald and Jean Barman, eds., *Vancouver Past: Essays in Social History* (Vancouver: UBC Press, 1986), p. 117.

205 *Vancouver Province*, January 16, 1911, and January 30, 1911.

206 Harland Bartholomew and Associates, *A Plan for the City of Vancouver, including Point Grey and South Vancouver*, 1929, p. 309.

207 *Vancouver Province*, November 11, 1928.

208 *Vancouver Sun*, October 18, 1928.

209 See Todd McCallum, "The Reverend and the Tramp, Vancouver, 1931: Andrew Roddan's *God in the Jungles*," *BC Studies* no. 147 (Autumn 2005), pp. 51–88, and Andrew Roddan, *Vancouver's Hoboes* (Vancouver: Subway Books, 2005), which is a reprint of *God in the Jungles* (Vancouver: First United Church, 1931).

210 Matthews, *Early Vancouver*, vol. 3, p. 304.

211 *Vancouver Sun*, September 4, 1931.

212 *Vancouver Sun*, December 21, 1929.

213 *Vancouver Province*, February 19, 1930; McCallum, "The Reverend and the Tramp," p. 62.

214 W.J. Barrett-Lennard, *Report on the Reorganization of Civic Administration of the City of Vancouver,* submitted to city council December 9, 1936, p. 56.

215 *Vancouver Province,* January 26, 1931.

216 Ivan Ackery, *Fifty Years on Theatre Row* (Vancouver: Hancock House, 1980), p. 107.

217 Anderson, *Vancouver's Chinatown,* p. 142.

218 *Vancouver Sun,* March 4, 1932.

219 Francis, *L.D.,* p. 178; Douglas C. Harris, "Property and Sovereignty: An Indian Reserve and a Canadian City," BC *Law Review* vol. 50, no. 2 (July 2017), p. 370.

220 Kheraj, *Inventing Stanley Park,* pp.146ff.

221 *Vancouver Sun,* December 7, 1933.

222 David Monteyne, "'From Canvas to Concrete in Fifty Years': The Construction of Vancouver City Hall, 1935–6," BC *Studies* no. 124 (Winter 1999/2000), p. 48.

223 Monteyne, "'From Canvas to Concrete," p. 55.

224 Francis, *L.D.,* p.183.

225 *Maclean's,* March 15, 1935, p. 18.

226 Lani Russwurm, "Constituting Authority: Policing Workers and the Consolidation of Police Power in Vancouver, 1918–1939," master's thesis, Simon Fraser University, 2007, p. 72.

227 *Vancouver Sun,* December 10, 1934.

228 *Vancouver Province,* December 12, 1934.

229 James Duncan, "Shaughnessy Heights: The Protection of Privilege," in Hasson and Ley, *Neighbourhood Organizations and the Welfare State,* p. 64.

230 Robin Fisher, *Duff Pattullo of British Columbia* (Toronto: University of Toronto Press, 1991), p. 222.

231 *Vancouver Province,* April 24, 1935.

232 *Vancouver Province,* May 29, 1935.

233 Wayne D. Madden, "Vancouver's Elected Representatives" (Vancouver: self-published, 2003, copy in City of Vancouver Archives), p.A-3-4.

234 *Vancouver Province,* December 7, 1935.

235 *Vancouver Sun,* December 9, 1935.

236 Andrea B. Smith, "The CCF, NPA and Civic Change: Provincial Forces Behind Vancouver Politics, 1910–1940," BC *Studies* no. 53 (Spring 1982), p. 61.

237 *Vancouver Star,* September 2, 1932.

238 Quoted in *Vancouver: Art and Artists, 1931–1983* (Vancouver: Vancouver Art Gallery, 1983), p. 20.

239 *Vancouver Sun,* June 14, 1932.

240 The following discussion is based on Daniel Francis, *Closing Time: Prohibition, Rum-runners and Border Wars* (Vancouver: Douglas & McIntyre, 2014), pp.127ff., and Rick James, *Don't Tell Nobody Nothin' No How: The Real Story of West Coast Rum Running* (Madeira Park, BC: Harbour Publishing, 2018).

241 *Vancouver Sun,* June 20, 1938.

242 *Vancouver Province,* June 20, 1938.

243 *Vancouver Province,* June 20, 1938.

244 *Vancouver News-Herald,* September 18, 1939.

245 From "About Being a Member of our Armed Forces" in *Beyond Remembering: The Collected Poems of Al Purdy* (Madeira Park, BC: Harbour Publishing, 2000), p. 169.

246 Pierre Berton, *Starting Out: 1920–1947* (Toronto: McClelland and Stewart, 1987), p. 184.

247 Marlatt and Itter, eds., *Opening Doors,* p. 23.

248 *Vancouver Sun,* September 16, 1937.

249 *Vancouver Sun,* February 2, 1941.

250 E.G. Perrault, *Tong: The Story of Tong Louie, Vancouver's Quiet Titan* (Madeira Park, BC: Harbour Publishing, 2002), p. 92.

251 Anderson, *Vancouver's Chinatown,* p. 169.

252 Ross Lambertson, "The Black, Brown, White and Red Blues: The Beating of Clarence Clemons," *Canadian Historical Review* vol. 85, no. 4 (December 2004), p. 763.

253 *Vancouver Province*, May 7, 1945.

254 Wayson Choy, *Paper Shadows: A Memoir of a Past Lost and Found* (Toronto: Penguin Canada, 1999), p. 149.

255 Eva Hoffman, *Lost in Translation: A Life in a New Language* (New York: E.P. Dutton, 1989), p. 101.

256 Harland Bartholomew and Associates, *A Preliminary Report Upon the City's Appearance* (Vancouver Town Planning Commission, 1947), p. 11.

257 Will Langford, "'Is Sutton Brown God?': Planning Expertise and the Local State in Vancouver, 1952–73," *BC Studies* no. 173 (Spring 2012), p. 32.

258 Quoted in David Ricardo Williams, *Mayor Gerry* (Vancouver: Douglas & McIntyre, 1986), p. 276.

259 *Vancouver Province*, August 12, 1947.

260 Jill Wade, "'A Palace for the Public': Housing Reform and the 1946 Occupation of the Old Hotel Vancouver," *BC Studies* nos. 69–70 (Spring/Summer 1986), p. 293–94.

261 *Vancouver Province*, November 16, 1948.

262 See Thomas Michael Thomson, "The Death and Life of the Little Mountain Housing Project: British Columbia's First Public Housing Community," master's thesis, UBC, 2010.

263 *Vancouver World*, November 27, 1889; *Vancouver News-Advertiser*, September 27, 1894.

264 *Vancouver World*, November 27, 1889.

265 Rolf Knight, *Along the No. 20 Line: Reminiscences of the Vancouver Waterfront* (Vancouver: New Star Books, 2011; orig. published 1980), p. 74.

266 Jacopo Miro, "*Visions of False Creek: Urban Development and Industrial Decline in Vancouver, 1960–1980*", master's thesis, University of Victoria, 2009, p. 19.

267 Harland Bartholomew and Associates, *A Plan for the City of Vancouver including Point Grey and South Vancouver*, 1929, p. 147.

268 Wayson Choy, *All that Matters* (Toronto: Doubleday Canada, 2004), p. 12.

269 *Vancouver Sun*, December 9, 1950.

270 *Vancouver Province*, September 28, 1957.

271 *Vancouver Province*, March 12, 1955.

272 Quoted in Rolf Knight, *Along the No. 20 Line*, p. 101.

273 *Vancouver Province*, March 15, 1955.

274 Lee Thiessen, "Protesting Smoke: A Social and Political History of Vancouver Air Pollution in the 1950s and 1960s," *Urban History Review* vol. 46, no. 1 (Fall 2017), pp. 60, 65.

275 *Vancouver Province*, November 13, 1952.

276 *Vancouver Sun*, June 28, 1966.

277 *Vancouver Province*, February 27, 1969.

278 Mike Harcourt and Ken Cameron with Sean Rossiter, *City Making in Paradise* (Vancouver: Douglas & McIntyre 2007), pp. 40–41.

279 Anderson, *Vancouver's Chinatown*, p. 189.

280 *Vancouver Province*, August 7, 1961.

281 *Vancouver Province*, September 26, 1960.

282 Hardwick, *Vancouver*, p. 86.

283 Ann McAfee, "Residence on the Margin of the Central Business District: A Case Study of Apartment Development in the West End of Vancouver, BC," master's thesis, Department of Geography, University of British Columbia, 1967, p. 7; John Punter, *The Vancouver Achievement: Urban Planning and Design* (Vancouver: UBC Press, 2003), p. 19.

284 Robert M. Walsh, "The Origins of Vancouverism: A Historical Inquiry into the Architecture and Urban Form of Vancouver, BC," PhD diss., University of Michigan, 2013, p. 177.

285 For Kanaka Ranch, see Barman, *Stanley Park's Secret*, pp. 46ff.

286 John Parminter, "Guardians in the Sky: Aircraft and their Use in Forestry in BC: 1918–1926," *Whistle Punk* vol. 1, no 4 (Spring 1986), p. 4.

287 *Vancouver Sun*, June 25, 1955.

288 Interview with Dorothy Nealy in *Opening Doors*, Daphne Marlatt and Carole Itter, eds. (Madeira Park, BC: Harbour Publishing, 2011; orig. published 1979), p. 217.

289 *Vancouver Sun*, July 19, 1952.

290 For a full discussion of the Clemons case, see Ross Lambertson, "The Black, Brown, White and Red Blues: The Beating of Clarence Clemons, *Canadian Historical Review* vol. 84, no. 4 (December 2004), pp. 755–76.

291 For the Mulligan investigation, see Betty O'Keefe and Ian Macdonald, *The Mulligan Affair: Top Cop on the Make* (Vancouver: Heritage House, 1997).

292 For a full discussion of the games, see Jason Beck, *The Miracle Mile: Stories of the 1954 British Empire and Commonwealth Games* (Halfmoon Bay, BC: Caitlin Press, 2016).

293 George Woodcock, *Beyond the Blue Mountains: An Autobiography* (Toronto: Fitzhenry & Whiteside, 1987), p. 47.

294 Quoted in Marian Penner Bancroft, "UBC in the Sixties," on the Vancouver Art in the Sixties website, www.vancouverartinthesixties.com.

295 See James Hoffman, "Sydney Risk and the Everyman Theatre." *BC Studies* no. 76 (Winter 1987/88), pp. 33–57.

296 Robert A. Campbell, *Demon Rum or Easy Money: Government Control of Liquor in British Columbia from Prohibition to Privatization* (Ottawa: Carleton University Press, 1991), p. 124.

297 Becki L. Ross, *Burlesque West: Showgirls, Sex and Sin in Postwar Vancouver* (Toronto: University of Toronto Press, 2009), pp. 9–12.

298 See Ross, *Burlesque West*, for a full discussion of Vancouver nightlife.

299 Robin Brunet, *Red Robinson: The Last Deejay* (Madeira Park, BC: Harbour Publishing, 2016), p. 75.

300 See Michael G. Young, "The History of Vancouver Youth Gangs, 1900–1985," master's thesis, Simon Fraser University, 1993.

301 Quoted in Marc Edge, *Pacific Press: The Unauthorized Story of Vancouver's Newspaper Monopoly* (Vancouver: New Star Books, 2001), p. 50.

302 For the history of Vancouver newspapers, see Marc Edge, *Pacific Press: The Unauthorized Story of Vancouver's Newspaper Monopoly* (Vancouver: New Star Books, 2001).

303 See Daniel Francis, *Operation Orca* (Madeira Park, BC: Harbour Publishing, 2007) and Jason Colby, *Orca* (New York: Oxford University Press, 2018).

304 Colby, *Orca*, pp. 126ff.

305 Lawrence Aronsen, *City of Love and Revolution: Vancouver in the Sixties* (Vancouver: New Star Books, 2010).

306 *Vancouver Sun*, March 8, 1967.

307 CBC Television, *7 O'Clock Show*, March 18, 1968. Transcript at www.cbc.ca/archives/entry/ vancouver-politicians-averse-to-hippies. Accessed November 12, 2019.

308 Hardwick, *Vancouver*, p. 184.

309 Anderson, *Vancouver's Chinatown*, pp. 207–209.

310 Marlatt and Itter, eds., *Opening Doors*, p. 184.

311 Jane Jacobs, *The Death and Life of Great American Cities* (New York: Modern Library, 1993, orig. published New York: Random House, 1961), p. 10.

312 *Vancouver Sun*, November 24, 1967.

313 *Vancouver Province*, December 2, 1967.

314 Kheraj, *Inventing Stanley Park*, pp. 193–95; Walsh, "The Origins of Vancouverism," pp. 262–63.

315 *Vancouver Sun*, January 10, 1972.

316 For a thorough discussion of this episode, see Jack Little, *At the Wilderness Edge: The Rise of the Antidevelopment Movement on Canada's West Coast* (Montreal: McGill-Queen's University Press, 2019), pp. 15–49.

317 Bruce Hutchison, *The Unknown Country: Canada and Her People* (Toronto: Longmans, Green & Co., 1942), p. 323.

318 Paul Tennant, "Vancouver Civic Politics 1929–1980," *BC Studies* no. 46 (Summer 1980), p. 16.

319 *Vancouver Sun*, February 4, 2012.

320 Tennant, "Vancouver Civic Politics," p. 15.

321 Tennant, "Vancouver Civic Politics," p. 27.

322 *Vancouver Sun*, December 14, 1972.

323 Conversation with Michael Francis, May 14, 2019.

324 Tennant, "Vancouver Civic Politics," p. 22.

325 Miro, "Visions of False Creek," p. 27.

326 *Vancouver Sun*, October 18, 1967.

327 *Globe and Mail*, April 20, 1978.

328 *Globe and Mail*, April 15, 1978.

329 *Vancouver Province*, March 29, 1981.

330 *Vancouver Sun*, May 9, 1980.

331 *Vancouver Sun*, April 7, 1982.

332 *Vancouver Sun*, August 7, 1980.

333 Ross, *Burlesque West*, p. 139.

334 Vancouver Art Gallery, *Vancouver: Art and Artists*, p. 146.

335 *Globe and Mail*, June 8, 2007.

336 Vancouver Art Gallery, *Vancouver: Art and Artists*, p. 268.

337 Douglas C. Harris, "Condominium and the City: The Rise of Property in Vancouver," *Law and Social Inquiry* vol. 36, no. 3 (Summer 2011), p. 695.

338 Harris, "Condominium and the City," pp. 705–6.

339 David Ley, Daniel Hiebert and Geraldine Pratt, "Time to Grow Up? From Urban Village to World City, 1966–91," in Wynn and Oke, eds., *Vancouver and Its Region*, p. 237.

340 Trevor J. Barnes, David W. Edgington, Kenneth G. Denike and Terry G. McGee, "Vancouver, the Province, and the Pacific Rim," in Wynn and Oke, eds., *Vancouver and Its Region*, p. 183.

341 *Vancouver Sun*, August 11, 1983.

342 Rod Mickleburgh, *On The Line: A History of the British Columbia Labour Movement* (Madeira Park, BC: Harbour Publishing, 2018), pp. 230ff.

343 Quoted in Kristopher Olds, "Planning for the Housing Impacts of a Hallmark Event: A Case Study of Expo 86," master's thesis, School of Community and Regional Planning, UBC, 1988, p. 132.

344 Olds, p. 134.

345 Olds, p. 109.

346 David Grierson, *The Expo Celebration* (North Vancouver: Whitecap Books, 1986), p. 4.

347 *The New Yorker*, July 14, 1986.

348 *Vancouver Sun*, April 27, 1997.

349 See, for example, *Business In Vancouver*, April 26, 2016.

350 *Vancouver Sun*, October 23, 1986.

351 *Vancouver Sun*, October 29, 1979.

352 Conversation with Michael Francis, May 14, 2019.

353 Daniel Hiebert, "The Changing Social Geography of Immigrant Settlement in Vancouver," Working Paper #98-16 (September 1998), Vancouver Centre for Research on Immigration and Integration in the Metropolis, p. 5.

354 Hiebert, p. 10.

355 Hiebert, p. 17.

356 *Vancouver Sun*, March 27, 2017.

357 John Punter, *The Vancouver Achievement: Urban Planning and Design* (Vancouver: UBC Press, 2003), p. 133.

358 David Ley, *Millionaire Migrants: Trans-Pacific Life Lines* (Chichester, UK: Wiley-Blackwell, 2010), p. 160.

359 Larry Beasley, *Vancouverism* (Vancouver: UBC Press, 2019).

360 Berelowitz, *Dream City*, p. 1.

361 Punter, *The Vancouver Achievement*, p. 346.

362 *Vancouver Sun*, October 11, 1989.

363 *Vancouver Sun*, February 12, 1990.

364 Punter, *The Vancouver Achievement*, p. 276.

365 Beasley, *Vancouverism*, p. 230.

366 Peter Trower, *Dead Man's Ticket* (Madeira Park: Harbour Publishing, 1996), p. 27.

367 *Maclean's*, March 1, 1958.

368 Larry Campbell, Neil Boyd and Lori Culbert, *A Thousand Dreams: Vancouver's Downtown Eastside and the Fight for Its Future* (Vancouver: Greystone Books, 2009), p. 39.

369 J.V. Cain, *Report on the Task Force into Illicit Narcotic Overdose Deaths in British Columbia* (Victoria: Office of the Chief Coroner, Ministry of Attorney General, 1994), p. vi.

370 Travis Lupick, *Fighting for Space: How a Group of Drug Users Transformed One City's Struggle With Addiction* (Vancouver: Arsenal Pulp Press, 2017), p. 327.

371 Beasley, *Vancouverism*, p. 232.

372 For a fuller discussion of this episode, see Daniel Francis, *Red Light Neon: A History of Vancouver's Sex Trade* (Vancouver: Subway Books, 2006), chapter five.

373 Douglas C. Harris, "Property and Sovereignty," p. 379.

374 *Globe and Mail*, July 25, 2000.

375 *Vancouver Province*, November 2, 1984.

376 *National Post*, November 2, 1999.

377 *Vancouver Province*, June 13, 2000.

378 See special Woodsquat issue of *West Coast Line*, no. 41 (Fall/Winter 2003–2004).

379 See Stan Douglas, *Abbott & Cordova, August 17, 1971* (Vancouver: Arsenal Pulp Press, 2011).

380 Robert Enright, ed., *Body Heat: The Story of the Woodward's Redevelopment* (Vancouver: Blueimprint, 2010), p. 42.

381 See Christopher A. Shaw, *Five Ring Circus: Myths and Realities of the Olympic Games* (Gabriola Island, BC: New Society Publishers, 2008).

382 *Toronto Star*, July 9, 2010.

383 *Toronto Star*, July 9, 2010.

384 Trevor Barnes and Tom Hutton, *Dynamics of Economic Change in Metro Vancouver*, report prepared for Metro Vancouver, November 2016, p. 6.

385 *Maclean's*, November 22, 2015.

386 *Vancouver Sun*, March 1, 2010.

387 British Columbia Coroners Service, *Illicit Drug Toxicity Deaths in BC, January 1, 2009–August 31, 2019*, p. 10.

388 *Vancouver Courier*, June 12, 2019.

389 Stephen Quinn, "New Normal," CBC News, September 7, 2019, available at newsinteractives. cbc.ca/longform/new-normal. Accessed September 18, 2019.

390 City of Vancouver, *Clouds of Change: Final Report of the City of Vancouver Task Force on Atmospheric Change* (June 1990), p. 1.

391 Beasley, *Vancouverism*, p. 304.

Sources

I made extensive use of historic newspapers at the Vancouver Public Library and on the news-papers.com website, including the *Vancouver Sun*, the *Province*, the *World* and the *Daily Colonist* as well as selected issues of the *Globe and Mail* and the *News-Advertiser*. References to specific issues and articles will be found in the notes. The following books, articles, reports and such are meant to be a select list of recommended readings about the history of the city, not an exhaustive bibliography.

Anderson, Kay J. *Vancouver's Chinatown: Racial Discourse in Canada, 1875–1980.* Montreal: McGill-Queen's University Press, 1991.

Baker, Simon. *Khot-La-Cha: The Autobiography of Chief Simon Baker.* Vancouver: Douglas & McIntyre, 1994.

Barman, Jean. "Erasing Indigenous Indigeneity in Vancouver." *BC Studies* no. 155 (Autumn 2007): 3–30.

———. *Stanley Park's Secret: The Forgotten Families of Whoi Whoi, Kanaka Ranch and Brockton Point.* Madeira Park, BC: Harbour Publishing, 2005.

Bartholomew, Harland and Associates. *A Plan for the City of Vancouver including Point Grey and South Vancouver.* 1929.

Bartlett, Eleanor A. "Real Wages and the Standard of Living in Vancouver, 1901–1929." *BC Studies* no. 51 (Autumn 1981): 3–62.

Bartroli, Tomas. *Genesis of Vancouver City: Exploration of its Site 1791, 1792 and 1808.* Vancouver: self-published, 1997.

Beasley, Larry. *Vancouverism.* Vancouver: UBC Press, 2019.

Beck, Jason. *The Miracle Mile: Stories of the 1954 British Empire and Commonwealth Games.* Halfmoon Bay, BC: Caitlin Press, 2016.

Belshaw, John, ed. *Vancouver Confidential.* Vancouver: Anvil Press, 2014.

Belshaw, John, and Diane Purvey. *Vancouver Noir: 1930–1960.* Vancouver: Anvil Press, 2011.

Berelowitz, Lance. *Dream City: Vancouver and the Global Imagination.* Vancouver: Douglas & McIntyre, 2005.

Blomley, Nicholas. *Unsettling the City: Urban Land and the Politics of Property.* New York: Routledge, 2004.

Burkinshaw, Robert K. *False Creek: History, Images and Research Sources.* Vancouver: City of Vancouver Archives, Occasional Paper #2, 1984.

Cain, Louis P. "Water and Sanitation Services in Vancouver: An Historical Perspective." *BC Studies* no. 30 (Summer 1976): 27–43.

Campbell, Lara. *A Great Revolutionary Wave: Women and the Vote in British Columbia.* Vancouver: UBC Press, 2020.

Campbell, Larry, Neil Boyd and Lori Culbert. *A Thousand Dreams: Vancouver's Downtown Eastside and the Fight for Its Future.* Vancouver: Greystone Books, 2009.

Campbell, Robert A. *Demon Rum or Easy Money: Government Control of Liquor in British Columbia from Prohibition to Privatization.* Ottawa: Carleton University Press, 1991.

Carlson, Keith Thor. "Rethinking Dialogue and History: The King's Promise and the 1906 Aboriginal Delegation to London." *Native Studies Review* vol. 16, no. 2 (2005): 1–38.

Chapman, Aaron. *The Last Gang in Town*. Vancouver: Arsenal Pulp Press, 2016.

———. *Liquor, Lust and the Law: The Story of Vancouver's Legendary Penthouse Nightclub*. Vancouver: Arsenal Pulp Press, 2012.

Choy, Wayson. *All That Matters*. Toronto: Doubleday Canada, 2004.

———. *Paper Shadows: A Chinatown Memoir*. Toronto: Penguin Canada, 1999.

City of Vancouver. *Clouds of Change: Final Report of the City of Vancouver Task Force on Atmospheric Change*, June 1990.

Conley, James. "Frontier Labourers, Crafts in Crisis and the Western Labour Revolt: The Case of Vancouver, 1900–1919." *Labour/Le Travail* 23 (Spring 1989): 9–37.

———. "'Open Shop' Means Closed to Union Men: Carpenters and the 1911 Vancouver Building Trades General Strike." *BC Studies* nos. 91–92 (Autumn / Winter 1991–92): 127–51.

Coupland, Douglas. *City of Glass*. Vancouver: Douglas & McIntyre, 2009.

D'Acres, Lilia, and Donald Luxton. *Lions Gate*. Vancouver: Talonbooks, 1999.

Davis, Chuck. *The Chuck Davis History of Metropolitan Vancouver*. Madeira Park, BC: Harbour Publishing, 2011.

Davis, Donald F. "Competition's Moment: The Jitney-Bus and Corporate Capitalism in the Canadian City, 1914–29." *Urban History Review* vol. 18, no. 2 (October 1989): 102–22.

Donaldson, Jesse. *Land of Destiny: A History of Vancouver Real Estate*. Vancouver: Anvil Press, 2019.

Edge, Marc. *Pacific Press: The Unauthorized Story of Vancouver's Newspaper Monopoly*. Vancouver: New Star Books, 2001.

Enright, Robert, ed. *Body Heat: The Story of the Woodward's Redevelopment*. Vancouver: Blueimprint, 2010.

Everitt, John and Warren Gill. "The Early Development of Terminal Grain Elevators on Canada's Pacific Coast." *Western Geography* nos. 15–16 (2005/2006): 28–52.

Ewert, Henry. *The Story of the BC Electric Railway Company*. North Vancouver: Whitecap Books, 1986.

Fisher, Robin. *Duff Pattullo of British Columbia*. Toronto: University of Toronto Press, 1991.

Francis, Daniel. *L.D.: Mayor Louis Taylor and the Rise of Vancouver*. Vancouver: Arsenal Pulp Press, 2004.

———. *Red Light Neon: A History of Vancouver's Sex Trade*. Vancouver: Subway Books, 2006.

———. *Seeing Reds: The Red Scare of 1918–1919, Canada's First War on Terror*. Vancouver: Arsenal Pulp Press, 2010.

Gilmour , Julie F. *Trouble on Main Street: Mackenzie King, Reason, Race and the 1907 Vancouver Riots*. Toronto: Penguin Canada, 2014.

Grainger, M. Allerdale. *Woodsmen of the West*. Toronto: McClelland and Stewart, 1964 (orig. published 1908).

Grierson, David. *The Expo Celebration*. North Vancouver: Whitecap Books, 1986.

Gutstein, Donald. *Vancouver Ltd*. Toronto: James Lorimer & Co., 1975.

Harcourt, Mike, with Wayne Skene. *Mike Harcourt: A Measure of Defiance*. Vancouver: Douglas & McIntyre, 1996.

Harcourt, Mike, Ken Cameron and Sean Rossiter. *City Making in Paradise: Nine Decisions that Saved Vancouver*. Vancouver: Douglas & McIntyre, 2007.

Hardwick, Walter. *Vancouver*. Toronto: Collier-Macmillan Canada, 1974.

Harris, Douglas C. "Condominium and the City: The Rise of Property in Vancouver." *Law and Social Inquiry* vol. 36, no. 3 (Summer 2011): 694–726.

———. "Property and Sovereignty: An Indian Reserve and a Canadian City." *UBC Law Review* vol. 50, no. 2 (July 2017): 321–92.

Hasson, Shlomo, and David Ley. *Neighbourhood Organizations and the Welfare State*. Toronto: University of Toronto Press, 1994.

Hayes, Derek. *Historical Atlas of Vancouver and the Lower Fraser Valley*. Vancouver: Douglas & McIntyre, 2005.

Hoffman, Eva. *Lost in Translation: A Life in a New Language*. New York: E.P. Dutton, 1989.

Hoffman, James. "Sydney Risk and the Everyman Theatre." *BC Studies* no. 76 (Winter 1987–88): 33–57.

Howard, Irene. *The Struggle for Social Justice in British Columbia: Helena Gutteridge, the Unknown Reformer*. Vancouver: UBC Press, 1992.

Johnston, Hugh. *The Voyage of the* Komagata Maru. Vancouver: UBC Press, 2014 (orig. published 1989).

Kazimi, Ali. *Undesirables: White Canada and the* Komagata Maru. Vancouver: Douglas & McIntyre, 2012.

Kelly, Brian, and Daniel Francis. *Transit in British Columbia: The First Hundred Years*. Madeira Park, BC: Harbour Publishing, 1990.

Kheraj, Sean. *Inventing Stanley Park: An Environmental History*. Vancouver: UBC Press, 2013.

Kluckner, Michael. *Vancouver Remembered*. North Vancouver: Whitecap Books, 2006.

———. *Vancouver, The Way It Was*. North Vancouver: Whitecap Books, 1984.

———. *Vanishing Vancouver*. North Vancouver: Whitecap Books, 2012.

Knight, Rolf. *Along the No. 20 Line: Reminiscences of the Vancouver Waterfront*. Vancouver: New Star Books, 2011 (orig. published 1980).

Lambertson, Ross. "The Black, Brown, White and Red Blues: The Beating of Clarence Clemons." *Canadian Historical Review* vol. 85, no. 4 (December 2004): pp. 755–76.

Langford, Will. "'Is Sutton Brown God?' Planning Expertise and the Local State in Vancouver, 1952–73." *BC Studies* no. 173 (Spring 2012): 11–39.

Lauster, Nathanael. *The Death and Life of the Single-Family House: Lessons from Vancouver on Building a Livable City*. Philadelphia: Temple University Press, 2016.

Leier, Mark. "Solidarity on Occasion: The Vancouver Free Speech Fights of 1909 and 1912." *Labour/Le Travail* 23 (Spring 1989): 39–66.

———. *Where the Fraser River Flows: The Industrial Workers of the World in British Columbia*. Vancouver: New Star Books, 1990.

Leonard, Frank. "'So Much Bumph': CPR Terminus Travails at Vancouver, 1884–89." *BC Studies* no. 166 (Summer 2010): 7–38.

Lewis, Alfred Henry. *South Vancouver Past and Present*. Vancouver: Western Publishing Bureau, 1920.Ley, David. *Millionaire Migrants: Trans-Pacific Life Lines*. Chichester, UK: Wiley-Blackwell, 2010.

———. *The New Middle Class and the Remaking of the Central City*. Oxford: Oxford University Press, 1996.

Liscombe, Rhodri Windsor. *The Modern Spirit: Modern Architecture in Vancouver, 1938–1963*. Vancouver: Douglas & McIntyre, 1997.

Lupick, Travis. *Fighting for Space: How a Group of Drug Users Transformed One City's Struggle with Addiction*. Vancouver: Arsenal Pulp Press, 2017.

Macdonald, Bruce. *Vancouver: A Visual History*. Vancouver: Talonbooks, 1992.

MacDonald, Norbert. "The Canadian Pacific Railway and Vancouver's Development to 1900." *BC Studies* no. 35 (Autumn 1977): 3–35.

———. "A Critical Growth Cycle for Vancouver, 1900–1914." *BC Studies* no. 17 (Spring 1973): 26–42.

Marlatt, Daphne, and Carole Itter, eds. *Opening Doors: Vancouver's East End*. Victoria: Ministry of Provincial Secretary and Government Services, Sound Heritage Series, 1979.

Matthews, J.S., comp. *Conversations with Khahtsahlano, 1932–1954*. Vancouver: City of Vancouver Archives, 1955.

Matthews, J.S. *Early Vancouver: Narratives of Pioneers of Vancouver*. Vols. 1–7, 1932–56. Reprint, Vancouver: City of Vancouver Archives, 2011.

McCallum, Todd. *Hobohemia and the Crucifixion Machine: Rival Images of a New World in 1930s Vancouver*. Edmonton: Athabasca University Press, 2014.

——. "The Reverend and the Tramp, Vancouver, 1931: Andrew Roddan's *God in the Jungles*." *BC Studies* no. 147 (Autumn 2005): 51–88.

McDonald, Robert A.J. "'Holy Retreat' or 'Practical Breathing Spot'? Class Perceptions of Vancouver's Stanley Park, 1910–1913." *Canadian Historical Review* vol. 65, no. 2 (June 1984): 127–53.

——. "Lumber Society on the Industrial Frontier: Burrard Inlet, 1863–1886." *Labour/ Le Travail* 33 (Spring 1994): 69–96.

——. *Making Vancouver: Class, Status and Social Boundaries, 1863–1913*. Vancouver: UBC Press, 1996.

——. "Victoria, Vancouver, and the Economic Development of British Columbia, 1886–1914." *British Columbia: Historical Readings*, W. Peter Ward and R.A.J. McDonald, eds. Vancouver: Douglas & McIntyre, 1981: 369–95.

McDonald, R.A.J., and Jean Barman, eds. *Vancouver Past: Essays in Social History*. Vancouver: UBC Press, 1986.

McDowell, Jim. *Uncharted Waters: The Explorations of Jose Narvaez, 1768–1840*. Vancouver: Ronsdale Press, 2015.

Mickleburgh, Rod. *On The Line: A History of the British Columbia Labour Movement*. Madeira Park, BC: Harbour Publishing, 2018.

Monteyne, David. "'From Canvas to Concrete in Fifty Years': The Construction of Vancouver City Hall, 1935–6." *BC Studies* no. 124 (Winter 1999–2000): 41–68.

Moogk, Peter N. *Vancouver Defended: A History of Men and Guns of the Lower Mainland Defences, 1859–1949*. Vancouver: Antonson Publishing, 1978.

Morley, Alan. *Vancouver: From Milltown to Metropolis*. Vancouver: Mitchell Press, 1961.

Morton, James W. *Capilano: The Story of a River*. Toronto: McClelland and Stewart, 1970.

O'Keefe, Betty, and Ian Macdonald. *The Mulligan Affair: Top Cop on the Make*. Vancouver: Heritage House, 1997.

——. *Dr. Fred and the Spanish Lady: Fighting the Killer Flu*. Vancouver: Heritage House, 2004

Parnaby, Andrew. *Citizen Docker: Making a New Deal on the Vancouver Waterfront, 1919–1939*. Toronto: University of Toronto Press, 2008.

Perrault, E.G. *Tong: The Story of Tong Louie, Vancouver's Quiet Titan*. Madeira Park, BC: Harbour Publishing, 2002.

Persky, Stan. *The House that Jack Built: Mayor Jack Volrich and Vancouver Politics*. Vancouver: New Star Books, 1980.

Price, John. "'Orienting' the Empire: Mackenzie King and the Aftermath of the 1907 Race Riots." *BC Studies* nos. 156–57 (Winter/Spring 2007–2008): 53–81.

Punter, John. *The Vancouver Achievement: Urban Planning and Design*. Vancouver: UBC Press, 2003.

Rae, Herbert [George Gibson, pseud.] *Maple Leaves in Flanders Fields*. Toronto: William Briggs, 1916.

Roddan, Andrew. *Vancouver's Hoboes*. Vancouver: Subway Books, 2005, with an introduction by Todd McCallum. (A reprint of *God in the Jungles*, Vancouver: First United Church, 1931.

Ross, Becki L. *Burlesque West: Showgirls, Sex and Sin in Postwar Vancouver*. Toronto: University of Toronto Press, 2009.

Roy, Patricia. *The Triumph of Citizenship: The Japanese and Chinese in Canada, 1941–1967*. Vancouver: UBC Press, 2007.

———. *Vancouver: An Illustrated History*. Toronto: James Lorimer, 1980.

———. "Vancouver: 'The Mecca of the Unemployed,' 1907–1929." In A.F.J. Artibise, ed., *Town and City*. Regina: Canadian Plains Research Centre, University of Regina, 1981: 393–413.

———. *A White Man's Province: British Columbia Politicians and Chinese and Japanese Immigrants, 1858–1914*. Vancouver: UBC Press, 1989.

Roy, Susan. *These Mysterious People: Shaping History and Archaeology in a Northwest Coast Community*. Montreal: McGill-Queen's University Press, 2010.

Russwurm, Lani. "Constituting Authority: Policing Workers and the Consolidation of Police Power in Vancouver, 1918–1939." master's thesis, Simon Fraser University, 2007.

Salloum, Sheryl. "John Vanderpant and the Cultural Life of Vancouver, 1920–1939." *BC Studies* no. 97 (Spring 1993): 38–50.

Schofield, Peggy, ed. *The Story of Dunbar: Voices of a Vancouver Neighbourhood*. Vancouver: Ronsdale Press, 2007.

Shaw, Christopher A. *Five Ring Circus: Myths and Realities of the Olympic Games*. Gabriola Island, BC: New Society Publishers, 2008.

Sleigh, Daphne. *The Man Who Saved Vancouver: Major James Skitt Matthews*. Victoria: Heritage House Publishing, 2008.

Smith, Andrea B. "The CCF, NPA and Civic Change: Provincial Forces Behind Vancouver Politics, 1910–1940." *BC Studies* no. 53 (Spring 1982): 45–65.

Smith, Lisa Anne. *Vancouver is Ashes: The Great Fire of 1886*. Vancouver: Ronsdale Press, 2014

Stanger-Ross, Jordan. "Municipal Colonialism in Vancouver: City Planning and the Conflict over Indian Reserves, 1928–1950s." *Canadian Historical Review* vol. 89, no. 4 (December 2008): 541–80.

Starkins, Edward. *Who Killed Janet Smith?* Toronto: Macmillan of Canada, 1984.

Stouck, David. *Ethel Wilson: A Critical Biography*. Toronto: University of Toronto Press, 2003.

Tennant, Paul. "Vancouver Civic Politics 1929–1980," *BC Studies* no. 46 (Summer 1980): 3–27.

Thiessen, Lee. "Protesting Smoke: A Social and Political History of Vancouver Air Pollution in the 1950s and 1960s." *Urban History Review* vol. 46, no. 1 (Fall 2017): 57–70.

Tippett, Maria. *Emily Carr: A Biography*. Toronto: Oxford University Press, 1979.

Trower, Peter. *Dead Man's Ticket*. Madeira Park, BC: Harbour Publishing, 1996.

Tuck, J. Hugh. "The United Brotherhood of Railway Employees in Western Canada, 1898–1905," *Labour/Le Travail* 11 (Spring 1983): 63–88.

Vancouver Art Gallery. *Vancouver: Art and Artists, 1931–1983*. Exhibition catalogue (October 15 to December 31 1983), Vancouver: Vancouver Art Gallery, 1983.

Wade, Jill. *Houses for All: The Struggle for Social Housing in Vancouver, 1919–1950*. Vancouver: UBC Press, 1994.

Walsh, Robert M. "The Origins of Vancouverism: A Historical Inquiry into the Architecture and Urban Form of Vancouver, BC." PhD thesis, University of Michigan, 2013.

Ward, W. Peter. *White Canada Forever: Popular Attitudes and Public Policy Toward Orientals in British Columbia*. Montreal: McGill-Queen's University Press, 1978.

Weaver, John C. "The Property Industry and Land Use Controls: The Vancouver Experience, 1910–1945." Peter Ward and R.A.J. McDonald, eds., *British Columbia: Historical Readings*. Vancouver: Douglas & McIntyre, 1981: 426–48.

Williams, David Ricardo. *Mayor Gerry: The Remarkable Gerald Grattan McGeer*. Vancouver: Douglas & McIntyre, 1986.

Wilson, Ethel. *The Innocent Traveller*. Toronto: The Macmillan Company of Canada, 1949.

Woodcock, George. *Beyond the Blue Mountains: An Autobiography*. Toronto: Fitzhenry & Whiteside, 1987.

Working Lives Collective. *Working Lives: Vancouver 1886–1986*. Vancouver: New Star Books, 1985.

Wynn, Graeme and Timothy Oke, eds. *Vancouver and Its Region*. Vancouver: UBC Press, 1992.

Yee, Paul. *Saltwater City: An Illustrated History of the Chinese in Vancouver*. Vancouver: Douglas & McIntyre, 2006 (orig. published 1986).

Yu, Henry. *Journeys of Hope: Challenging Discrimination and Building on Vancouver Chinatown's Legacies*. Vancouver: UBC Initiative for Student Teaching and Research in Chinese Canadian Studies, 2018.

Index

Page numbers in **bold** refer to photographs, maps or illustrations

A

Abbott, Harry, 38
Abbott & Cordova, 7 August 1971 (photo), 226–27
Abyssinia (ship), 36
AIDS crisis, 219–20
Air Pollution Control Society, 160–61
Air Raid Precautions (ARP), 144
Alexander, R.H., 28, 31–32
Allerdale Grainger, Martin, 62
Alsbury, Tom, 164
anti-Asian riots (1907), 73–75, 109
architecture, 152
Art, Historical and Scientific Association, 113
Arts Club, 171
Arts of the Raven (exhibition), 201
Asahi (baseball club), **139**, 140
Asiatic Exclusion League (AEL), 73, 75, 108
Athenia (ship), 142–43
Athletic Park, 139
Aunt Sally, 80
Ay-yul-shun (English Bay Beach), 10, 61

B

Bailey, Nat, 106
Baker, Simon, 113
Balkind, Alvin, 171
Bannister, Roger, 167–68, **169**
Barrett, Dave, 204
Bartholomew, Harland, 114
Bartholomew Report, 115, 159
Basford, Ron, 193–94
Baxter, Truman, 93
Bayshore Inn, 165
BC Breweries Ltd., 54
BC Electric Railway Company, 42, **44**, 45, **48**, 49, 51, 59, 65, 97
    building, 152, **153**
BC Government Employees' Union, 205
BC Mills, Timber and Trading Company, 37
BC Place, 209–10
BC Sugar Refining Company, **39**

Beasley, Larry, 216, 218, 221
Beaven, Robert, 28
Bell-Irving, Henry, 38
Bennet, W.A.C., 154
Bennett, Bill, 204, 205, 206, 209, 210, 212, 213
Bennett, R.B., 126, 157
Bennettville, 157, **158**
Berton, Pierre, 144
Better Vancouver League, 131
Bill Haley and the Comets, 173
Bingham, W.J., 125
Bird, J. Edward, 76
Birney, Earle, 171
bissett, bill, 200
Black, George, 26
Black community, 39–40, 112, 166
Black Spot, 200
Board of Administration, 152–53
Bobak, Molly, 171
Boeing Canada, 148
Bowman, Will, 112
Boyd, Denny, 197
Branca, Angelo, 147
Brighouse, Samuel, 18, **19**
Brighton Hotel (Maxie's), 29, **30**
British Columbia Art League, 112
British Properties, 129
Brockton, Francis, 18
Brodie, Steve, 141
Brown, Bob, 139, 140
Bullen, Harry, 45
Burnaby, Robert, 22
Burns, Mrs. Charles, 59–60
Burns, Pat, 176
Burrard Dry Dock, 148
Burrard Inlet, 15, 105, 154
Burrard Street Bridge, 128
Burrell, Martin, 76

C

Cain, Vince, 220
Campbell, Gordon, 212, 217

Campbell, Larry, 219, 221, 226, 227
Campbell, Tom, 181, 184, 185, 186, 187, **189–90**, 191, 200
Canada Place, 210
Canadian Literature (journal), 201
Canadian Northern Pacific Railway, 62, 64
Canadian Northern Railway, 46, 127
Canadian Pacific Railway (CPR), 35–36, 63, 84–85
    and city development, 26–28, 46
    and economy, 28, 36, 39, 130
canneries, 43
Capilano Reserve, 7
Capilano Stadium, 140
Capilano, Joe, 11
Capilano, Mary Agnes, 113
Capilano River, 41
Carlisle, John, 40
Carnegie Community Centre, 212, 221
Carnegie Library, 190
Carr, Emily, 59–60, 112, 136
Carter-Cotton, Francis, 61
Cave Supper Club, 173
Cellar (jazz club), 200
Celona, Joe, 111, 131, 132
centennial, Vancouver, 211, 214
Central Mortgage and Housing Corporation (CMHC), 155, 194
c̓əsnaʔəm (Marpole Midden), 16–17
Chan, Mary, 184
Chan, Shirley, 184
Chan, Walter, 184
Charles, Prince of Wales, 213
Chay-chil-wuk (Seymour Creek), 10
Chaythoos (Prospect Point), 7, 10
Chinatown, 70, 71, **72**, 74, 83, 109–10, 146, 149
    as heritage district, 194–95
    redevelopment attempts, 162–65, 184–87
Chinatown Property Owners Association, 164
Chinese Benevolent Association, 109, 127, **186**
Chinese community, 31, 70–71, 110, 127, 146, 184–86, 195
        discrimination against, 39, 69–71, 146, 195
Chinese Cultural Centre, 195
Chinese head tax, 69, 71, 72, 73
Chip-kay-um, Chief (Chief George), 7
Choy, Wayson, 149, 159
Christ Church Cathedral, 81
city hall, Vancouver, 129

CityPlan, 217
Clarke, G.H., 141
Clemons, Clarence, 165–66
Clifford J. Rogers (ship), 154
Clough, John, 40
Clutesi, George, 201
Coal Harbour, 18, 165
Committee of Progressive Electors (COPE), 190, 226
Commodore Ballroom, 105, 138
Con, Harry, 184
Con Jones Park, 139
Consolidated Exporters, 137, 138
Consolidated Railway and Light Company, 49
Co-operative Commonwealth Federation, 102
Cornett, Jack, 149
coronavirus pandemic, 235–37
Coughlan's shipyard, **98**
counterculture, Vancouver, 180–81
Coupland, Douglas, 5
Crane's Shipyards, 165
Cranmer, Doug, 201
Crease, Henry, 22
Crofton House School for Girls, 51, 55
Cromie, Don, 175, 176
Cromie, Sam, 175
Cumyow, Won Alexander, 109–10

D

Davies, Libby, 190
Deadman's Island, 2, 11, 41
Deighton, John (Gassy Jack), 13–14, 23
Denman Arena, 96
Deva, Jim, 199
Diana, Princess of Wales, 213
Doering, Charles, 54
Dominion Trust Building, 50, 67
Don, Lee, **72**
Douglas, Charles, 86, 93
Douglas, Stan, 226–27
Downtown Eastside Residents Association (DERA), 190, 212, 220
Dr. Peter Centre, 220
Dr. Sun Yat-Sen Classical Chinese Garden, 195
drugs in Vancouver, 109–10, 181, 182–84, 218–21
Ducharme, Frederick, 157
Dunbar, Charles Trott, 119

E

East End, 4, 110–11, 161–62, 190–91, 212, 218–19, 239

Eburne, Harry, 116

Ecstasy of Rita Joe, The (play), 201

Edmonds, H.V., 51

Edmonds, Jane, 51

Eihu (Granville resident), 26

Eihu, Mary, 165

electoral system, Vancouver, 134–35, 192

Electors Action Movement, The (TEAM), 190, 191–92, 194

Elizabeth (the Queen Mother), 141, 142

Emery, Tony, 199

Emily Carr College of Art and Design, 194

Empire Stadium, 168, 174, 205

Employers' Association of Vancouver, 85

Englesea Lodge, 115

English Bay, 55–56

environmentalism in Vancouver, 160, 182, 234–35

Erickson, Arthur, 162, 188, 217

Eriksen, Bruce, 190

European exploration of Vancouver, 14–18

Evans, Liz, 220

Everyman Theatre Company, 171–72

Expo 86, 209–10, **211**, 212, 213–14

E-yal-mough (Jericho), 10, 22

F

Faces (nightclub), 198

Fairview, 54

False Creek, 63, 148, 157–**58**–59
photos, **160**, **178**, **193**, **208**
redevelopment, 192–94, 203, 209, 210, 229

Farley, Lilias, 136

Fertig, Mona, 201

Findlay, James, 87

Findlay, Walter, 103

fine arts in Vancouver, 112–13, 136–37, 170–71, 172, 199–202

fire department, Vancouver, 40, 41, 65

First United Church, 123, 212

Fisher, Blanche, 157

Flynn, Errol, 196

Foikis, Joachim, 200

Fortes, Seraphim "Joe," 55–56, **57**

Foster, W.W., 132, 133–34

Fotheringham, Alan, 191

Fraser, Simon, 17

Furlong, John, 227

G

Gagnon, Sandra, 221

Gale, Harry, 99

Gallagher, William, 23, 26, 32

gangs in Vancouver, 131, 174

Garden, James, 2, 73

Gardiner, Dick, 45, 46

Gastown, 7, **12**, 13, **24**, 32–35, 38, 40, 194

Gastown Smoke-In, 182–**83**–84

gay community, 198–99

George, Dan, 201

George, Henry, 88–89

George VI, 141, 142

Georgia Auditorium, 96, 102

Georgia Straight (newspaper), 181

Georgia Viaduct, 187

Gleason, Mrs., 56

Gold, Emma, 26

Gold, Louis, 26

Goodwin, Albert "Ginger," 99

Grandview, 59–60

Granville Island, 64, 148, **193**–94, 203

Granville Street Bridge, 159

Granville townsite, 23, 26, 27

Great Depression
protests, 125, 133–34, 140–41
unemployment, **122**, 123–24, **126**–27, 129, 140
and Vancouver economy, 127–28, 132–33
work camps, 127, 133

Great Northern Railway (GNR), 46, 62, 63–64

Green, Jim, 226, 227

Green Hill Park explosion, 149

Greenpeace, 182

Greer, Sam, 41, 56

Greer Hall, Jessie, 41

Griffiths, Arthur, 227

Group of Seven, 113, 136

Gutteridge, Helena, **101**–2

H

Hailstone, William, 18, **19**

Hamber, Eric, 43, 142

Hamersley, Alfred St. George, 38

Hamilton, Don, 214

Hamilton, Lachlan, 37, 42

Harcourt, Mike, 184, 190, 191, 197, 209, 214

Hardwick, Walter, 3, 184, 193
Harland Bartholomew and Associates, 152
Harlem Nocturne, 173
Harlow, Robert, 171
Hastings Mill, 13, 23, **24–25**, 31, 37, 85
Hastings Townsite, 29, 30
Hendry, John, 37, 63
Henry, Bonnie, 236
Henry, Janet, 221–22
Hill-Tout, Charles, 10
HMS *Plumper* (ship), 18
Hoffar, Irene, 136
Hoffar Motor Boat Company, 165
Hoffman, Eva, 151, 170
Hogan's Alley, 39, 110, **163**, 165–66, 187
Hopkinson, William, 79
Hotel Vancouver (first), 37–38
Hotel Vancouver (third), 127, **128**, 142–43
Houdini, Harry, 112
housing, 58, 154–59, 203–4, 218, 225, 233–34
Hudson, Charles, 138
Hudson's Bay Company, 18, 38
Hume, Fred, 159
Humulcheson (Capilano), 10, 15
Hunter, Bob, 182, **183**
Hutt, Debra, 196–97

I

Imperial Roller Rink, 55
incorporation of Vancouver, 28–29
Indian Names for Familiar Places (map), **8–9**,
    10, 11
Indigenous art, 113, 201–2
Indigenous communities, discrimination
    against, 7, 79–81, 221–22, 223
Indigenous place names, 8–9, 10, 11
Industrial Workers of the World (IWW), 87, 88
Intermedia, 199

J

Japanese community, 58, 71, 73, 75, 116, **139**,
    140, 144, **145**, 146
        internment of, 144–46, 195
Jefferson Airplane, 180
Jepson-Young, Peter, 219
Jericho, 10, 22
Jewish community, 156
Jewish Community Centre, 156
Joe, Mathias, 10, 11

Johnson, Pauline, 11, 65–66, 81
Joint Indian Reserve Commission, 80, 81
Jones, Con, 139
Jung, Douglas, 195
Juvenile Detention Home, 174

K

Kanaka Ranch, 165
Keefer, George Alexander, 41
Kerrisdale, 118
Khahtsahlano, August Jack, **6**, 7, 10, 16, 80
Khahtsahlanogh, Chief, 7, 58
Khanamoot, 29
Kidd, George, 133
Killam, Larry, 194
King, William Lyon Mackenzie, 75, 107,
    109, 154
Kitsilano, 56, 181, 203–4
Kitsilano Agreement, 223
Kitsilano Beach, 14, 58
Kitsilano Point, **6**, 10
Kitsilano Reserve, 128, 223, 224
Ki-wah-usks, 54
Klondike gold rush, 49, 85
Knight, Rolf, 157
Komagata Maru (ship), 4, 76, **77**, 79
Kum-kum-lye (Hastings Sawmill), 100, 22
Kwakwaka'wakw People, 113

L

labour disputes, 84–88, 97–100, 146, 204–6
Landy, John, 167–68, **169**
Langlois, Thomas Talton, 59
Laurier, Wilfrid, 75
Lee, Bessie, 184, 185
Legends of Vancouver (book), 11
Leipzig (ship), 92
Lennie, Beatrice, 136
Lennie, R.S., 111
Lennie Commission, 111–12, 120, 131
Li, Ka-shing, 213
Lindbergh, Charles, 128
Linton, Andy, 157
Lions Gate Bridge, 129, 186
Literary Storefront, 201
Little Mountain Housing Project, 156–57
Little Sister's bookstore, 199
logging, 22–26, 36, 43, 49–50, 85–86
Lost Lagoon, 65–67

Louie, Geraldine, 146
Louie, Tong, 146
Lower Mainland Regional Planning Board
    (LMRPB), 153
Lowndes, Joan, 199
Ludgate, Theodore, 2
Luk'luk'I (Maple Tree Square), 26
Lyons, Teddy, **44**, 45, 46

M
Macdonald, Jock, 136
MacDuff, Jeannie, 123
MacLean, Malcolm, 31–32, 33, **35**, 82
MacLennan, Malcolm, 111
MacPherson, Donald, 221
Macpherson, R.G., 73
Malkin, William, 49, 120, 128, 136
Mallard, Derrick, 182
Mallard, Gwen, 182
Manhattan Apartments, 164
maps and images of Vancouver, **52–53**, **121**
Marathon Realty, 191, 194, 209
Mariah (daughter of Aunt Sally), 80
Marine Building, 105
Marsh, Leonard, 162
Martin, Joseph "Fighting Joe," 93, 94
Martin, Mungo, 201
Marzari, Darlene, 184, 191
Matthews, James, 7, 10
Mawson, Thomas, 66–67
McAfee, Ann, 216
McBride, Richard, 92, 93, 100, 102
McCarthy, Grace, 210
McCleary, Fitzgerald, 116
McCleary, Samuel, 116
McDonald, Robert, 43, 49, 85
McDougall, John, 69–70
McGeer, Gerry, 111, 130–32, 133–34, 136,
    140, 154
McLagan, Sara, 61
McLung, Nellie, 102
McNair, James, 50
McNair, Robert, 50
McNair, William, 50
McNeill, Alex, 154
McRoberts, Hugh, 116
Melvin, Grace, 113
Menchions, W.R., 165
Michaud, Maximilian, 29

Midgley, Victor, 99
Miller, Jonathan, 26, 40, 42
Miracle Mile, 167–68, **169**
missing and murdered Indigenous women,
    221–23
Mitchell, John, 199–200
Mitchell, Margaret, 184
Miyasaki, Matsuhiro, 140
Moby Doll (killer whale), 179
Mole, Samuel, 116
Moody, Richard, 19
Moody, Sewell, 22–23
Moore, W.J., 124
Mortimer-Lamb, Harold, 113
Morton, John, 18–**19**
Moscarella, Arthur, 175
Mount Pleasant, 51, 54
Moy, Shue, 111
Mr. Peanut, 199–200
MST Partnership, 224
Mulligan, Walter, 154, 165, 166
Murphy, Emily, 110
Musqueam Park, 224
Musqueam People, 14, 17–18, 80, 115, 116,
    223–24

N
Narváez, José María, 14–15
Nat Bailey Stadium, 140
National Harbours Board, 157
Nealy, Dorothy, 165–66
Neel, Ellen, 201, **202**
New Design Gallery, 171
New Station Café, 165–66
News-Herald (newspaper), 175
newspapers, Vancouver, 61, 175–76
Newman, Murray, 179–80
Nichol, Walter, 61–62
1913 recession, 92–93, 96–97
Nitta, George, 108, 146
Non-Partisan Association (NPA), 135–36, 149,
    184, 190, 191, 192
Norgan, George, 137
Norris, Len, 175

O
Oakridge Centre, 156
Oberlander, Peter, 185
Odlum, Edward, 60

Odlum, Victor, 135, 176
Olympics, Vancouver, 227–28–29, 232–33
On-to-Ottawa Trek, 134, 141
Operation Solidarity, 204–6, **207**
Oppenheimer, David, 38, 43, 47, 61
O'Rourke, Mickey, 134
Orpheum Theatre, 105, 112
overdose crisis in Vancouver, 233, 236
Owen, Philip, 220–21, 221, 222

P

Paapee-ak (Brockton Point), 14
Pacific Centre, 188
Pacific Coast Hockey Association, 96
Pacific National Exhibition, 30
Parks Board, 3, 65–66, 80
Patricia Hotel, 112
Patrick, Frank, 94, **95**, 96
Patrick, Joe, 94, 96
Patrick, Lester, 94, 96
Pattison, Jim, 212
Pattullo, Duff, 131, 141
Paull, Andy (Qoitchetahl), 10, 15
Pedgrift, Sam, 40
Penthouse Cabaret, 195–96, 197
Peters, Jim, 168
Philliponi, Joe, 195–96
Phillips, Art, 191, 200
Pickton, Robert "Willy," 222
Point Grey, 14, 17, 117–19
police department, Vancouver, 40, 111–12, 132, 165–67, 182–**83**–84
Poole, Jack, 227
population of Vancouver, 93, 105, 153, 204
Portland Hotel Society, 220
pre-contact history of Vancouver, 10–11, 14
Presley, Elvis, 174
pride parade, Vancouver, **198**
prohibition, 102–3
Province (newspaper), 61–62, 175, 176
Provincial Industrial School for Girls, 74
Puckahls, 36
Puil, George, 200
Punjabi Market (area), 215
Purdy, Al, 144

Q

Quahail-ya, 13, 23
Queen's School, 55

Quinn, Stephen, 233

R

racial demographics of Vancouver, 4, 79, 107–8, 214–15
racism, 107–9, 173, 215–17
Radford, John, 136
Rankin, Harry, 190, 219
Rat Portage Sawmill, 58
Raymur, James, 23
Reid, Bill, 201
Reifel, George, 137–38
Reifel Bird Sanctuary, 138
Reid, Malcolm, 76
Relief Camp Workers' Union, 133
Renfrew Heights, 155
residential neighbourhoods, 51–55, 58, 59. *See also* individual neighbourhoods
Richards, Dal, 142
Richards, George Henry, 18
Risk, Sydney, 171–72
Riverview Hospital, 218
Robert Kerr (ship), 32, 33
Robinson, Red, 173–74
Robson, John, 29
Robson Square, 188
Roddan, Andrew, 123–24, **126**
Rogatnick, Abraham, 171
Rogers, Benjamin Tingley, 39
Rogers, Frank, 84
Rogers, Jeremiah (Jerry), 22, 23, 26, 56
Rogers, Jonathan, 51
Royal City Planing Mills, 37, 68, 71
Rubin, Jerry, 180
rum-running, 137–38
Russell, Frankie, 111
Ryga, George, 201

S

Salmonbellies, 159
Sasamat, 16
Save the Downtown Eastside Committee, 212
Scott, Charles, 113
Scott, Jack, 175
Sea Foam (ferry), 30
Second Narrows bridge, 106, 129, 170
Sen-ákw (Burrard Bridge), 7, 10, 81, 157, 223
sex work in Vancouver, 82–83, 173, 196–97, 223–24

Shadbolt, Doris, 171, 201
Shadbolt, Jack, 171
Shaughnessy Heights, 117, 132
Shaw, Chris, 227
Sherman, Maud, 136
shipyards, Vancouver, 148
Sick, Emil, 140
Silvey, Portuguese Joe, 26
Simon Fraser University, 192
Singh, Bela, 79
Singh, Gurdit, 76
Singh, Mewa, 79
Singh, Munshi, 76
single tax, 88–89
Skana (killer whale), 179–80
Skwa-yoos (Kitsilano Beach), 56
Sky Bungalow, 152
SkyTrain, 170, 210
Slah-kay-ulsh (Siwash Rock), 14
smallpox, 16, 41–42
Smilin' Buddha, 173
Smith, Janet, 108–9
Society for Promoting Environmental
    Conservation (SPEC), 182
Sockeye Limited, 119
Solidarity Coalition, 205, 206
South Asian community, 58, 73, 75–76, 79, 215
South Vancouver, 115–17, 120
Spanish flu pandemic, 103–4
Spaxman, Ray, 216, 218
Spencer, Nelson, 131, 135
Spong, Paul, 179–80, 182, **183**
sports in Vancouver, 94–96, 138–40, 167–68,
    172, 227–**28**–29, 232–33
Squamish People, 16, 18, 27, 80, 113
    forced relocation, 80, 81, 128–29
    territorial rights, 11, 223
St. Paul's Hospital, 50
Stait-wouk (Second Beach), 10
Stamp, Edward, 13, 22, 23, 30
Stanley, Lord, 42, 94
Stanley Cup, 94
Stanley Park, 1–2, 42–43, 65–66, 129,
    80, **230–31**
Stark, James, 64
State Theatre, 173
Stevens, H.H., 93
Stewart, Birdie, 26, 82
Stewart, Kennedy, 233, 236

Stewart, John, 40
Stone, Henry, 113, 136
Strata Titles Act, 203
Strathcona, 38–39, **90**, 112, 147, 162, 164, 184
Strathcona Property Owners and Tenants
    Association (SPOTA), 184, 190
Strathcona School, **90**
Street, Bill, 191
Sullivan, Josephine, 26
Sullivan, Philip, 26
Sun (newspaper), 175, 176
Supple Jack (Khaytulk), 7
Sutton Brown, Gerald, 162, **163**, 185, 192
Swanson, Jean, 190
Sylvia Hotel, 173

T
Tait, Robert, 111
Tallman, Ellen, 200
Tallman, Warren, 200
Tauber, Harry, 136
Taylor, Austin, 133
Taylor, Fred "Cyclone," **95**, 96
Taylor, Jim, 176
Taylor, Louis, 54, 61–62, 75, 97, 111–12, 120
    as mayor, 128, 130
    mayoral campaigns, 93–94
    socialism, 86, 88–89
Telford, Lyle, 148
Tennant, Paul, 189, 191
Thompson Berwick Pratt, 152
Three Greenhorns, 19, 38
TISH group, 200
Totem Arts Studio, 201
totem poles, 201, **202**
town planning, 114, 115, 120, 216–17, 218
Town Planning Commission, 114
Townsend, Mark, 220
transportation in Vancouver
    automobiles, 64–65, 105–6
    bicycles, 64
    buses, 170
    Canada Line, 228
    electric streetcars, 45, 46–49, 65, 168, 170
    interurban trains, 59, 119, 170
    railways, 46
    SkyTrain, 170, 210
    See also BC Electric Railway Company
Trasov, Vincent, 199

Trower, Peter, 218–19
Tsleil-Waututh People, 16, 18
Tupper, Reginald, 166–67
Turvey, John, 220

U
Ulksen (Point Grey), 14, 17
unemployment, 47, 67, 92, 106–7, 125,
    127, 129, 205
Union Steamship Company, 40, 63, 161
United Brotherhood of Railway Employees
    (UBRE), 84–85
University of British Columbia, 105
Ustlawn (North Vancouver), 10
utilities, Vancouver, 40–43

V
van Bramer, James, 30
Van Horne, William Cornelius, 14, 27–28,
    29, 39
Vander Zalm, Bill, 213
Vancouver, George, 15, 16
Vancouver Aquarium, 179–80
Vancouver Archives, 10
Vancouver Area Network of Drug Users
    (VANDU), 220
Vancouver Art Gallery, 50, 113, 136, 199, 201
Vancouver Charter, 135
Vancouver Club, **118**
Vancouver Daily World, 61
Vancouver Electric Illuminating Company, 42
Vancouver Electric Railway and Light
    Company, 47
Vancouver General Hospital, 50
Vancouver Housing Authority, 156
Vancouver Improvement Company, 38
Vancouver Lawn Tennis Club, 55
Vancouver Millionaires, 94, **95**, 96
Vancouver News-Advertiser, 61
Vancouver School of Decorative and
    Applied Arts, 113
Vancouver Special, 215–16
Vancouver Times (newspaper), 176
Vancouver Trades and Labour Council
    (VTLC), 73, 99, 100
Vancouver Veterans (Beavers, Maple Leafs,
    Capilanos), 139–40
Vancouver Water Works Company, 41
Vancouverism, 216–17, 218

Vanderpant, John, 113
Vanderpant Galleries, 113, 136
Varley, Fred, 113, 136–37
Victory Square, 105
Volrich, Jack, 191, 197, 214
von Alvensleben, Alvo, 51, 65
von Alvensleben, Edith, 51

W
Wade, F.C., 89
Walker, Michael, 212
Warren, Val, 176
Wasserman, Jack, 175
Water Street, **12**, 23, 26, 194
Weatherbie, Vera, 137
Webster, Jack, 167, 176
West Coast Shipbuilders, **147**, 148
West End, 19, 38, 55, 152, 164, 197, **198**–99
Western Front Lodge, 199, 200
Westminster and Vancouver Tramway
    Company, 49
W.H. Malkin & Co., 49
White, Frank, 160
White Spot, 106
Whiteway, William Tuff, 94
Wilson, Ethel, 35, 50, 56, 82
Wilson, Halford, 146
Women and Girls Protection Act, 146
women's suffrage, 100–102
Wong Foon Sing, 108
Woodcock, George, 171–72, 201
Woodsquat, 225–**26**
Woodward, Charles, 60
Woodward, W.C., 136
Woodward's Department Store, 50, 225–27
World (newspaper), 61
World Building, 51, 67, 175
World War I, 91, 92, 97, 103–5
World War II, 142–44, 147, 148, 149
Writing on the Wall, The (book), 108

X
Xway'xway (Lumberman's Arch), 10, 15, 17, 22,
    49, 80, 81, 113, 214, 223

Z
Zaria, 200

Harbour Publishing Co. Ltd.
P.O. Box 219, Madeira Park, BC, V0N 2H0
www.harbourpublishing.com

Jacket: Jack Shadbolt, "Granville at Night," 1946, watercolour. Private collection. Copyright © courtesy of Simon Fraser University Galleries, Burnaby. Image courtesy of Waddington's Auctioneers and Appraisers, Toronto.
Page ii—iii photo: Vancouver Tourist Association map, City of Vancouver Archives, AM54-S4-: Trans P155 N104
Page iv photo: *Province Newspaper* photograph, Vancouver Public Library 43364

Edited by Mary Schendlinger
Indexed by Nicola Goshulak
Text design by Roberto Dosil
Printed and bound in Canada
Printed on FSC-certified paper with 30% recycled content

Excerpt(s) on pages xi, 35, 50, 56, and 82 from THE INNOCENT TRAVELLER by Ethel Wilson, copyright © 1990 University of British Columbia, by arrangement with Macmillan of Canada. Reprinted by permission of McClelland & Stewart, a division of Penguin Random House Canada Limited. All rights reserved.
Excerpt on page 59 from THE EMILY CARR OMNIBUS, Emily Carr, 1993, Douglas and McIntyre. Reprinted with permission from the publisher.
Excerpt on page 144 from "About Being a Member of Our Armed Forces" by Al Purdy, BEYOND REMEMBERING: THE COLLECTED POEMS OF AL PURDY, edited by Sam Solecki, 2000, Harbour Publishing
Excerpt on page 144 from STARTING OUT: 1920-1947 by Pierre Berton, McClelland and Stewart, 1987.
Excerpt(s) on page 149 from PAPER SHADOWS by Wayson Choy, Copyright © 1999 Wayson Choy. Reprinted by permission of Penguin Canada, a division of Penguin Random House Canada Limited. All rights reserved.
Excerpt(s) on page 159 from ALL THAT MATTERS by Wayson Choy, Copyright © 2004 Wayson Choy. Reprinted by permission of Anchor Canada/Doubleday Canada, a division of Penguin Random House Canada Limited. All rights reserved.
Excerpt on page 171 from BEYOND THE BLUE MOUNTAINS: AN AUTOBIOGRAPHY by George Woodcock, Fitzhenry & Whiteside, 1987.
Excerpt on page 219 from DEAD MAN'S TICKET by Peter Trower, 1996, Harbour Publishing

Harbour Publishing acknowledges the support of the Canada Council for the Arts, the Government of Canada, and the Province of British Columbia through the BC Arts Council.

Library and Archives Canada Cataloguing in Publication
Title: Becoming Vancouver : a history / Daniel Francis.
Names: Francis, Daniel, author.
Description: Includes bibliographical references and index.
Identifiers: Canadiana (print) 2021027025X | Canadiana (ebook) 20210270268
  | ISBN 9781550179163 (hardcover) | ISBN 9781550179170 (EPUB)
Subjects: LCSH: Vancouver (B.C.)—History. | LCSH: Vancouver (B.C.)—Biography—Anecdotes.
Classification: LCC FC3847.4 .F73 2021 | DDC 971.1/33—dc23